PENGUIN BOOKS

THE RISE AND FALL OF MONETARISM

David Smith is economics editor of the *Sunday Times*. He has also been economics correspondent of *The Times*, economics and deputy editor of *Financial Weekly*, economics and business writer for *Now!* magazine, a forecaster with the Henley Centre and an economic report writer for Lloyds Bank.

He studied economics at the universities of Cardiff, Oxford and London, having been introduced to the subject while at West Bromwich Grammar School.

He was born and brought up in the West Midlands but now lives in London. He is married with two children.

D1333933

THE RISE AND FALL
OF MONETARISM

DAVID SMITH

For Jane

PENGUIN BOOKS

Published by the Penguin Group
Penguin Books Ltd, 27 Wrights Lane, London w8 5TZ, England
Viking Penguin a division of Penguin Books USA Inc,
375 Hudson Street, New York, New York 10014, USA
Penguin Books Australia Ltd, Ringwood, Victoria, Australia
Penguin Books Canada Ltd, 2801 John Street, Markham, Ontario, Canada L3R 1B4
Penguin Books (NZ) Ltd, 182–190 Wairau Road, Auckland 10, New Zealand

Penguin Books Ltd, Registered Offices: Harmondsworth, Middlesex, England

First published in Pelican Books 1987
Reprinted in Penguin Books 1991
1 3 5 7 9 10 8 6 4 2

Printed in England by Clays Ltd, St Ives plc
Filmset in Monophoto Ehrhardt

CONTENTS

INTRODUCTION

Monetarism, like sport and religion, is a subject on which people take sides. Apparently innocuous ideas about relationships between money and other variables in the economy have generated a huge amount of intellectual and political heat.

Monetarism means different things to different people. To the economist it means the belief that there exists a stable relationship between the growth of the stock of money in the economy and national income. To the general public it means, more often than not, hospital closures and unemployment.

This book is an attempt to lift the veil on some of the mysteries of monetarism, and to conduct a post mortem on the monetarist experiments of the 1970s and 1980s. Although sitting on the fence for too long can be uncomfortable, the book is critical but is intended to be fair. Monetarists may disagree. So may unreformed Keynesians.

In the 1950s, any economist who stood up in polite company and announced that he was a monetarist risked the outraged reaction faced by the man in the famous Bateman cartoons. Twenty-five years later, those who had not embraced monetarism to some degree were regarded as intellectual dinosaurs.

Monetarism's rise, as we see in the first part of the book, was slow and painful for most of the post-war period, taking two steps forward and one back. But when victory came, the monetarists found, as so often, that they were pushing on an open door.

Politicians need simple ideas to present to voters. When the twin conditions of recession and sharply rising prices began to emerge in the 1970s, monetarism fitted the bill. Inflation, it was said, occurred because the printing presses were working overtime turning out pound, or dollar, notes.

To a Margaret Thatcher, or a Ronald Reagan, this was a self-evident truth. Putting it into practice might involve a few short-term sacrifices, but the politician who was determined to succeed through monetarism would do so. Unfortunately, it was not as easy as that.

By the time this book was written, monetarists had lost most of their bounce. The image of the Bateman character had begun to return. Having been accustomed to seeing themselves as the eunuchs in the harem, monetarists found, when invited to join in, that it was not nearly as much fun as they had imagined. The trials and tribulations of practical monetarism form most of the second half of this book.

The title, *The Rise and Fall of Monetarism*, deserves a little explanation. That monetarism rose is incontestable. That it has fallen is rather more controversial. When I began researching and writing this book, monetarism was certainly not what it was, but it was clinging on with some tenacity. As it progressed, the steady drizzle of monetarism falling started to turn into a thunderstorm.

Monetarists are a cunning lot. They will tell you that what they believe now is what they always believed and that the experience of the past several years has changed nothing. They will also tell you that events turned out in a way they had fully expected before the monetarist experiments got under way. Monetarist politicians, particularly in Britain, will tell you that the policies they are pursuing now are fully consistent with what went before.

As the story unfolds, the reader may care to set such claims against the facts as related in this book. For that is the best way to judge whether, and by how much, monetarism has fallen.

I

OLD IDEAS

Every movement has a leader. The leadership of the movement that came to be known as monetarism is in no doubt. Milton Friedman and the Chicago School led the monetarist assault on the post-war conventional wisdom in economics and, in the process, Friedman became the best-known economist of his day.

The economic debate since the war has been an intellectual battle, between Friedman and John Maynard Keynes, although they never crossed swords directly. Friedman and the monetarists lined up on one side, against the followers of Keynes on the other. Divided on economics, Friedman and Keynes could hardly have presented a more striking contrast as individuals.

Friedman, a small man, was born in Brooklyn in 1912, of poor, first-generation Jewish immigrant parents. Lack of money almost prevented him from continuing his studies in economics. His approach has always been from outside the establishment, worrying away at accepted ideas with terrier-like tenacity. Keynes, born thirty years earlier into a well-to-do academic family in Cambridge, was tall, educated at Eton, and moved between Cambridge, the City and the Treasury with the ease of the gentleman amateur. He attacked the establishment from within, often in the pages of *The Times*, traditionally the establishment newspaper in Britain.

The struggle for supremacy between Friedman and the ideas of Keynes (Keynes himself died in 1946) makes up much of the story of the rise of monetarism as a born-again force in modern economics. For it is important to remember that the monetarism that emerged from Chicago was the product of a very long tradition in economics.

Monetarism – Old and New

Although the description is a modern one, monetarist ideas have been around in economics for a very long time. Philosopher economists such as John Locke and David Hume were expounding a monetarist view of the economy in the late seventeenth and eighteenth centuries. The tradition extends back for 300 years, pre-dating the industrial revolution and the enormous economic and social changes that revolution brought about.

It is important to remember, too, that the tradition goes back to the days when ideas about money were rather different. In the seventeenth century, money was as likely to be a bag of gold coins as a piece of paper. And if it was a piece of paper, it could be exchanged for gold at the bank. Nowadays, money is not generally regarded in terms of gold or other precious metals. Modern paper currency cannot be exchanged for gold – we have moved away from what economists describe as a commodity currency system.

This brings us to the first plank of monetarism, in both its older and newer versions. This is that there is something called money, which can be defined and measured. It sounds so straightforward that it hardly bears consideration and, in the old days when the banking system was backed by gold, this was the case. But, as economies have become more sophisticated and the banks more expert and bolder in the creation of credit, defining and measuring money has grown ever more difficult.

Consider for a moment what most individuals would now regard as money, in terms of spending power. There are, as before, bank notes and coins, although they are not linked to gold or any other precious metal. There are cheques that can be drawn on bank or building society accounts, although it is the case that if everyone wanted to withdraw all the money in their accounts at once there would not be anything like enough notes and coin to go round. This is because the banks create credit on the basis of the relatively small amount of currency they hold.

Even this does not get us far enough along the road towards a complete modern definition of money, which should perhaps also include company and individual overdraft facilities, a variety of savings instruments and – of increasing importance to the spending power of the individual – plastic credit cards.

The point is that there is no single, all-purpose definition of money. In the ten years from 1976, at least seven different definitions of money were measured and monitored in Britain, ranging from very narrow measures comprising little more than notes and coin to very broad measures of credit and liquidity.

Monetarists have been inclined to emphasize narrow definitions of money as the appropriate measure, representing the base of what could be described as an inverse pyramid of credit and liquidity in the economy. Credit and liquidity, they argue, tend to move in line with the money base.

The second and most crucial element of monetarism is the belief that changes in the amount of money in the economy, assuming measurement difficulties can be overcome, are the source of other economic changes. In particular, monetarists believe that there is a close relationship between changes in the stock of money and changes in national income, increases in money leading to increases in national income.

National income, the value of all incomes in the economy combined (which is also equivalent to the value of national output and the total spending on domestically produced goods) can increase for one of two reasons. It can rise because more is being earned, produced and spent in real terms, or it can increase simply because prices have gone up between one year and the next.

Monetarists have tended to link changes in the stock of money with this second reason for an increase in national income, higher prices. This is because, for early monetarists, the world they observed was one of full employment and full utilization of capacity. A surplus or glut, either of labour or of goods, did not feature in their scheme of things.

And so David Hume, writing in 1750, offered the following description of the effects of an increase in the stock of money, or specie: 'At first, no alteration is perceived; by degrees the price rises, first of one commodity, then of another; till the whole at last reaches a just proportion with the quantity of specie which is in the kingdom.'

Later monetarists accepted that changes in money affected both real output and prices, but believed that the link between money and prices would always be the most obvious and dramatic. Thus the message from Friedman, writing more than 200 years after Hume, was essentially the same: 'The central fact is that inflation is always and everywhere a monetary phenomenon. Historically, substantial changes in prices have always occurred together with substantial changes in the quantity of money relative to output. I know of no exception to this generalization ...'

With these two planks of monetarism in place – that money can be defined and measured and that changes in money cause changes in prices – the structure is almost complete. To finish it off, all we need is the third plank, which is also the monetarist prescription for economic policy. This is that governments can and should control changes in the stock of money – the money supply – in order to prevent inflation.

The prescription is common to old and new monetarism alike. But monetary control was a lot easier in the old days. Under the Gold Standard before the First World War (and briefly after it), notes issued by the Bank of England were backed by and fully convertible into gold. Let us start from a position where the money supply in Britain has been increased so as to permit higher prices. The result is that British goods become less competitive on world markets and there is a balance of payments deficit.

This deficit has to be cleared by a shipment abroad of Britain's gold reserves. The loss of gold automatically results in a contraction of the money supply and the inflation is eliminated. In practice, things did not work quite as smoothly as this, but a semi-automatic framework for monetary control was there.

In the modern era, without such automaticity, many have questioned whether it is within the power of governments to control the money supply. Critics of monetarism argue that, in a modern credit economy, the money supply expands to meet the needs of the economy and that there is a limited amount the central bank can do about it.

Monetarists say that such control is possible, if there is the will to achieve it. Friedman in particular has advocated monetary rules as the way for governments to proceed. Under these rules, a target would be set for the growth of the money supply, appropriately measured, which would allow for real growth in the economy in line with the expansion of productive capacity. But the monetary rule would be set so as not to allow any extra money into the economy to create inflation.

The world has changed a lot since the pre-industrial days, but the monetarist manifesto has had a consistency about it. It is that money can be defined and measured; that money changes lead to changes in national income; and that money can and should be controlled.

The Traditional Quantity Theory

We have come this far without mentioning the quantity theory of money and, for the reader who is put off by anything resembling a mathematical equation, this section is mercifully brief. A more detailed description of the development of the quantity theory is provided in the Appendix.

The quantity theory of money forms the basis of monetarism, and the sharp-eyed reader will have noticed that there is something missing from our description of monetarism above. We have said that money (M) is related to prices (P) and real national income or output, which we can call Y.

The problem is that the stock of money existing at any one time will never be sufficient to be equivalent to national income in current prices (PY). This is because each unit of money is not simply used once and then stored away. One person's spending is another person's income, which in turn is spent to form someone else's income. Every pound or dollar note changes hands on a number of occasions within a given time period.

The missing link is what the quantity theorists called the velocity of circulation (V) – the speed at which money circulates around the economy, or the number of times a unit of currency changes hands within a given period. Prices and output must therefore be linked not just to money, but also to the speed at which that money moves around.

This gives us the familiar quantity theory equation, whereby money (M) multiplied by its velocity (V) gives us national income in current prices (PY). Or, $MV = PY$.

That is the end of the brief mathematical interlude. But the introduction of the velocity of circulation raises an important question. How did monetarists know that changes in money and not changes in velocity caused prices and output changes? If money suddenly started working harder, if its velocity increased, then inflation could occur even if the money supply was held down.

The answer to this was a straightforward one. It was that the velocity of circulation was determined by factors which, by their nature, were very slow to alter, such as the structure of the banking system, and whether people were paid on a weekly or monthly basis.

Another difficulty emerges when the quantity theory is presented in equation form. What is there to say that it is money changes that cause price and output changes, and not the other way round? The best answer to this was provided in the earlier part of this century by the two great Cambridge professors of economics, Alfred Marshall and Arthur Pigou.

According to them, the cash that people hold for transactions and as a precaution against the unforeseen will be a stable proportion of each individual's income. Now, suppose that there is a sudden increase in the amount of money in the economy. Everyone finds that they are holding more money in proportion to their income than they would like. Their response is to go out and spend it. And if the economy is operating at full employment and full capacity as Marshall, Pigou and the earlier 'classical' economists assumed, the result is higher prices.

In providing an explanation of the link between money and prices, the Cambridge economists also underlined the monetarist belief in a stable velocity of circulation. If the behaviour of individuals is fixed in the sense of wanting a certain proportion of income to hold in money, then the velocity of circulation, which is the sum of these individual decisions, will also be stable.

The Keynesian Revolution

When John Maynard Keynes set out to challenge the existing economic orthodoxy in the 1920s and 1930s, he operated under two major advantages. As a distinguished Cambridge economist who had helped develop that existing orthodoxy, he was familiar with both its strengths and weaknesses. More importantly, Keynes was working at a time when conventional economic wisdom appeared to have run out of explanations and solutions to the dire economic imbalances which had emerged after the First World War.

The combination of Keynes's theoretical insight and the economic devastation of the inter-war years dealt a crushing blow to the quantity theory. 'The quantity theory of money,' Milton Friedman wrote in 1956, 'fell into disrepute after the crash of 1929 and the subsequent Great Depression and only recently has been slowly re-emerging into professional respectability.'

The knock-out blow to the quantity theory having been dealt by actual events, it was only too easy for Keynes to trample over its prostrate form. Thus Friedman again, this time in 1959: 'The obvious disorders in the economy and the urgent need for a remedy made the world in general and the economics profession in particular receptive to new ideas. John Maynard Keynes was the chief architect of the subsequent intellectual revolution.'

Keynes's great work, *The General Theory of Employment, Interest and Money*, was published in 1936. However, the challenge mounted by Keynes began much earlier, even as the quantity theory was being refined at Cambridge in the years immediately after the First World War.

It will be recalled that a central assumption of classical economics was full employment. The economy tended towards an equilibrium in which supply equalled demand at a full employment level of national income. This cosy theoretical assumption was one of the many casualties of the First World War. In Britain, the unemployment rate reached 10 per cent in 1921 and did not fall back into single figures until the eve of the Second World War. In the 1920s and 1930s, the level of unemployment in Britain ranged from one million to just over three million. Keynes's awareness of the 'obvious disorders' in the economy came long before the Great Depression of 1929–33. Britain's slump occurred well before the Great Depression in the United States. As importantly, Keynes had a ready target to aim at in the so-called Treasury view which dominated British economic policy in the 1920s.

The application of the Treasury view, which Lord Kaldor described as the first full-scale example of monetarist dogma dominating economic policy in Britain (the second being Margaret Thatcher's economic experiment of 1979), was savagely attacked by Keynes. The drive to return to the Gold Standard, urged by the Cunliffe Committee and the City of London, resulted in a monetary policy that Keynes labelled as 'simply a campaign against the standard of life of the working classes', operating through the 'deliberate intensification of unemployment'.

In 1929, seven years before the *General Theory* appeared, Keynes proposed, through Lloyd George's Liberal Party manifesto, a public works programme costing £100 million annually and taking 500,000 men off the dole queues. But the Treasury view, rigid on monetary policy, was also fixed in its perception of the powers of fiscal policy. The view, as then defined, was that: 'Whatever might be the political or social advantages, very little additional employment can, in fact, and as a general rule, be created by State borrowing and State expenditure.'

This, which was echoed, almost to the word, by ministers in Margaret Thatcher's government and, for that matter, by the Labour Prime Minister James Callaghan in 1976 in his speech to his party's conference, confirms the clear similarities, noted by Kaldor, in economic policy in the two periods. The main difference of course is that, in the earlier period, there was an unemployment but not an inflation problem.

Keynes's response in the 1920s and 1930s was to establish a new theoretical framework which accommodated and explained the situation of mass unemployment, and which set economic policy moving in a new direction. Concerned as we are with the development of monetarist thinking, it is necessary to focus on only one, admittedly central, element of the Keynesian revolution: his treatment of money and the rate of interest.

In the quantity theory of money, the motive for holding cash was clear. Money itself was held to have no value except as a means of facilitating transactions, although in addition some might be held as a precaution against unforeseen circumstances. To these traditional transactions and precautionary demands for money, Keynes added a third – the speculative demand for money. Money held for speculative investment clearly differed in its determinants and effects from that held for the purpose of buying goods and services.

In Keynes's scheme, the speculative demand for money was principally determined by the rate of interest. This was because individuals, in Keynes's model, were faced with a choice between holding money or interest-bearing bonds. The amount of money held at any one time depended on their view of the future course of bond prices, in turn determined by expectations about interest rates. Thus Keynes saw the demand for money as split into that for active balances, cash needed for transactions or precautionary purposes, and idle balances, those required for speculation.

In adopting this approach, Keynes delivered two body blows to the traditional quantity theory. The first was that demand for active balances, while determined as before by income, was now related to an overall income level for the economy which could fluctuate sharply because full employment was no longer guaranteed, as had once been assumed by classical economists. The second and perhaps more important blow was the introduction of idle balances, the level of which depended on interest rates.

With these now included in the wider demand for money, Keynes could put forward a very different 'transmission mechanism', from changes in money to other economic changes. In his view, the cog in this mechanism was the interest rate – the lower the interest rate, the greater the demand for idle balances.

In the economy, Keynes argued, there will be a spectrum of views about the likely future course of interest rates. At very high interest rates, most people will anticipate a downward move in rates and a rise in bond prices, and so the speculative demand for money will be low and bond holdings high. At low interest rates, in contrast, the general expectation will be for a rise in rates and a consequent fall in bond prices. This, allied to the fact that the yield on bonds may be insufficient for it to be worth giving up the convenience of holding cash, means that speculative demand for money will be high and bond holdings low. This spectrum of bond and cash holdings, known as the liquidity preference schedule, was highly sensitive to interest rates.

Keynes took things further with his observation that, at very low rates of interest, all investors are likely to take the view that a rise in rates is inevitable. In this situation, which he called the liquidity trap, changes in the quantity of money do not work through the economy. Rather, the more money that is pumped in, the more speculative balances increase. And as long as this situation persists, monetary policy is rendered impotent. He envisaged a situation where the interest rate could be simultaneously too high to encourage investment and too low to break out of the liquidity trap. Expanding the money supply would be ineffective as a means of restoring full employment: it would be like 'pushing on a piece of string'. It followed from Keynes's monetary analysis that there will be circumstances when the economy is stuck in a position of unemployment and excess capacity. With monetary policy unable to help, fiscal policy and public investment programmes were required to step into the breach.

This was the familiar policy prescription of Keynes, often but wrongly associated with Roosevelt's New Deal in the 1930s in the United States (there is little evidence that Roosevelt or his advisers were directly influenced by Keynes), and more accurately described as the basis for policy during and after the Second World War. The damage to monetary policy in general, and the quantity theory in particular, was severe. The followers of Keynes in the post-war years emphasized the primacy of fiscal policy, to an extent that Keynes would have been unlikely to do himself. Monetary policy was accorded, in theory if not always in practice, a minor role.

The innovations of Keynes, apart from demonstrating the ineffectiveness of monetary policy in certain circumstances, also rocked the very foundations of the quantity theory. Armed with the concept of idle or speculative balances, it is easy to see how the stable and predictable link between money and prices could break down. Imagine Keynes's formulation of the demand for money under conditions of full employment. There is no difficulty with the transactions and precautionary demands for money. They will be related, as before, in a stable way to full-employment income. But the speculative demand for money creates a problem. At any time, people can move money in or out of these idle balances. If people move money out of idle balances for spending, at full-employment national income, then a rise in prices can occur without a prior, or at least an immediately prior, increase in the money supply.

Alternatively, as in the example above, a rise in the money supply, even under classical conditions of full employment, may not lead to a rise in prices, because it is absorbed into larger idle balances. Keynes had broken down the stable quantity theory link between money and prices. The link, such as it was, would be indirect and often very muted.

Modern monetarists have laboured to demonstrate that, in many respects, Keynes did not abandon the quantity theory. *The General Theory of Employment, Interest and Money* runs to nearly 400 pages and running through it, while stronger in some places than others, is the conviction that money does indeed matter.

Keynesians may indeed have chosen to ignore the 'money' in the *General Theory* and earlier works such as Keynes's *Treatise on Money*. Even so, Keynes ushered in a completely new way of approaching economics and economic policy. It was nothing less than a revolution.

In the dire economic conditions of the inter-war years, old-style economics was seen to have run out of answers. New ideas were needed and Keynes offered them. But as Robert Lekachman, a biographer of Keynes, observed: 'The laboratory experiment of the efficacy of Keynesian remedies occurred not in the 1930s but during the enormous war-time surge in national output and the post-war boom in consumer goods which ensued.'

Friedman's Counter-Attack

In these conditions of post-war rebuilding and recovery, one may wonder why, in Chicago, economists chose to mount a counter-attack aimed at reviving the old and, to the majority of the economics profession, obsolete quantity theory of money. The answer is twofold. Firstly, some economists, mainly in the United States, were already worried that, as the power and influence of the trade unions increased and with no firm hand on the monetary tiller, the creeping inflation of the 1950s could all too easily turn into galloping inflation. Associated with this was the fear, again more in the United States than in Britain, that Keynesian economic policies meant unacceptably big government.

Friedman himself provided a second reason. At Chicago, whatever was happening elsewhere, the tradition of the quantity theory had not been usurped by Keynesian thinking. He was simply continuing with that tradition. He wrote:

Chicago was one of the few academic centres at which the quantity theory continued to be a central and vigorous part of the oral tradition throughout the 1930s and 1940s, where students continued to study monetary theory and to write theses on monetary problems. At Chicago, Henry Simons and Lloyds Mints directly, Frank Knight and

Jacob Viner at one remove, taught and developed a more subtle and relevant version, one in which the quantity theory was connected and integrated with general price theory and became a flexible and sensitive tool for interpreting movements in aggregate economic activity and for developing relevant policy prescriptions.

Friedman set himself the task of capturing this oral tradition on paper, apologizing in advance for the fact that a model of the quantity theory could not hope to take in all the subtleties of the Chicago tradition. He also determined to rebut the attack on the quantity theory mounted by the joint forces of Keynes and the Great Depression.

Friedman had returned to the University of Chicago in 1946, having attained an MA in economics there in the early 1930s. On leaving Chicago after taking his degree, he became a research fellow at Columbia University before moving to the US National Resources Committee in 1935. From there he moved to the National Bureau of Economic Research in 1937, continuing his association with the Bureau, apart from a three-year break between 1945 and 1948, until 1981. It was at the NBER that he developed the strong bias towards empirical testing of theory characteristic of his work.

Until his return to Chicago, there was little to suggest that Friedman would emerge in the role of monetarist counter-revolutionary. From 1941 to 1943 he was seconded to the US Treasury's tax division. In the years 1943 to 1945 he was associate director of the statistical research group in the Division of War Research at Columbia.

His doctorate, eventually awarded in 1946, was for a project called 'Income from Professional Practice', which had as its main and controversial conclusion that entry restrictions into the professions pushed up costs to the consumer.

Friedman's first major contribution to the macro-economic debate was in 1948, the year he became, at the comparatively early age of thirty-six, a professor of economics at Chicago. Friedman set out 'A Monetary and Fiscal Framework for Economic Stability', which drew heavily on an article published twelve years earlier by one of his mentors, Henry Simons. Simons had advocated rules for monetary policy which would help to minimize fluctuations in economic activity, keeping the economy on a stable course.

Simons's article of 1936, 'Rules versus Authority in Monetary Policy', was largely swept away in the excitement over the publication of Keynes's *General Theory* in the same year. Simons proposed 100 per cent reserve banking, removing the ability of the banks to create 'money' through the traditional process of credit creation. This, argued Simons, would remove the instabilities inherent in the banking system, and greatly enhance the ability of the monetary authorities to control the quantity of money in circulation.

Friedman took on the Simons idea of 100 per cent reserve banking and allied to it a proposal for stabilization through fiscal policy. In contrast to the Keynesian approach, Friedman said that governments should stick to pre-arranged plans for stable public spending, allowing all the adjustment to come through government revenues. In an economic downturn, at fixed tax rates, a fall in revenues would produce a budget deficit. Because of the 100 per cent reserve banking system, this would produce an increase in the money supply which would push the economy back towards a stable growth path. An economic boom would produce the opposite situation of budget surplus, monetary contraction, and a move back down to stable growth.

This early thrust in the debate, parried with little difficulty by the new Keynesian orthodoxy, stood apart from Friedman's later work in two important ways. The first was that it was firmly embedded in the ivory tower of academic economics. The concept of 100 per cent reserve banking, while acceptable as a theoretical nicety, had little practical significance. It was asking, in modern sophisticated economies, for the clock to be turned back to the time when banks could only issue paper backed by an exactly equivalent amount of gold in their vaults. The second element was that it ascribed an equal role in economic management to fiscal policy, albeit a role that, unlike in the Keynesian framework, was based on strict rules rather than discretion. The later Chicago emphasis was on the impotence of fiscal policy, and the primacy of monetary policy.

While pushing it into the background, Friedman did not abandon his 1948 idea of stable fiscal policy rules. In the debate over Britain's monetarist experiment and the role of the PSBR (public sector borrowing requirement), it was still present. In evidence to the House of Commons Treasury and Civil Service Committee in 1980, he said : 'The PSBR should be allowed to vary automatically over the cycle in response to cyclical variations in the nominal volume of government spending for a stable expenditure programme and of government receipts for a stable tax structure. Neither expenditure programmes nor tax structures should be varied in response to cyclical variations.'

The Modern Quantity Theory

By the early 1950s, Friedman was embarking on a course which was to lead, eventually, to a fully-fledged monetarist counter-attack on Keynes. The breakthrough came in a 1956 article, 'The Quantity Theory of Money: A Restatement'.

This was published in a collection edited by Friedman. The collection also contained a piece by Friedman's Chicago colleague, Philip Cagan, on hyperinflation. This both highlighted the extreme dangers of what could happen when inflation really took hold, and provided evidence of the causes of inflation. Cagan, after defining hyper-inflation as a situation in which prices are rising by 50 per cent or more per *month*, assembled some remarkable historical data. In Hungary, between August 1945 and July 1946, prices rose by an average of 19,800 per cent a month. At the end of the period, prices were 3,810 million million million million times their August 1945 level. The more famous German inflation of the 1920s was slightly less dramatic but still stunning. Between August 1922 and November 1923, prices rose by an average of 322 per cent a month, to give a price level at the end of the period 10,200 million times that at the start. The common experience of these and several other examples of hyper-inflation was that sharp increases in the quantity of money preceded the very rapid price rises.

The impetus for increases in the money supply came from the desire of governments to maintain revenues during periods of economic dislocation. Governments were prepared to allow the money supply to rise to preserve the real value of revenues. In Cagan's words, 'they inflated at ever increasing tax rates'.

Friedman also drew on the experience of rapid inflation to support the quantity theory. In his investigation of the monetary history of the United States, he found five such periods – around 1776, 1812, the American Civil War of the 1860s and the First and Second World Wars. Like Cagan, he found that changes in the quantity of money in these periods clearly provided the basis for sharp price increases. He also cited examples of inflation brought to heel by control of the money supply, such as in Italy in 1947, Germany in 1948, the United States and Britain in 1951 and France in 1960.

In describing his version of the quantity theory simply as a 'restatement', Friedman was displaying undue modesty. The modern quantity theory developed by Friedman was a very different animal from its ancestors.

Keynes had struck at the heart of the old quantity theory with his introduction of the idea that individuals hold speculative balances of money for the purpose of investing in interest-bearing bonds, and that, as a result, the demand for money will vary according to the rate of interest. This innovation appeared to destroy the quantity theory view that the demand for money, and by implication the velocity of circulation, was stable. If it varied with something as volatile as interest rates then the demand for money was not stable at all. According to Keynesians, demand and velocity were 'will o' the wisps', which flitted around.

Friedman's task, therefore, was to re-establish the old view that both the demand for money and its velocity were stable. Otherwise, the monetarist relationships between money and national income broke down irretrievably.

Friedman recognized that Keynes's monetary analysis was an important and valuable contribution to the debate. And so, as is often forgotten, he endeavoured to build upon it rather than to knock it down. Like Keynes, he saw that the important question was what determined the demand for money. 'The quantity theory of money is in the first instance a theory of the demand for money,' he wrote.

Keynes's innovation was to regard money as an asset which could be substituted for another asset – interest-bearing bonds. Friedman saw the logic of treating money as an asset, but thought that Keynes had not gone nearly far enough in considering the range of assets for which money could be substituted.

To Friedman, the range of choices faced by the individual was a very wide one. The choice could be between holding money and bonds, but it could also be between money and a washing-machine or television set, or between money and a larger house. 'The most fruitful approach is to regard money as one of a sequence of assets, on a par with bonds, equities, houses, consumer durables,' he wrote. Friedman's Chicago stew contained a larger number of ingredients.

But in complicating the quantity theory in this way, Friedman was also taking it back to its traditional roots. There was method in his madness, and the method was to demonstrate that the rate of interest, so important in Keynes's destruction of the old quantity theory, was a comparatively insignificant element in the modern version. In fact, so insignificant would the rate of interest be, since it influenced only one of a large number of asset decisions, that Friedman asserted it would exert very little influence on the demand for money. This assertion, as we will see later, did not stand up very well to testing.

However, for the time being Friedman had resurrected the relationship in which money was one of a range of assets held, the dominant factor in determining the demand for money being the wealth of the individual, as measured by his long-run stable income, which he called 'permanent income'. The demand for money, the result of a large number of separate choices conveniently pulling in opposite directions so as to cancel one another out, would be a stable proportion of income.

It was back to the old explanation, albeit in slightly more elaborate form, of the transmission mechanism from changes in the money stock to changes in national income. An increase in the money supply gives individuals more money, in relation to their total portfolio of assets, than they wish to hold. The response is to shift this money into other assets – into bonds, equities, washing-machines, cars, houses and so on. And the sum of these spending decisions is a higher level of national income, expressed in current prices, than we started with.

Some of this increased spending would produce extra output. But Friedman, like his predecessors, thought that the main effect would be observed in higher prices. Increases in the money supply mainly lead to higher prices.

There was still a long way to go. Friedman had to prove that his version of the quantity theory, constructed as a theoretical response to Keynes's demolition of the old quantity theory, stood up in practice. But even in 1956, before completing his lengthy process of testing, he was fairly sure of his ground. 'There is perhaps no other empirical relation in economics,' he wrote,

> that has been observed to recur so uniformly under so wide a variety of circumstances as the relation between substantial changes in the stock of money and in prices; the one is invariably linked with the other and in the same direction; this uniformity is, I suspect, of the same order as many of the uniformities that form the basis of the physical sciences.

The monetarist counter-revolution had begun.

2

IN THE WILDERNESS

The revival of the quantity theory at Chicago in the 1950s attracted much interest in the academic world. It also produced a lively response, most of it sceptical. But its impact on policy was negligible. This was hardly surprising. Time lags between ideas and practice are inevitable. Only later did Friedman acquire the ready access to newspapers, magazines and television that helped speed the dissemination of his ideas.

Indeed, in the United States, Keynesian economic policies – having been adopted rather more cautiously than in Britain after the war – were gaining ground. The contrast between the conservatism of policy in the Eisenhower years of the 1950s, after the cheap money experiment of the immediate post-war period had broken down, and the robust Keynesianism of Kennedy and Johnson in the 1960s was striking. This culminated in President Johnson's Great Society programme, launched in 1965.

Richard Nixon, elected president in 1968 on a manifesto of balanced budgets and responsible monetary policy, similar in several important respects to that put forward by Margaret Thatcher in Britain eleven years later, changed tack dramatically. In 1971, Nixon declared: 'I am now a Keynesian', an apparent abandonment of sound money principles which, whatever he did later, was an impeachable offence as far as monetarists were concerned.

In Britain, the Conservative government elected in 1951, after six years of Labour rule, embarked on a policy of tightening monetary policy through raising bank rate (the rate of interest at which the Bank of England lends to the banking system), eschewing the cheap money policies of Clement Attlee's Chancellors. Policy was eased for the 1955 General Election, but was tightened again under the chancellorship of Peter Thorneycroft.

After the 1955 election, despite restrictive Budgets and direct instructions from the Chancellor of the Exchequer to the banks to restrict lending, monetary growth continued strong. British policy in the mid 1950s is regarded by some as a test run for the post-1979 monetarism of Margaret Thatcher, although the evidence of a direct link between Chicago ideas and policy in Britain at that time is weak. The experiment, if that is what it was, came to an end with the resignation of Thorneycroft, together with two junior Treasury ministers,

Enoch Powell and Nigel Birch, over the Treasury's failure to persuade the Cabinet that cuts in public expenditure were needed.

But this little local difficulty, to use Prime Minister Macmillan's phrase, did have wider consequences. Some months earlier, the clear lack of success in controlling monetary growth, despite the use of all the weapons in the authorities' armoury, had resulted in the establishment of a special committee 'to inquire into the working of the monetary and credit system and to make recommendations'. The Radcliffe Committee, which reported in 1959, was to set the cause of monetarism in Britain back for over a decade.

The Radcliffe Committee

Under the chairmanship of Lord Radcliffe, a distinguished judge, a nine-man committee conducted a remarkably detailed two-year investigation. Its report, distilled from hundreds of hours of evidence and about 150 written submissions, could hardly have been more out of spirit with the monetarist ideas emerging in the United States.

The August 1959 'Report of the Committee on the Working of the Monetary System' was unanimous. Its nine members – Lord Radcliffe himself, Professor A. K. Cairncross, Sir Oliver Franks, Lord Harcourt, W. E. Jones, Professor R. S. Sayers, Sir Reginald Verdon Smith, George Woodcock and Sir John Woods – came out against straightforward monetarist ideas about money supply control. 'Though we do not regard the supply of money as an unimportant quantity,' the report said, 'we view it as only part of a wider structure of liquidity in the economy . . . It is the whole liquidity position that is relevant to spending decisions and our interest in the supply of money is due to its significance in the whole liquidity picture.'

The committee believed that monetary measures would, in normal times, play no more than a subordinate role in directing the economy. They would not in themselves be sufficient to keep the economy in balance. The only area where money supply control was likely to be important was in the management, by the authorities, of government debt. And the report came out strongly against the principle that, in return for sticking to some pre-arranged path for the money supply, governments should be prepared to accept highly volatile interest rates.

Instead, the committee urged a positive policy towards interest rates, because of their effect on investment and stock-building, although it was admitted that the evidence pointed to these effects being weak. An interest rate policy was also needed to avoid undue pressure on the pound. Money supply statistics should be collected, said the report, and co-ordination of policy between the Treasury and the Bank of England should be closer. Hire-purchase and other quantitative controls on bank lending should be brought in when needed although they were not, in the normal run of things, desirable.

The report set the tone for monetary policy in Britain in the 1960s. It was a period dominated by pressure on sterling, and the need to raise interest rates in response to each new crisis. Running against this was the view that interest rates should be kept as low as possible in support of fiscal policies, which were the chief means of stimulating growth in the economy.

The money supply in itself had no role in policy and, indeed, was rarely mentioned. Sir Alan Walters, Margaret Thatcher's personal economic adviser from 1981 to 1983, has recalled applying to the Bank of England in the early 1960s for a research grant to develop statistics on the quantity of money in Britain. (The quantity of money is the stock existing at any one time; the money supply is the increase in that stock over a given period.) The application was turned down because, he claimed, statistics on the money stock were of little practical use in formulating policy.

To be fair to the Bank of England, such statistics were developed during the 1960s in response to one of the recommendations of the Radcliffe Report. The Bank also started publishing its *Quarterly Bulletin*, making information on money, together with its own interpretation of financial and monetary trends, available to a wider public. For practical purposes, however, the money supply was allowed to vary; it was not even maintained within informal limits. Until events started to turn in its favour towards the end of the decade, the Chicago revival of the quantity theory of money – for its impact on policy in Britain under both Conservative and Labour governments – might never have happened.

The Radcliffe Committee included two academic economists, Richard Sayers and Alec Cairncross. Cairncross later became government chief economic adviser. Neither man, then or subsequently, was sympathetic to the monetarist approach. It was therefore surprising, but no less devastating, that as well as steering economic policy in Britain away from monetarist ideas the Radcliffe Report also directed its fire at the central principle underlying the revival of the quantity theory.

This was the notion of a stable demand for money which in turn produces a velocity of circulation which is also stable, or at least moves in a predictable way. Changes in velocity will mean that the effects of an increase in the money supply on prices are uncertain, and that practical control of the money supply may not serve the intended purpose.

An increase in the money supply accompanied by an offsetting decline in velocity will have no effect on prices or income – as in the case outlined by Keynes, when such money is just absorbed into idle balances. Or a rise in the velocity of circulation could mean that prices start to increase without a prior increase in the quantity of money.

The Radcliffe Committee dismissed the monetarist claim of stable or predictable velocity of circulation. 'The fact that spending is not limited by the amount of money in existence is sometimes argued by reference to the velocity of circulation of money,' said the report.

> It is possible for example to demonstrate statistically that during the last few years the volume of spending had greatly increased while the supply of money had hardly changed; the velocity of circulation of money had increased. We have not made more use of this concept because we cannot find any reason for supposing, or any experience in monetary history indicating, that there is any limit to the velocity of circulation; it is a statistical concept that tells us nothing directly of the motivation that influences the level of total demand.

Attempts to manage the economy by control of the money supply were thus doomed to failure. In a modern economy with a sophisticated financial structure, ways will be found to make money work harder, to counter a monetary squeeze by the authorities, the velocity of circulation will be forced higher. The more efficient the financial system, the committee said, the more that velocity could be stretched in this way.

Friedman's Researches

While a grand committee of inquiry in Britain was busy consigning the quantity theory – in either its traditional or restated forms – to the dustbin of noteworthy but impracticable ideas, Friedman was conducting a painstaking programme of research to demonstrate that the theory could hold over a long period, including the modern era.

Econometrics, the testing of theories using statistical methods, has become *de rigueur* among modern economists. Friedman made it a central element of his work from the beginning. In this respect, his association with the National Bureau of Economic Research, which began in 1937 when he was twenty-five, was fundamental.

Friedman's most notable research work was *A Monetary History of the United States*, published in 1963. The work, and the authorship, was shared with his long-time NBER colleague, Anna Schwarz. Friedman and Schwarz's *Monetary History*, set against the limited scope and cautious conclusions of most econometrics research, was breathtakingly ambitious.

It covered the period from 1867 to 1960 and involved more than just taking available data and examining what relationships were supported. Figures for the money stock had to be prepared, on the basis of available banking statistics, for the early years. Since the Federal Reserve System was not established until 1913, this was far from easy. The method employed was to take the derived data for the money stock and, by means of regression analysis, to discover what were the relationships between it and other economic variables. If the results turned out to be 'wrong' in the sense of not matching the theory, the equations were re-worked. If the statistical fit was poor, adjustments such as 'dummy' variables were inserted into the data, to cover unusual events. There is a sense, running through Friedman's research work, of reading a 'whodunnit' having already glanced at the final page.

This criticism of Friedman – that his research was biased towards achieving certain results – was present in the early 1960s and gained strength later, as mathematical methods came to dominate economics. But the grandness of the scale of the work, and the fact that nobody had attempted anything quite like it before, meant that much of the initial criticism could be dismissed as carping.

Friedman, at least, had no doubts about the significance of the proof he had uncovered in economic history. The *Monetary History* contained three main conclusions: firstly, that changes in the money stock were associated with changes in economic activity – money income and prices – over a long period; secondly, that there was a stable relationship between monetary changes and economic changes; and thirdly – anticipating a Keynesian criticism – that changes in the money stock often occurred independently, and were not the result of changes in economic activity.

Apart from these three general conclusions, Friedman and Schwarz cast an entirely new light on the sources of the 1929–33 Great Depression in the United States. The Great Depression, they argued, had nothing to do with the liquidity trap postulated by Keynes, or with some fundamental disequilibrium affecting capitalist economies which could only be corrected by programmes of public investment. It was, they said, purely and simply a direct result of the ineptitude of the United States equivalent of a central bank, the Federal Reserve Board.

In 1928, the 'Fed', concerned that the stock market boom, and the tidal wave of share speculation taking place, was bound to end in tears, decided to impose a policy of monetary restraint. A modest contraction of the money supply, begun in 1929, gave way to a much more substantial fall over the following three years.

The Fed, having no experience of the sort of financial crash it had inadvertently helped to set in train, responded to the collapsing economy, not by easing monetary policy and injecting liquidity, but by a further contraction. Over the period 1929 to 1933, the stock of money fell by more than a third. According to Friedman,

> It fell because the Federal Reserve System forced or permitted a sharp reduction in the monetary base, because it failed to exercise the responsibilities assigned to it in the Federal Reserve Act to provide liquidity to the banking system. The Great Contraction is tragic testimony to the power of monetary policy – not, as Keynes and so many of his contemporaries believed, evidence of its impotence.

More importantly, in his view, with nearly 10,000 banking failures and the most severe recession in United States economic history, the period demonstrated the fallibility of discretionary economic policies in general, and of discretionary monetary policy in particular. Had the Fed been pursuing a pre-arranged growth path for the money stock – monetary rules – the Great Depression would at best never have happened at all, and at worst would have been confined to a short-lived downturn, quickly reversed.

In five other recessions covered in the *Monetary History* – those of 1875–8, 1892–4, 1906–8, 1920–21 and 1937–8 – a prior decline in the stock of money was discovered. This, along with the evidence during periods of inflation, convinced Friedman that the direction of causation ran from monetary change to variations in economic activity, and not the other way round.

On average, peaks in the growth rate of the money stock were found to precede peaks in economic activity by 16 months. Troughs in monetary growth preceded cyclical low points for the economy by an average of 12 months. In each case, the lag was found to vary considerably. The lag before peaks varied from 6 to 29 months; that before troughs, from 4 to 22 months. So, as Friedman was the first to admit, a monetarist model will not be of much use in predicting, to the month, when a given change in the money supply will feed through to income and prices.

The introduction of cycles in economic activity into the debate raises again the question of the direction of causation. The peak in monetary growth now recorded could as well be the response to the last high point in activity as the forerunner of the next one. This criticism, later refined by Friedman's Keynesian critics, has never been satisfactorily answered.

Another criticism of the quantity theory, echoed in the Radcliffe Committee's report, was that the velocity of circulation is not stable but varies in response to economic conditions. Usually it was thought that velocity acted to neutralize changes in the money stock – rising when it was contracting, and vice versa.

Friedman's results did not fully support the existence of unchanging velocity of circulation. In the long term, it was discovered, there was a steady fall in the income velocity of circulation. A later work, also written with Anna Schwarz, *Monetary Trends in the United States and the United Kingdom* (1982), found that, over the period from 1867 to 1975, every 1 per cent rise in real income per head was accompanied by a rise of 1.8 per cent in real cash balances per head. But a steady long-term fall in velocity posed no great problems for Friedman or the quantity theory. He explained it by reference to the status of money as a luxury good – the more prosperous people become, the more they will be prepared to pay for the convenience of holding money. Interestingly, declining long-term velocity runs counter to what the Radcliffe Committee intuitively expected. The committee argued that velocity would tend to rise during periods of economic development, because of increasing financial sophistication.

Friedman's other main finding on velocity was more problematical. Velocity tended to rise during upswings in the business cycle, and fall during the downswings. The effects of an increase in the money supply would thus be exaggerated during a period of expansion, while a contraction in the money stock, its effects compounded by declining velocity, would accentuate the downturn.

Cyclical fluctuations in velocity, while not operating in such a way as to neutralize changes in the money stock, were a difficulty. They appeared to upset the quantity theory view of a stable demand for money function, and hence stable velocity.

But Friedman was nothing if not tenacious. The cyclical behaviour of velocity, he said, fitted perfectly his concept that permanent income, rather than actual income, formed the basis of spending decisions. Permanent income, a concept invented by Friedman, is the individual's notion of long-run sustainable income, after removing the short-term, or transitory, influences on income. During the upswing of the cycle, actual income rises above permanent income; in the downswing the opposite occurs. Therefore, the permanent income velocity of circulation is in the first place much more stable than velocity measured on actual income. And secondly, those movements that remained over cycles were consistent with the long-term trend for velocity, slowly declining as income rises.

In the early 1960s, the period of his most intensive research, Friedman conducted another celebrated study, this time collaborating with David Meiselman. It presented the economics equivalent of a championship boxing bout. A Keynesian model and a monetarist model were set up against one another to see which, over the sixty-one-year period covered, best explained events. The results were criticized, mainly because the authors were deemed to have chosen a Keynesian model with which no self-respecting Keynesian would have wished to be associated. The conclusions were, however, clear. There was a clear and stable link between growth in the money stock and growth in money income (national output in money terms). On the other hand, the Keynesian links between government spending and money income were weak and unstable.

Keynesian economists, faced with such a direct attack, hit back. Friedman and Meiselman, they said, had not even achieved a technical knock-out. The results were suspect and the contest invalid, a lean and fit monetarist challenger having been put into the ring against a weak parody of the Keynesian champion. But Friedman had put his opponents on the defensive, shifting the onus of proof away from the emerging monetarist model and on to the Keynesian conventional wisdom.

This was to stand him in good stead for his next major challenge to the existing orthodoxy. This was his attack on the principle, underlying economic policy decisions in this period, that there was a trade-off between unemployment and inflation. This belief was so widespread that it hardly needed any theoretical support. But it had such support, in the form of the Phillips curve.

The Phillips Curve

Professor Alban Phillips, an engineer turned economist, worked on long runs of data. In this respect, at least, he was like Friedman. But his most important work, published in 1958, came to sharply differing conclusions about the nature and causes of inflation. Phillips tested the hypothesis that the price of labour – wage rates – depends upon its demand. The relationship could be expected to reveal itself in two main ways. When the level of unemployment is very low, employers will outbid one another for workers. The workers are in a sellers' market; their services go to the highest bidder. But when unemployment is high and demand for labour slack, workers will be reluctant to accept wage reductions, but will accept either smaller wage rises, or no increases at all.

Alongside the level of unemployment, Phillips argued, its rate of change was likely to be very important, providing an indicator of the rate of change of demand for labour. So the effect on money wage rates will differ, depending on whether a given level of unemployment is steady, rising, or falling.

Phillips added a third, complicating factor. This was the impact on money wages of changes in the cost of living, as measured by retail or consumer prices. But this effect, he said, was only likely to be important when prices have been pushed up sharply by higher import costs, perhaps resulting from some overseas disturbance.

Phillips split his historical data into three time periods – 1861 to 1913, 1913 to 1948, and 1948 to 1957. He found, as the hypothesis suggested, that the relationship between money wages and unemployment was not a straight line. There were limits at both ends of the scale. Even at very low levels of unemployment, employers called a halt to the process of outbidding each other, perhaps because they could see the next cyclical downturn on the horizon. Workers, too, even at very high levels of unemployment, were only occasionally prepared to accept reductions in money wages.

Examples of such wage reductions occurred in the late nineteenth century and in the inter-war period, but not in the post-war years. This was because unemployment in the period from 1948 to 1957 averaged 2 to 3 per cent in Britain, and because the Welfare State was in operation, providing workers with an alternative, in the form of benefits, to unacceptable wage cuts.

There were periods, during the American Civil War of the 1860s and the Korean War of the early 1950s, when big increases in import costs emerged as the driving force for wage rises. But in general the Phillips curve, running from low unemployment and rapid money wage rises to high unemployment and low rises in wages, held.

Having established that the hypothesis fitted the data over ninety-six years, Phillips was able to draw some lessons for policy, based on the most recent data. These were that, with productivity growing at its post-war average rate of 2 per cent a year, the level of unemployment 'needed' for stable prices was just under 2.5 per cent of the workforce. If for some reason productivity stopped growing, or the goal of policy was stable wage rates, the unemployment rate would need to be rather higher – around 5.5 per cent.

The message was clear. There were inflationary consequences for economic policy directed towards employment. A policy which achieved too low an unemployment rate, say 1 per cent, would result in inflation. On the other hand, a policy which deliberately brought about 7 or 8 per cent unemployment would be unnecessarily harsh, producing zero inflation, no better than with 2.5 per cent unemployment, assuming the presence of productivity growth.

The Keynesian framework of policy in the post-war years was therefore a framework for both unemployment and inflation. By ensuring a level of aggregate demand consistent with 2.5 per cent unemployment and topping it up or reducing it where necessary through government spending, policy-makers could ensure price stability, except in the rare instances where import costs rose sharply. With this sort of power implicit in fiscal policy, there was no need for the sort of monetary discipline urged by the monetarists.

The Natural Rate of Unemployment

During the 1960s, Friedman's work on the quantity theory and the consumption function, together with his ambitious empirical researches, had earned him a considerable reputation and following. He was elected president of the American Economic Association in 1967, and chose the occasion of his presidential address in December of that year to attack the simple Phillips curve. The Phillips relationship had in any case begun to show signs of strain, reflected in the condition of simultaneously rising unemployment and inflation, without an obvious explanation in the form of sharply higher import costs.

Friedman borrowed and adapted a concept from the Swedish economist, Knut Wicksell. Wicksell had described a 'natural' rate of interest at which an economy without inflation will settle. The actual rate can only be pushed below the natural rate if the monetary authorities embark on a policy of inflation. It can only be forced above it by means of deflation.

The concept, Friedman said, was directly applicable to the rate of unemployment. At any one time there is a natural rate of unemployment for the economy, determined by factors such as the ease with which individuals can move to find work and the amount of information that is available on job vacancies. The natural rate will tend to be lower in economies where the labour market is efficient, and vice versa. It may be higher the more generous the system of state benefits, which permit individuals to take longer to look for another job. Unemployment below the natural rate was an indication of a tight labour market, and in this situation real wage rates were likely to be bid up. Unemployment above the natural rate would produce declining real wages.

It looked, on the face of it, like the Phillips curve in slightly different language. But it was not. The crucial distinction missed by Phillips, Friedman claimed, was that between real and money wages. In everyday world conditions of rising prices, the difference between money and real, or inflation-adjusted, wages could be important.

Friedman described what would happen should the government decide to push unemployment below its natural rate of, say, 3 per cent. This is achieved by expanding the money supply, and the initial effects are favourable. Through the usual quantity theory route, cash balances become higher than people want them to be. The surplus cash is spent, and there is higher spending and income in the economy. As Friedman explained in his 1967 AEA address:

> To begin with, much or most of the rise in income will take the form of an increase in output and employment rather than in prices. People have been expecting prices to be stable, and prices and wages have been set for some time in the future on that basis. It takes time for people to adjust to a new state of demand. Producers will tend to react to the initial expansion in aggregate demand by increasing output, employees by working longer hours, and the unemployed by taking jobs at former nominal (money) wages. This much is pretty standard doctrine.

But then the adverse effects start to creep in. Because of the rise in demand for their products caused by the monetary expansion, firms put up prices. Rising prices have the effect of reducing real wages. Workers notice the decline in their real wages that has resulted from unanticipated inflation and are determined not to get caught out again. Their former belief in stable prices turns into an expectation of rising prices. In the next round of wage negotiations, the expectation of rising prices leads to wage demands which will compensate, and more, for higher prices. And the effect of these higher wage demands is to push up unemployment.

The story does not end here. The government, if still aiming to keep unemployment below the natural rate of 3 per cent, has to go through the same process again, but this time in an economy where expectations of rising prices already exist.

The trick can only be repeated if the next monetary expansion embarked upon by the authorities provides for, not just the inflation that everyone has built into their expectations, but more: to give a degree of unanticipated inflation. A policy of keeping unemployment below its natural rate has to involve, if the analysis is correct, not simply inflation but an accelerating rate of inflation.

Friedman had not quite demolished the Phillips curve. There was, he admitted, always a temporary trade-off between unemployment and inflation. But there was no permanent trade-off. The point is illustrated by returning to the example where the natural rate is 3 per cent. The government's first effort at achieving unemployment below the natural rate is at the expense of, say, 2 per cent inflation. Assuming the next effort has to include the same amount of unanticipated inflation, it is achieved at the cost of 4 per cent inflation.

The two points, unemployment below 3 per cent and 2 per cent inflation, and the same unemployment rate but with 4 per cent inflation, cannot be on the same Phillips curve. For the Phillips relationship to hold, other things being equal, 4 per cent inflation would have to be associated with a lower unemployment rate.

The explanation is that, between the two periods, the Phillips curve has moved upwards and outwards. And next time, when 6 per cent inflation is needed for the same, sub-natural unemployment rate, the curve will have moved again. And so on. The long-term relationship between inflation and unemployment cannot therefore be couched in terms of a single Phillips curve, but by means of points on a series of different curves. This was Friedman's famous long-run vertical Phillips curve, capturing the impotence of the authorities in attempts to drive unemployment below its natural rate by expanding the economy.

Each attempt is doomed to dissipate itself in ever-increasing rates of inflation. The solution, Friedman concluded, is not to try. A far better approach is to control the money supply in order to achieve the desired outcome for the price level, using other methods, if necessary, to reduce unemployment.

As Friedman was aware, the expression 'natural rate of unemployment' had a certain depressing inevitability about it which could make it difficult for

Fig. 1 Phillips curves

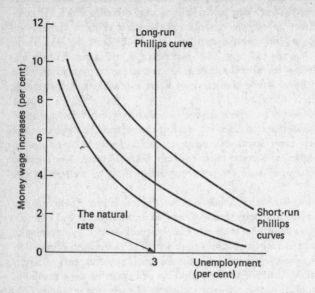

many people to accept. 'Let me emphasize that by using the term "natural" rate of unemployment, I do not mean to suggest that it is immutable and unchangeable,' he wrote.

> On the contrary, many of the market characteristics that determine its level are man-made and policy-made. In the United States, for example, legal minimum wage rates ... and the strength of labour unions all make the natural rate of unemployment higher than it would otherwise be. Improvements in employment exchanges, in availability of information about job vacancies and labour supply, and so on, would tend to lower the natural rate of unemployment.

Later variations on the concept of the natural rate of unemployment adopted less controversial but decidedly clumsier names. These included the 'constant inflation rate of unemployment' and the 'non-accelerating inflation rate of unemployment', or NAIRU, which came into general usage in the 1980s.

NAIRU, while unlikely to win any prizes for elegance, captured the idea that the monetarists were trying to get across more effectively. It could not be confused with the idea of some unchangeable long-term unemployment equilibrium for the economy as, despite Friedman's protestations, the natural rate often was. Rather, NAIRU was self-explanatory. All it said was that in the conditions existing at the time, and in particular the organization and efficiency of the labour market, there was a rate of unemployment at which there was no tendency for inflation to accelerate. NAIRU was the minimum level of unemployment that could be achieved by the expansion of demand – any attempt to drive unemployment below NAIRU will be punished by higher inflation.

It was thought that the way to lower NAIRU was to make the labour market operate more efficiently, for example by abolishing minimum wage legislation and curbing the power of the unions. However, in the 1980s a more powerful factor appeared to be at work in the opposite direction, that is, in raising NAIRU. This was the existence of high unemployment itself. The indications are that when unemployment is high and long-lasting, many of the unemployed cease to exert an influence on the wage bargaining process. Britain's long-term unemployed, for all their influence on the wages of those in employment, could as well have been in another country.

Whether it was called the natural rate or NAIRU, there was a fundamental question for Friedman and the other protagonists of the doctrine to answer. What if a government, deciding that the natural rate is an acceptable level of unemployment to aim for, adopts it as a target? Cannot monetary and fiscal policy then be used, without adverse consequences, to prevent the actual rate from departing from the natural rate?

Friedman's answer to this was a firm 'No'. Targeting the natural rate was not possible because there is no good way of knowing exactly what it is at any one time. Changes in the structure of the labour market, or increases in union power, can have the effect of shifting the natural rate around. There is evidence that during prolonged periods of high unemployment, the natural rate itself also increases.

In addition, the actual rate may depart from the natural rate for any number of reasons, and such departures may be only temporary. Attempting to tackle these through a general economic expansion or contraction may only introduce extra instability. The time lag between policy-makers noticing that un-employment is higher than it should be and expansionary policy taking effect may mean that the economy is boosted just at the time when unemploy-ment is falling independently. The consequences would be seen in higher inflation.

Like Keynes in the 1930s, Friedman's explanation enjoyed the advantage of fitting, much better than the simple Phillips curve, the conditions emerging at the time he was writing. In the 1960s, in several major economies a pattern had developed in which governments, while generally successful in targeting un-employment at low levels, only did so at the expense of higher inflation.

In the United States, consumer price inflation in 1960 was 1 per cent and the unemployment rate 5.5 per cent. Ten years later, unemployment was virtually unchanged at 5 per cent, but inflation had risen to a rate of 6 per cent.

In Britain a far more worrying condition had emerged. Britain, like the United States, had a 1 per cent inflation rate in 1960. By 1970, again matching the experience across the Atlantic, it had risen to a little over 6 per cent. But in the meantime unemployment had nearly doubled. The level of unemployment, excluding school-leavers, rose from 370,000 in 1960 to 600,000 in 1970. This was the first intimation of 'stagflation'.

The natural rate hypothesis could offer an explanation, or rather a choice of explanations, for the twin woes of inflation and unemployment afflicting Britain. Simultaneously rising inflation and unemployment could be due to the fact that the government, having tried to target a low rate of unemployment, was forced to draw back when the inflationary consequences became too severe, until the next attempt to force unemployment below its natural rate. But each successive effort to reduce unemployment began from a higher point, both for inflation and unemployment, than the one before it.

Alternatively, and this may offer a better explanation of the British experience, the natural rate itself may have been increasing, because of growing union power and the introduction of policies which obstructed the free workings of the labour market.

Friedman was cautious in 1967 about the time that it would take for damaging inflationary expectations to exert themselves. The initial favourable effects of an unemployment-reducing expansion could last for two to five years, he suggested, and expectations might take twenty years to work through fully. In the 1970s, as we shall see, expectations could wreak havoc over a much shorter time scale.

3

THE END OF CONSENSUS

The late 1960s was a time of growing strain and imbalance for the world economy. Inflation rates in the Western industrialized countries were rising. At the beginning of the decade average inflation was less than 2 per cent; at the end it was 5 per cent.

The Bretton Woods system of fixed exchange rates was cracking up. Sterling's devaluation in 1967 was one major blow and the system was to fail completely six years later. Doubt and dissatisfaction were widespread, despite the achievement of 4 or 5 per cent a year growth rates in the industrialized world. Among economists, there was increasing concern about the frequent resort to artificial devices such as prices and incomes policies.

The tensions came from a number of quarters. America's involvement in the Vietnam war, with its increasing demands on the Federal budget, was one scapegoat. As well as draining the United States financially, the war appeared to sap the morale of the world's leading economy, with damaging knock-on effects for other countries. Others saw the effects of the war as compounding the dangers of policy in the Kennedy–Johnson years, with ambitious Keynesian plans for the economy.

The Great Society programme of 1965 was certainly ambitious, although many of its goals were submerged in budgetary pressures. It set a tone of expansionary fiscal policy, which was echoed in a number of countries. There was a general trend for the public sector to take up an increasing share of the economy. This, whatever the underlying explanation for it, was enough, in the view of many economists, to produce instability and, because of the rising tax burden, to lead to slower, less healthily based economic growth.

The years of post-war recovery had been impressive, so much so that the world economy may have done too well for its own good. Expectations of growth and prosperity had built up, perhaps to unsustainable levels. Something had to give. There was a steady increase in the power of organized labour. The trade unions, particularly in Britain, were roundly blamed for a variety of economic woes – those actually occurring and those that seemed about to occur.

To the monetarists, all these supposed explanations were, in fact, just symptoms of a deeper problem. The world was paying the price, quite literally, for ignoring money. It was therefore no surprise that inflation was rising and that the pressure of too much money in the system was causing damaging currency instabilities.

The Collapse of Bretton Woods

The post-war system of fixed exchange rates, known as the Bretton Woods system after the village in New Hampshire where it was hammered out in 1944, finally collapsed in March 1973. Its survival for nearly thirty years, from the end of the war to the rise of the Organization of Petroleum Exporting Countries, evokes a modern golden age of strong growth and steady prices. Re-assemble Bretton Woods, it is said, and those conditions would return.

The system, to be fair, has had rather too good a press, conditioned by comparisons with the sharp currency swings and persistent instability of the floating rate era of the late 1970s and 1980s. It is often forgotten that the system envisaged in 1944 did not begin operating properly until the early 1960s, when the countries of Western Europe, as well as Japan, allowed free access to the foreign exchange markets for current account transactions. Even then, exchange controls on capital transactions remained firmly in place and, indeed, may have been essential for the preservation of fixed exchange rates.

In Britain, a fierce debate over devaluation dominated economic policy for much of the 1960s, to an extent that, in retrospect, is hard to believe. The eventual decision to devalue the pound from $2.80 to $2.40, taken with a heavy heart by the Prime Minister, Harold Wilson, in November 1967, came after years of soul-searching. It provided the first major wrinkle in the Bretton Woods system. The decision to float the pound by the Conservative Prime Minister, Edward Heath, in June 1972 was the system's death knell.

Even the staunchest monetarist supporters of free markets have conceded that fixed exchange rates acted as a discipline on policy in the post-war years. Nigel Lawson, the second of Margaret Thatcher's Chancellors, accepted that the Bretton Woods system brought effective pressure to bear on policy, admittedly in a less satisfactory way than self-imposed monetary discipline. 'During this period foreign exchange crises served as a proxy for monetary disciplines,' he wrote in 1980.

After the Radcliffe Committee's rejection of monetarism in 1959, the exchange rate retained its central role in monetary policy in Britain. The aim of policy was to produce low and stable interest rates, in support of government funding and a fiscal policy directed towards full employment. All too often, pressures on sterling, with frequent balance of payments crises, thwarted this aim. The result was a monetary policy which, while intended to be fully accommodative, was not loose enough to do too much damage. Professor Michael Artis has written of the 1960s: 'It seems unlikely that monetary policy did very much for good or bad in this period; it did not do very much at all, and was not supposed to.'

Elsewhere the exchange rate also played a key role, although not always so traumatically as in Britain. In Germany, for example, monetary policy had to be relaxed on several occasions in response to upward pressure on the exchange rate. In 1960, at the height of a boom, a tight monetary policy was abandoned because capital inflows were threatening to force a Deutschmark revaluation.

The inherent weakness of the Bretton Woods system, recognized long before its demise, was that, while imposing policy disciplines on others, whether they were strong or weak currency countries, it failed to do so at the heart of the system – in the United States. The post-war framework of fixed exchange rates was a dollar system, at the insistence of the Americans. Keynes had attended the Bretton Woods conference of 1944 armed with a plan under which a new paper currency, Bancor, would form the basis of a system administered by a new international central bank. But proposals for a dollar-based system, put forward by the US Treasury Secretary, Harry Dexter White, won the day. The dollar, it is true, was pegged to gold, at a fixed price of $35 an ounce, but all other parities were in terms of the dollar. The task of ensuring that their currencies stayed at these parities fell to the countries concerned. The dollar was not required to adjust.

This was not the only bias in the Bretton Woods framework. There was also, and damagingly, a bias towards dollar weakness built into the arrangements. This was because, in order to have the weaponry to hand to preserve the dollar parities of their currencies, central banks needed dollar reserves. And, at a time when flows across the exchanges were increasing strongly – initially through sharply rising world trade – central banks needed, not just a fixed stock of dollars, but an increasing supply.

The Bank of Japan, for example, could only achieve adequate growth in reserves by buying dollars in the foreign exchange markets. If the dollar was already strong, the effect of this would be to push it up further, threatening the yen's parity against the dollar. Therefore the Bank of Japan could only buy when the dollar was weak, and an adequate build-up of Japanese central bank reserves required that the dollar was generally weak. Extending this to all other central banks produces the Bretton Woods paradox – the dollar, the basis of the system, also had to be its weakest currency.

Monetary policy in the United States was conducted in this context. Freed from the disciplines faced by others, indeed almost obliged to run a loose policy to ensure an adequate supply of dollars to the world, the authorities could happily concentrate on the domestic objective of full employment, followed – some way behind – by price stability.

There were occasions when dollar outflows became too large, even for a system hungry for dollars. These were generally tackled with special measures, not a shift in overall policy. Between 1960 and 1962, the Federal Reserve Board attempted Operation Twist, raising short-term interest rates relative to long rates, to stem capital outflows. In 1963 the Interest Equalization Tax was introduced and extended into the Foreign Credit Restraint Program, adopted in 1965. But such measures failed to achieve the desired objective. The rapid growth of the Eurodollar market during the 1960s was testimony to capital's ability to by-pass official controls.

The Bretton Woods system, creaking by the late 1960s, finally collapsed in March 1973, but not before wreaking havoc. As the system went through its death throes and a last-ditch effort was made to maintain fixed rates, massive dollar outflows resulted in major rises in money supply around the world. The United States exported loose money policies.

The fixed rate system did not go down without a fight. On 15 August 1971, excessive pressure on the dollar forced President Nixon to suspend the convertibility of the dollar into gold. Four months later, finance ministers and central bankers of the major countries met at the Smithsonian Institution in Washington to conclude an agreement to devalue the dollar against all currencies and raise the official gold price from $35 to $38.50 an ounce, although dollar inconvertibility remained.

The Smithsonian Agreement put the pound back to $2.60, partially reversing the difficult but necessary devaluation of 1967. It did not last. Britain, with Ireland and Denmark, temporarily joined the currency 'snake' set up by the original six EEC members in May 1972.

One month later, embarrassingly, the pound had to be allowed to float free of both the dollar and the semi-fixed EEC snake. The Bretton Woods system, now clearly held together with sticking plaster, survived for another nine months. But in early 1973, the Swiss franc, Italian lira and Japanese yen were unpegged from the dollar. And on 16 March 1973, at the second of two meetings that month in Paris, the major industrialized countries agreed to abandon fixed parities and adopt floating exchange rates.

Labour's Monetary Targets

When people think of Britain's Labour Party in connection with monetarism and monetary targets, it is usually in the context of their adoption, in 1976, by the then Chancellor of the Exchequer, Denis Healey. There was, however, an earlier episode.

Immediately following the devaluation of sterling in November 1967, a Letter of Intent to the International Monetary Fund committed the government to growth in the money supply in 1968 at or below its rate of increase in 1967. The Letter, published on 30 November 1967, the day after Roy Jenkins had replaced James Callaghan as Chancellor of the Exchequer, was chiefly concerned with the balance of payments, and how quickly the devaluation would act on Britain's current account deficit. But it also represented the first formal commitment to monetary targets by a post-war British government.

While the achievement of the balance of payments target set out in the Letter of Intent proved difficult – the Chancellor promised a shift into current account surplus in the second half of 1968 – the monetary targets were achieved. The M1 measure of money (notes and coin plus sight deposits in sterling – narrow money) grew by 5.6 per cent in 1968, down from its 8.6 per cent rise in 1967. Growth in the broader money measures also slowed.

It was typical of the period, however, that this slow-down in monetary growth was achieved mainly through a sharp tightening of fiscal policy. Cuts in planned public expenditure were announced shortly after the devaluation, to be followed, in the spring of 1968, by a tax-raising Budget. Roy Jenkins's March 1968 Budget stood out, at the time, as among the most deflationary in the post-war era, raising taxation by nearly £1 billion overall.

The bold fiscal measures brought about a sharp reduction in the budget deficit. A slower rate of monetary growth was thus achieved without prohibitively high interest rates. Bank rate, having been increased from 6 to 8 per cent in November 1967, was brought down slowly during 1968, to 7.5 per cent in March and 7 per cent in September.

The initial success in controlling the money supply was little noticed outside the official circles of the Treasury, the Bank of England and the International Monetary Fund in Washington. However, it coincided with the first major stirrings of interest in monetarism in Britain, and the beginnings of the idea that the economics of Milton Friedman could be highly relevant. Then, as later, Britain was a fertile breeding-ground for such ideas. The traumas of the 1967 devaluation and the many indications of relative economic decline produced a widespread dissatisfaction with economic policy, and the view that the post-war Keynesian consensus was not delivering the goods in Britain.

Samuel Brittan, the principal economics commentator for the *Financial Times*, had begun to take an interest in the Chicago revival of the quantity theory. Brittan, who had left journalism temporarily to advise the short-lived Department of Economic Affairs, was aware of the shortcomings of existing policy from the point of view of both practitioner and observer. During 1968 and 1969 he described the nature of the Chicago alternative and helped produce a shift of thinking, particularly in the City of London. Economists at the Bank of England, brought up in the traditions of the Radcliffe Committee, started to take an interest.

Peter Jay, then economics editor of *The Times,* was well connected in the Labour Party – as son of Douglas Jay, a minister in the Wilson government, and son-in-law of James Callaghan, the former Chancellor and later Prime Minister. He also began to shift towards monetarism at this time. In May 1968, he wrote an article entitled 'Inflation – Is the Money Supply Crucial?'. In October 1968, *The Times* carried a leading article, by tradition anonymous but written by Jay, headlined 'Understanding the Role of the Money Supply'.

In December 1968, the British magazine the *Banker* devoted an issue to monetarism, including contributions from Friedman as well as from the eminent financial journalist Harold Wincott. The Institute of Economic Affairs, founded in 1957 with the aim of countering the drift towards state control of the economy and regulatory interference in the workings of markets, provided an outlet for monetarist views. The monetarist view of macro-economics fitted in with the IEA's philosophy on micro-economics and the free market. A paper published in 1969 by the IEA examined the behaviour of the British economy in quantity theory terms. 'Money in Boom and Slump', by Alan Walters, later personal economic adviser to Margaret Thatcher, set the tone for the IEA's stronger pro-monetarist influence during the 1970s.

The flurry of interest in monetarism at this time, while sowing the seeds for the counter-revolution of the 1970s was not accompanied by an economic policy that could remotely be described as textbook monetarism. The 1968 success in reducing monetary growth was achieved, as we have seen, principally through fiscal policy. A prices and incomes policy, anathema to monetarists, was firmly in place.

This was not an elevation of monetary policy to pre-eminence in economic policy-making. Rather, the post-devaluation period was a temporary injection into policy of the discipline needed to protect the pound's new parity of $2.40 which, during 1968, came under periodic pressure.

The fact that monetary policy remained firmly directed towards preserving the parity of sterling could be seen even more clearly in 1969. The Treasury wanted to renew $1 billion of a special International Monetary Fund stand-by credit facility, taken out in 1965. After some months of negotiation, a second Letter of Intent was sent to the IMF in June 1969. It specified a new monetary target for the fiscal year 1969/70. Domestic credit expansion was to be limited to no more than £400 million.

Domestic credit expansion, a concept devised at the IMF, is, despite its name, particularly geared towards the external target of maintaining the exchange rate. It measures the broad money stock, adjusted for changes in foreign exchange reserves and official overseas borrowing. As it turned out, Roy Jenkins was able to announce in his April 1970 Budget that the target for domestic credit expansion had been easily achieved. The return of the current account to surplus in 1969, and the restoration of confidence in sterling, produced a fall in the domestic credit expansion measure in 1969/70. A £900 million limit on domestic credit expansion was announced for 1970/71, and the Chancellor predicted that broad money would rise by less than this.

It was not to be. Two months after the April 1970 Budget, Labour was toppled from office by the Conservatives, led by Edward Heath. Jenkins, who became one of the founder members of the Social Democratic Party in the early 1980s, had achieved substantial success in financial policy, with help from the IMF. The pressure was off the pound; the current account of the balance of payments was in surplus; and, perhaps most notably, the budget deficit had been eliminated and the public sector borrowing requirement was negative when he left office. But what was good for the Exchequer was not necessarily good for the party. Excessive fiscal caution was blamed for Labour's poor showing in the June 1970 election.

Heath's New Conservatism

Edward Heath was a new style of Conservative Prime Minister. Educated at a grammar school – the first Tory leader not to have emerged from one of the great public schools, he approached the task of government in the style of a marketing manager planning a new product launch. Weekend meetings and conferences were held, the most famous at Sundridge Park in September 1969 and at Selsdon Park (hence the soubriquet 'Selsdon Man') in January 1970.

Each potential minister went through what amounted to an intellectual assault course to overcome opposition to Conservative policies: opposition not from the electorate, but from the Civil Service. Defeat of the bureaucracy and a more efficient government machine was a key aim, but rolling back the frontiers of the state was perhaps central to policy. The aim was to reduce state involvement in all areas, including many of the nationalized industries. 'Lame ducks', as loss-making concerns came to be described, would not be helped along. The individual was to become more self-reliant. Excessive trade union power was to be reined back through a programme of industrial relations legislation. Taxation would not necessarily be cut drastically, but direct taxes, which acted against incentive and enterprise, were to be reduced in favour of higher indirect taxes. It was, in short, very similar to the programme adopted by Margaret Thatcher nine years later, with one essential difference. There was no commitment to control the money supply.

This, however, was hardly remarkable at the time. Labour's experience with monetary targets, if it was noticed at all, was seen as the necessary medicine to take for getting the country through a temporary malaise brought on, in part, by Labour policies. Under the Conservatives, who were confident enough to reject prices and incomes policies, these problems were not expected to arise.

The new Conservative Chancellor of the Exchequer, Iain Macleod, was one of the most respected politicians of his time. The City trusted him, although he was from the moderate wing of the party. Macleod had supported Heath in his climb to Conservative Party leadership. He had been a key influence on the formation of policy ideas in opposition. It was, therefore, a blow of incalculable magnitude when in July 1970, just a month after the election, he died from a heart attack after an operation for appendicitis, at the early age of fifty-six.

Macleod was a hard act to follow, even if he had hardly begun his work as Chancellor. It is impossible to assess how, or if, subsequent events would have differed had he lived. The man given the unenviable task of taking over was Anthony Barber.

Although the financial position inherited from Labour was a strong one, there were a number of worrying signs for the economy, notably the combination of rising unemployment and inflation. One of Barber's first acts as Chancellor was to authorize an instruction from the Bank of England to the banks to slow down the pace of lending. But his first Budget, in October 1970, was a modest and neutral one, cutting public spending and income tax by almost exactly equivalent amounts.

Wages were rising sharply at the time of the election in the summer, and they accelerated over the following pay round, as the new government left pay determination to employers and the unions. The pay surge, while meriting concern, was viewed as a reaction to several years of incomes control, a storm which would quickly blow itself out. In 1970 and 1971, average earnings rose by nearly 12 per cent a year. But there was worse to come.

To monetarists, a sharp increase in wages is not the cause of inflation, it is one of the symptoms. And there was a parallel between the post-incomes policy surge in wages and the sharp increases in the money supply in the early 1970s. Just as incomes policies had kept the lid on wages, with the inevitable result that a head of steam would build up and blow it off, so controls on bank lending had done the same for money and credit.

Two institutional changes under Barber's chancellorship opened the floodgates for a monetary expansion of fearsome proportions. The first was the 1971 change in the Bank of England's system of monetary management to new arrangements known as Competition and Credit Control. The second was the decision to float the pound in June 1972. Either of these changes, taken alone, could have been enough to remove the monetary anchors. Together, they were a lethal combination.

Competition and Credit Control

The system of monetary management that had developed since the publication of the Radcliffe Report in 1959 was one which relied increasingly on quantitative controls on bank lending and hire purchase. The clearing banks, faced with lending ceilings throughout most of the 1960s, could derive no gain from competing on prices. The interest rate cartel between the major banks was thus firmly in place. But the big banks and the finance houses regarded the system, as it had evolved, as manifestly unfair. It produced a situation in which much of the growth in lending was conducted by a new breed of institution, the so-called secondary banks. The Bank of England sympathized.

The Bank's proposals for change, published in a document called 'Competition and Credit Control' in the spring of 1971 and brought into effect in the autumn, contained several elements. There was to be a move away from quantitative controls, and any controls, principally qualitative, which remained would extend to a wider range of institutions than just the clearing banks and finance houses.

A report by the National Board for Prices and Incomes in 1967 had come out strongly against the banks' interest rate cartel, and this was echoed in the 1968 Monopolies Commission report on the proposed merger between Barclays Bank, Lloyds Bank and Martins Bank. The Bank of England's 1971 changes abolished the cartel.

Competition and Credit Control also introduced a change in the rules governing the liquid assets that the banks were required to hold. From 1963, banks had to hold at least 28 per cent of their deposit liabilities in liquid assets, with a minimum of 8 per cent in cash. The 1971 changes introduced a new concept: reserve asset ratios. Reserve assets were defined as those assets readily convertible to cash, but not cash itself. They included balances at the Bank of England, money at call in the money markets, and most short-term bills. The reserve asset ratio was set at 12.5 per cent. The clearing banks were required to hold the equivalent of 1.5 per cent of liabilities in the form of non-interest-bearing Special Deposits at the Bank of England, to be included in their reserve asset ratio. The significance of these Special Deposits will be seen later.

Finally, it was announced that the Government Broker – the Treasury's agent in the gilt-edged market – would end his practice of supporting the market in government stocks, except in the case of stocks with less than a year to run until maturity. During the 1960s the Government Broker had operated a policy of buying stock whenever selling pressure threatened to drive down prices too sharply. The argument was that only by thus ensuring a stable market could the Government Broker proceed with his main task of funding government borrowing. But the practice had the undesirable consequence of, in effect, giving traders a one-way option. They could buy stock in the expectation of a price rise, knowing that it was possible to withdraw, with minimal losses, if the market began to weaken. From 1971, this guarantee was removed.

The essence of Competition and Credit Control was a freeing of the markets in money, credit and government debt, in line with Conservative free market philosophy. It was recognized, and accepted, that one result would be greater volatility for interest rates and the price of government stocks.

Control over credit would be exerted through its price, and not through direct controls which distorted the market. The Bank of England was aware that, as the new system came into play, there would be a short-term, and possibly quite sharp, expansion of the money supply; but in 1971 this was not thought to be an unwelcome side-effect.

The Barber Boom

During 1971 unemployment began to rise strongly, outweighing concern about rising inflation. Unemployment increased by more than 250,000 in 1971 and the 'headline' total, including school-leavers, rose above 900,000 late in the year, and threatened to break through one million – then an unheard-of figure for the post-war period – over the winter months. Inflation also edged up, to more than 9 per cent by the end of 1971.

To economists brought up in the tradition of the Phillips curve, the combination of rising unemployment and inflation and, in particular, strongly rising wages, was a puzzle that could only be rationalized by reference to the distorting effects of years of pay policy. To politicians brought up in the post-war full-employment tradition, there was only one response: unemployment had to be tackled.

The natural monetary expansion anticipated with the new Competition and Credit Control freedoms for the banks was helped along by two cuts in bank rate – from 7 to 6 per cent in April 1971; and from 6 to 5 per cent in September, on the eve of the introduction of the new system. These reductions, at a time of rising inflation, meant that the era of negative real interest rates had begun. It was to last for most of the next decade.

These moves towards looser monetary policy were seen as complementing – for this was still very much the time of Keynesian policy ideas – expansionary measures on the fiscal side. The 1971 Budget cut personal and company taxation by over £500 million, and was followed by an expansion of public works programmes and the repayment of post-war credits – compulsory personal savings for the 1939-45 war effort. These later measures injected a further £500 million into the economy.

Some expansion of the money supply was planned, but nowhere was it intended that there would be a huge explosion of money and credit. The banks, freed from the fetters of controls, immediately began to make up for lost time. New bank lending to the private sector, £1,320 million in 1970, rose to £1,860 million in 1971. In 1972 it surged to £6,430 million, and in 1973 to £6,830 million.

Chancellor of the Exchequer Barber dropped domestic credit expansion targets in 1971. His argument was that large inflows of short-term capital from abroad – 'hot money' – were rendering it misleading and inappropriate. No alternative monetary target appeared in its place.

Had there been monetary targets in the following two years, it is difficult to believe that they could have been set so generously as to accommodate what happened. At this time, although no official targets were published (or unofficial targets monitored within the Bank of England until 1973), M3 was regarded as the most appropriate broad money measure. M3 included notes and coins and all sterling sight and time deposits (current and deposit accounts). Unlike sterling M3, later to achieve prominence, it also included bank deposits by the private sector in foreign currencies.

By coincidence, its growth rates over 1972 and 1973 were identical. The figures might suggest close control by the authorities were it not for the fact that, in each case, the rise was 28 per cent. In other words, in just two years, the broad money stock in Britain had risen by more than 60 per cent.

When the money supply goes wildly out of control, and even without the benefit of monetary targets casual observation confirmed that something was amiss, there are two options open to the authorities.

The first is to take steps – and, clearly, draconian ones would have been required – to bring it to heel. Bank rate was raised from 5 to 6 per cent in June 1972 and, in a number of steps, to 9 per cent by the end of the year. But initially this reflected concern for the exchange rate rather than domestic monetary conditions. Only in 1973, when bank rate was pushed up to 13 per cent by the end of the year, could domestic factors be cited as the main cause. The second approach is to lay stress on the distortions present in the monetary aggregate concerned, distortions which permit the authorities to tolerate very rapid rates of increase. During the Thatcher experiment with monetarism, this approach was extensively adopted.

In 1972/3 several reasons were advanced for not taking too much notice of the M3 explosion. Part of it, probably most of it, was due to the banks taking back market share from other deposit-taking institutions, including the 'fringe' or secondary banks. This had the effect of boosting M3 but not broader measures of money, although the 1971 changes had in fact widened the definition of the monetary sector. As well as regaining market share, the banks were seen as innovating with new types of deposit, again producing a once-for-all, but not necessarily worrying, M3 rise.

Another factor was that the banks and their customers, rightly as it turned out, saw the new freedoms as temporary, so that there was an element of rushing to borrow ahead of the inevitable clamp-down by the Bank of England. Finally, the new volatility of interest rates allowed large corporate customers to take advantage of gaps between the banks' lending rates and money market interest rates. This practice of bill arbitrage – borrowing on overdraft from the bank and re-lending by issuing money market bills – added an unspecified, but possibly substantial, amount to M3.

Even allowing for distortions, growth in broad money was very considerable. The removal of the constraint of the fixed rate for sterling in June 1972, while not, as we have seen, removing the performance of sterling from the policy arena, did provide an opportunity to let the money supply rip.

The pound was floated on 23 June 1972, six months after the agreement at the Smithsonian Institution in Washington. It immediately fell by an average of 7 per cent and the cry went up that the pound was not so much floating as sinking. Anthony Barber had provided a forewarning of the decision to float in his March Budget, when he said that faster growth was more important than preserving sterling's fixed parity.

Clearly, the Conservatives were not going to repeat the mistakes of the previous Labour government, when the economy was sacrificed on the altar of an inappropriately high exchange rate. The 1972 Budget was heavily expansionary, cutting taxes by £1,200 million and setting a 5 per cent target for real economic growth. The decision to float the pound was a popular one, having been urged by a number of commentators.

Unfettered monetary growth initially worked wonders for the economy. Gross domestic product, in real terms, had risen by only 2 per cent in 1970 and a dismal 1.5 per cent in 1971. In 1972, growth picked up to 2.7 per cent, and in 1973 surged by an almost unprecedented 7.1 per cent. Unemployment fell back from nearly a million during the winter of 1971/2 to just over 500,000 in 1973.

It was all to end in tears. Monetarist economists were predicting that inflation, 7 per cent in 1972 and 9 per cent in 1973, would leap to rates that threatened the preservation of democracy, as we shall see in the next chapter.

The Secondary Banking Crisis

More immediately, and of greater concern at the time, was the emerging crisis in Britain's financial system. The easy money conditions of the early 1970s and the recapture by the banks of their traditional markets following Competition and Credit Control had encouraged the fringe banks to seek new areas of activity. The area they chose above all others was property development. The Bank of England, reflecting on the crisis some years later,* described the situation as follows:

> There was no other general area of economic activity which seemed to offer as good a prospective rate of return to an entrepreneur as property development. The conse-quence was that, with the necessary finance so readily to hand, far too much of it was undertaken all at once. This was given particular encouragement at that time of generally rising inflation by the widely held belief that property was the inflation hedge *par excellence*, a belief which was adhered to in some quarters with blind assurance.

The fringe banks obtained their deposits mainly from the rapidly expanding money markets – from funds placed there by banks, blue-chip companies and conservative financial institutions – and lent on to property companies and speculators. The bubble grew bigger and bigger until, following the tightening of monetary conditions by the Bank of England from the middle of 1973 onwards, and exacerbated by the freezing of business rents at the end of 1972, it burst.

The first casualty was the publicly quoted London and County Securities which had, unusually, a high proportion of its deposits from the general public. In November 1973, London and County, whose problems were known in the City, found that it could no longer obtain funds from the money markets. The City started to cast a critical eye over other, similar organizations, and found that they were in more or less the same position. There was a clear danger of panic and a complete collapse of confidence.

Even the major banks were not immune from this – at one stage National Westminster had to issue a public statement to say that it was safe – because of the fear of large-scale withdrawal of deposits by foreigners concerned about the stability of the British financial system. In the Bank of England's words: 'The problem was to avoid a widening circle of collapse through the contagion of fear.' And so, over the Christmas and New Year holiday at the end of 1973, the Control Committee of the Bank of England and the London and Scottish Clearing Banks, popularly known as 'the lifeboat', was set up.

The aim of 'the lifeboat' was quite straightforward: to provide liquidity for

* Bank of England *Quarterly Bulletin*, June 1978.

fringe banks and other organizations in cases where the markets had lost confidence. The scale of the support needed, however, could hardly have been envisaged in December 1973.

In the summer of 1974, market doubts began to emerge over major finance companies with large property interests and, in particular, the First National Finance Corporation and United Dominions Trust. These companies represented a very different proposition from the fringe banks, and threatened to swamp the lifeboat. In August 1974, the clearing banks informed the Bank of England that they were setting a limit of £1,200 million on lifeboat support – equivalent to 40 per cent of combined capital and reserves. Above that, the Bank was politely told, it was on its own.

The Bank shouldered this responsibility, carrying the sole risk for some of the liquidity support over the winter of 1974/5. In March 1975 the lifeboat totalled £1,285 million. But the storm was blowing itself out and the panic was subsiding. The Bank subsequently undertook two rescues, of Slater Walker Securities at the end of 1975 and of Edward Bates & Sons in May 1976. But from the March 1975 high point, the size of the lifeboat declined.

It was a time of widespread financial fears, and not just in Britain. The Franklin National Bank in New York came near to closure in 1974. The Bankhaus Herstatt in Germany did close, following large foreign exchange losses. In the new era of exchange rate volatility, these were rife. Large losses were reported at the Westdeutsche Landesbank, the Union Bank of Switzerland and the Lugano branch of Lloyds Bank International, the latter due to fraud.

To monetarists, the message was clear. Apart from setting in motion a train of events that was bound to lead to substantially higher inflation, a world-wide monetary binge had brought the international financial system within a whisker of collapse. The system survived, but only just. The case for prudent monetary control was stronger than ever.

4

THE RISE OF MONETARISM

For monetarists, and in particular British monetarists, the early 1970s were what the Great Depression had been for Keynes and his followers. Existing ideas about economic policy had been dealt a savage blow by actual events. The Keynesians could neither predict accurately what was going to happen, nor offer a convincing way out of the morass into which Western economies were sinking.

The nightmare of stagflation – simultaneous sharply rising prices and unemployment – had arrived. Keynes's recipe for dealing with unemployment looked inappropriate because of the dangers it held of setting off even higher inflation. The fine-tuning and touches on the tiller associated with post-war Keynesian demand management may or may not have been right in dealing with small changes in unemployment or the inflation rate. But once the Phillips curve trade-off between unemployment and inflation had, quite literally, disappeared off the edge of the page, policy-makers were left groping. It was rather like trying to find one outfit to wear in both blazing sunshine and a blizzard. It was small wonder that there was nothing quite right in the wardrobe.

In 1970, Friedman saw the economics profession in Britain as woefully behind the times, the latter having largely failed to see the writing on the wall for Keynesian economics. He was only too pleased to take on the role of missionary, taking his teaching to the natives. In his Wincott lecture of that year, 'The Counter-Revolution in Monetary Theory', he said:

> The debate about monetary effects in Britain is pursuing the identical course that it pursued in the United States about five or so years ago.
>
> I am sure that the same thing must have happened in the 1930s. When the British economists wandered over to the farther shores among their less cultivated American brethren, bringing to them the message of Keynes, they must have felt, as I have felt coming to these shores in the opposite direction, that this was where they came in. I am sure they then encountered the same objections that they had encountered in Britain five years earlier. And so it is today. Criticism of the monetary doctrines in this country today is at the naive, unsophisticated level we encountered in the USA about five or more years ago.

The time lag between the rise of monetarism in academic circles in the United States and Britain was longer than Friedman suggested. British monetarists at this time were faced with putting together a challenge akin to that mounted by Friedman in the 1950s.

Friedman's star continued to rise. In 1976, he was awarded the Nobel Prize in Economics. In his Nobel lecture, delivered in Stockholm in December of that year, he tackled the question of why rising inflation was associated with increasing levels of unemployment. After all, the natural rate hypothesis allowed for rising prices, but as a consequence of efforts to push unemployment below its natural rate.

The new condition, which Friedman described as 'slumpflation', could, he said, be explained within the context of the natural rate hypothesis. Governments responded to the onset of higher inflation by introducing controls on wages and prices. Such controls distorted the operation of markets, creating economic inefficiency and pushing the recorded rate of unemployment higher. Thus it was possible to explain unemployment and inflation rising together in the short term. But Friedman still believed that the central element of the natural rate hypothesis – the vertical long-run Phillips curve – would still hold.

One thing was certain, in Friedman's view. The state of affairs existing in the mid 1970s was dangerous and untenable. 'The present situation cannot last,' he concluded. 'It will either degenerate into hyper-inflation and radical change; or institutions will adjust to a situation of chronic inflation; or governments will adopt policies that will produce a low rate of inflation and less government intervention into the fixing of prices.'

This last provided a rallying-call for monetarists everywhere.

Beginnings of the Academic Backlash

Why do ideas gain and lose acceptance in the universities? Is it because there are genuine new discoveries or interpretations of both theory and evidence? Or is it another, often equally powerful factor, whereby a younger generation of academics feels bound to challenge the wisdom handed down by their teachers, in the manner of children rebelling against their parents?

In British universities in the 1970s, both factors played their part. For most of the 1960s, to be a monetarist in Britain was like having an unfortunate but embarrassing affliction which people were usually too polite to mention. It is overstating the case to talk of a debate between monetarists and Keynesians in Britain at this time. The majority of Keynesians were so confident of their position, and its immunity from any serious challenge, that they did not even bother to examine closely the monetarist case.

Sir Alan Walters has the longest monetarist pedigree of any British economist, although most of his later career has been occupied with other areas of economics. Walters ploughed a lonely furrow during the years of Keynesian policy, as he recalled in 1977:

> In the late 1950s and early 1960s only a handful of British economists – for the most part associated with the Institute of Economic Affairs – began to swim against the mainstream of conventional wisdom of [the] Cambridge, National Institute, Treasury and Bank of England establishment. At first, the establishment ignored them – expecting, I suppose, that they would become weary and rejoin the mainstream.

Walters did not become weary. Despite a lack of official interest, he produced a historical series for the money stock in Britain, to which Friedman later paid generous tribute. He attempted his own, admittedly much less ambitious, version of Friedman and Schwarz's *Monetary History of the United States*, applied to Britain. Walters's 'Money in Boom and Slump' was published as a pamphlet by the Institute of Economic Affairs in 1969.

The few lonely voices pressing the monetarist case in Britain made progress, but it was painfully slow. Any monetarist counter-revolution in the universities was clearly not going to occur without some additional help. It arrived, appropriately, in the form of the US cavalry; the call to charge had gone up, just as fittingly, at the University of Chicago. Towards the end of the 1960s, Harry Johnson became Professor of Economics at the London School of Economics, while retaining his professorship at Chicago. Canadian by birth, he was a brilliant and prolific advocate of monetarism. Moreover, because of his unique position straddling Chicago and London, he helped speed the dissemination in Britain of monetarist thinking from the other side of the Atlantic. He died at an early age in the mid 1970s, before seeing his considerable influence bear fruit in policy.

Johnson was the moving force behind the creation in 1969 of the Money Study Group at the London School of Economics, which has continued to provide a forum for debate on monetary theory and policy. His teaching undoubtedly moulded the thinking of a generation of LSE students, who then went out into the City of London, or the Government Economic Service, or who became teachers themselves. At this time, the exposure of LSE students to monetarism was greater than at any other British university. From 1968 to 1976, Alan Walters was also a professor there.

Among other things, Johnson was associated with the monetary approach to the balance of payments, later developed and refined into the 'international monetarist' ideas of the London Business School. This general approach holds that the effects of monetary changes, and in particular differential rates of growth of money between countries, show themselves first in the performance of the balance of payments and the exchange rate.

Other centres of monetarist thinking were developing. In 1971, at Manchester University, Professors David Laidler and Michael Parkin, with the help of a grant from the Social Science Research Council, embarked on a major study of the nature and causes of inflation. The Manchester Inflation Workshop, as it was called, produced empirical results consistent with the monetarist case. One of the two professors, Michael Parkin, had earlier produced research demonstrating the ineffectiveness of incomes policies. David Laidler started from a position of some sympathy with the view of inflation as a monetary phenomenon.

Laidler saw the Manchester results, although often highly tentative, as sound enough on which to base forecasts. In 1974, in evidence to the House of Commons Expenditure Committee, he accurately predicted that the rate of inflation would exceed 20 per cent in 1975, as a result of the sharp rises in the money supply in 1972 and 1973. His 'back of the envelope' calculations, as he described them, also forecast that the monetary slow-down of 1974 would lead to a big rise in unemployment.

It was something of a vintage period for the 'back of the envelope' monetarist forecasters. In early 1972, Alan Walters predicted that the acceleration in the money supply would result in a 1974 inflation rate of 'over 10 per cent and perhaps as high as 15 per cent'. Both Walters and Laidler came close: the actual inflation rates were 15.9 per cent in 1974 and 24.2 per cent in 1975.

Some of Laidler's predictions around this time were more far-reaching. In 1975, he argued that inflationary expectations had become so deeply embedded that only a long period of pain for the economy would exorcise them. He wrote:

> My own guess is that inflationary expectations are now so much more deeply embedded in the economy than they were in 1972 that unemployment of one million will not have so large an initial impact on the inflation rate now as it did then. And, given the speed of the current contraction, I have serious doubts about our ability to prevent unemployment going substantially above that figure in the next eighteen months. Even if we prevent the current recession turning into a major depression, and avoid over-reacting to unemployment with expansionary policies that, in bringing unemployment down, set up a yet more violent burst of inflation than we have experienced, we shall nevertheless see an average of a million unemployed for five years or more if we are to get the inflation rate below, say, five per cent by 1980.

Unemployment broke through one million during 1975 and subsequently stayed comfortably above that level, reaching two million in 1980, when the rate of inflation was, in fact, 18 per cent. The inflation rate, however, had been down to 8.2 per cent in 1978.

The Manchester Inflation Workshop supported Friedman's natural rate hypothesis and the demolition of the traditional Phillips curve. The natural rate of unemployment for Britain was tentatively estimated to be 'a little less than 2 per cent' in the mid 1970s. To put this in perspective, an unemployment level of one million was equivalent to a rate of between 4 and 5 per cent.

Laidler's lasting contribution to the economic policy debate in Britain, and one which was embodied in the Medium Term Financial Strategy adopted by the Thatcher government in 1980, was the concept of gradualism.

The idea that the right way to deal with inflation is to announce, and adhere to, a programme of gradually reducing the rate of growth of money rested, according to Laidler, on the fact that, in a situation where inflationary expectations are high, the initial effects of a monetary contraction will be felt in lower output and employment. A sudden and severe fall in the money supply could, therefore, impose an unacceptable squeeze on the real economy, slashing output and forcing up unemployment. The gradualist approach produces expectations of declining inflation and – or so it was argued – could achieve lower inflation with far less pain. As we shall see, policies which were gradualist in intent could, when carried out, also result in a great deal of pain.

Politicians and Pundits

A small group of monetarist economists sniping away at the establishment would not, on its own, have produced a revolution in economic policy. But monetarism was beginning to become fashionable in the two key centres of power and influence in Britain – the House of Commons and Fleet Street.

During 1972, when Edward Heath and Anthony Barber embarked on the breakneck expansion that was, albeit temporarily, to lift growth and cut unemployment, the right wing of the Conservative Party began to get restless. The sequence of events that began with the miners' strike of January and February 1972 – the first since the General Strike of 1926 – and ended with the Prime Minister's declaration of a ninety-day statutory freeze on prices, wages, rents and dividends on 6 November 1972 had disenchanted many Conservatives.

Having fought to erase the memory of the Wilson years of pay and price controls, they were faced with the sight of their own government doing a complete policy U-turn, with as savage a set of statutory controls as any introduced under Labour. The U-turn on a prices and incomes policy was preceded, also to the dismay of many Conservatives, by a switch to a policy of active industrial intervention and support, most notably with the rescue of Upper Clyde Shipbuilders in February 1972.

The government's rationale for introducing a prices and incomes policy was based on a straightforward application of the Keynesian conventional wisdom of the time. The economy had to be boosted, through an expansion of demand, to reduce unemployment to an acceptable level of around half a million. But the normal Phillips curve relationship was not working, perhaps because of a rise in union power under Labour. State interference in prices and incomes was therefore justified, if only as a temporary measure.

To monetarists, this reasoning was badly flawed. The government was introducing the paraphernalia of controls to try to deal with something that was caused, purely and simply, by allowing the money supply to grow too fast.

A pamphlet was put together, mainly by Harry Johnson and Alan Walters, and co-ordinated by the Conservative MP, Richard Body. It was signed by most of the prominent British monetarists, numbering eight in all. The group called itself the Economic Radicals and pulled no punches in its assault on the policy errors that had produced the drift towards controls. It also stated clearly the monetarist prescription for retrieving the economy from the loose money quagmire into which it was sinking. The pamphlet, 'A Memorial to the Prime Minister', published on 2 November, was nicely timed. It drew support from about forty Conservative MPs and formed the basis for subsequent protests over the government's policy U-turn.

At this time the right wing of the Conservative Party was known as the Powellite wing, after Enoch Powell. He was better known in the country for his forthright views on immigration, but had established his pedigree in economics by resigning, as a junior Treasury minister, with the Chancellor, Peter Thorneycroft, in January 1958. In June 1973, Powell said: 'The flow of money is increasing by such a pace that it would increase by a fifth in a single year. There is no doubt what this means – inflation.'

Other prominent dissidents in the party included John Biffen, Jock Bruce-Gardyne, Nicholas Ridley, Neil Marten, Hugh Fraser and Anthony Fell. Ridley, Biffen and Bruce-Gardyne were later to become Treasury ministers under Margaret Thatcher. Terence Higgins, the Financial Secretary to the Treasury in the Heath/Barber years, also made it known that he was unhappy with the direction that policy was taking, and the rapid rise in the money supply in which the government was acquiescing, indeed encouraging.

The protest, in the manner typical of backbench revolts in mid-term, had little effect on policy. The monetary boom, as we have seen, gathered strength. Edward Heath, once he had the prices and incomes policy bit between his teeth, was determined to make it succeed. Stages 1, 2 and 3 of a prices and incomes policy of nightmarish complexity, including relativities boards, followed.

The Economic Radicals went public again, this time with a letter to Edward Heath early in 1974. But too much water had flowed under the bridge, and too much money into the economy. The miners called a second strike in February 1974 and Heath called a General Election on the question of who was running the country, government or miners. In two elections that year, the electorate decided, narrowly, that Labour and the miners were.

The ignominious end of what had begun as an ambitious attempt to transform the economy along free market lines served to swell the ranks of the Powellite right wing of the Conservative Party. This wing, united by dissent and disappointment, was for the most part easily re-directed, in the subsequent contests for the party leadership, towards Margaret Thatcher.

Moreover, the Heath/Barber years had given monetarism a power base among the opinion formers. The influence of newspapers on opinion is often over-stated. A great many ideas that are advocated in newspaper columns stay, often quite rightly, on the printed page. But journalists undoubtedly played a major part in the rise of monetarism during the 1970s.

Samuel Brittan and Peter Jay, friends and rivals as, respectively, principal economics commentator of the *Financial Times* and economics editor of *The Times*, had described monetarism to their readers in the late 1960s. In the early 1970s, they realized that the situation developing in Britain could usefully be analysed within the monetarist framework. Description turned to analysis and, in time, to open advocacy of monetarism.

Under the sympathetic editorship of William Rees Mogg, who yearned for the stability of the Gold Standard, Jay took *The Times* on to a position of forthright support for monetarism. In May 1973, he wrote of 'the boom that must go bust'. In 1975, he wrote, in strictly Friedmanite terms, of the conse-quences of an attempt by the authorities to reduce unemployment by injecting money into the economy:

> Before long consumers and pay bargainers, indeed everyone involved in the econ-omy, get used to continuing inflation. It becomes built into their expectations; and so the stimulative effects of any given amount of governmental reflation are discounted and so eroded. Governments then begin to have to increase the dose; and there is no end to this process of trying to keep the actual inflation rate ahead of constantly catching-up expectations, until the stage of hyperinflation and breakdown is reached.

Jay, after leaving *The Times* in 1977, first to become British Ambassador in Washington and later to concentrate on a career in television, largely dropped out of the economic debate. Brittan, however, remained at the forefront of the development of monetarism in Britain. In the period after 1979, he continued to worry away at policy, at least once a week, in the pages of the *Financial Times*.

Before long, Jay and Brittan were joined by many others. City and financial editors found a ready market for monetarist-type critiques of economic policy during the latter years of the Heath government. The financial community in the City of London, in particular, was highly sympathetic.

Keynesian Defences

To view the rise of monetarism as a series of easy victories over disillusioned and demoralized Keynesians is misleading. Keynesians were aware that their model appeared to have broken down in the first half of the 1970s. But their response, quite naturally, was to revise rather than abandon it.

Once economists, particularly in the United States, became aware of the seriousness of the monetarist challenge, they began to offer a whole series of criticisms of the monetarist case, and defences of the Keynesian conventional wisdom.

The criticism fell under a number of different headings, variously hitting at the heart and the detail of the propositions of monetarism. The most basic of these criticisms centred on the concept of money itself. A modern, sophisticated economic system clearly differs from the classical, gold-based economy. There is a wide variety of measures of 'money' in the economy, from notes and coins to very broad measures of liquidity.

Monetarists have tended to emphasize the monetary base – notes and coins plus bankers' balances at the central bank – and to distinguish between money and credit. But policies aimed at controlling the money supply have, in practice, been geared towards both broad and narrow measures of money.

Two principal difficulties arise. The first is the problem of definition when different measures of money are not behaving uniformly, and perhaps even moving in opposite directions. The second is the appropriate policy response in such situations. This was a particular problem during the early years of the Thatcher government. Steps were taken to bring fast-growing broad money, sterling M3, under control, imposing a severe financial squeeze on the economy. And yet the evidence from narrow money, M1, was that monetary growth was not excessive.

A second strand of criticism concerned the nature of the demand for money. It had been necessary, it may be recalled, for Friedman, in restating the quantity theory of money, to specify a whole range of factors, including rates of return on a spectrum of assets, in the demand for money. The rate of interest, representing the rate of return on just one of these assets, was included but was considered to be relatively unimportant. This contrasted sharply with Keynes's formulation of the demand for money, in which interest rates played a key role.

Friedman's demand for money function, with interest rates playing a minor part, looked implausible. Monetarist economists such as David Laidler found that it could not be supported with empirical research. A more accurate formulation, according to Laidler, was one in which interest rates played an important role. 'There is an overwhelming body of evidence in favour of the proposition that the demand for money is stably and negatively related to the rate of interest,' he wrote. Later, looking back on the first few years of Margaret Thatcher's monetarist experiment, he was to doubt whether even this stable relationship still held.

While finding against the view that interest rates were unimportant, Laidler and others such as Karl Brunner and Allan Meltzer were equally adamant that Keynes overstated the consequences of interest-sensitive demand for money, and that the liquidity trap described in the *General Theory* was not supported empirically.

Keynesian critics, as might be expected, went somewhat further in their assault on the demand for money, as set out by Friedman. Not only were interest rates important, they argued, but the demand for money was inherently unstable. The introduction of the concept of permanent income to explain apparently contradictory movements in the demand for money, and hence the velocity of circulation, over the cycle was regarded as sleight of hand.

Studies by Latané, and by Bronfenbrenner and Mayer, had found a strong interest rate relationship, and concluded that the velocity of circulation did move sharply over the cycle. The explanation was that a rise in income resulting from an expansion of economic activity forced up interest rates which, in turn, reduced the demand for money, and increased velocity. People substituted money for interest-bearing assets, and so a rise in the stock of money was associated with an increase in velocity, and vice versa.

The admission, even by monetarist economists, that interest rates helped determine the demand for money was important when taken in conjunction with a third area which, to Keynesians, looked particularly suspect in the new quantity theory. To Friedman and his followers, the rate at which the money stock increased was in the gift of the policy-makers.

Again, empirical research dealt considerable damage to the monetarist case. As early as 1964, Teigen conducted a study which showed that, in the United States, the supply of money tended to increase with the rate of interest. There are two ways of assessing such results, duplicated in later research for other countries. The one that is kindest to monetarism is that governments, in the absence of monetary rules, tend to draw back from restricting growth in the money supply, because they do not want to see interest rates rise too much in response to any relative rise in the demand for money.

The other interpretation, and one which attacks the very foundations of monetarism, is that the stock of money in a modern credit economy cannot be determined by the authorities. Instead, the money stock increases in response to the growth of the economy and changes in the price level. It responds, in the language of the nineteenth-century critics of the quantity theory, to the needs of trade.

In either case, the first because of institutional arrangements which presumably could be changed and the second because of some underlying economic reality, the money supply is endogenously, rather than exogenously, determined.

Friedman's defence, that changes in the stock of money always precede changes in the economy (on the face of it evidence of the direction of causation), was, to Keynesian critics, no defence at all. Lord Kaldor, in fine knockabout form in a 1970 article attacking what he described as the 'new monetarism', described the phenomenon of the rise in the money supply which takes place in November every year. This increase, associated with a seasonal increase in consumer spending, is followed, a few weeks later, by Christmas. Monetarist logic, he pointed out, would require that the increase in the money supply was the cause of Christmas.

Later, he described his response on hearing that concrete evidence had been unearthed in Chicago that changes in the money stock, M, cause changes in money national income, Y. 'When I first heard of Friedman's empirical findings, in the early 1950s,' he wrote,

> I received the news with some incredulity, until it suddenly dawned on me that Friedman's empirical results must be read in reverse; the causation must run from Y to M, and not from M to Y. And the longer I thought about it the more convinced I became that a theory of the value of money based on a commodity-money economy is not applicable to a credit-money economy. In the one case money has an independent supply function, based on production cost, while in the other case new money comes into existence in consequence of, or as an aspect of, the extension of bank credit. If, as a result, more money comes into existence than the public . . . wishes to hold, the excess will be automatically extinguished – either through debt repayment or its conversion into interest-bearing assets – in a way which gold could not be made to disappear from existence.

James Tobin, later a Nobel Prize-winner in economics, took the Keynesian attack right into Friedman's court by re-working the results obtained in Friedman and Schwarz's *Monetary History of the United States*. By assuming that the money supply was endogenously determined (that is, called forth by changes in the economy), Tobin found an almost perfect fit to explain the apparently incontrovertible evidence that money changes always preceded changes elsewhere in the economy. The lags of the *Monetary History* – an average of sixteen months between peaks in monetary growth and economic activity, and twelve months between troughs – emerged just as well when the money supply was assumed to be endogenous.

Friedman would have little truck with most of the criticisms. He accused Kaldor of being a 'Johnny-come-lately' with an attack which, by implication, most sensible people had discarded as unrealistic long before. He went as far as conceding that there would be feedback effects on monetary growth from changes in economic activity, but claimed that these would be dwarfed by the far stronger effects running in the direction implied by the quantity theory.

There were other important criticisms of monetarism. The empirical results assembled in its support did not make up a consistent whole. But, as with the economics of Keynes in the 1930s, monetarism was gathering momentum. The defence mounted by the old guard could be seen as a desperate attempt to prop up a failed model of the economy. Friedman and his followers were nothing if not determined fighters. The Keynesians, either in hand-to-hand combat or by sniping, faced a formidable assault. The monetarists scented victory.

5

RELUCTANT MONETARISTS

The emergence of significantly higher inflation and the traumas of the first oil price shock of 1973/4 frightened most of the major countries into deflationary economic policies. But in Britain, partly because of the change of government which occurred in 1974, things were different. In the manner of the bon viveur determined to stay around long after the rest of the guests have departed, expansionary fiscal policies held on longer in Britain than anywhere else, even though the champagne had gone distinctly flat.

The Heath government had been defeated, narrowly but ignominiously, in February 1974. The gamble of holding what was essentially a referendum on a single issue, the miners' strike, was always a risky one. The sharp rise in the price of oil, the threat of a cut in the supply lines for imported energy and the implied increase in the value of Britain's domestic coal reserves, served to increase that risk.

The subsequent attempt to reflate out of the oil crisis by the Labour government under Harold Wilson was, with the benefit of hindsight, a clear and major mistake. But two things should be remembered about the background to the decisions taken by the Chancellor of the Exchequer, Denis Healey, at this time. The first was that, while there had been commodity price rises before, during the Korean war in the 1950s and, indeed, for the majority of non-oil commodities from the late 1960s or early 1970s, the exertion of market power by the oil-producing countries in 1973 and 1974 was a new phenomenon.

Secondly, there was an inflationary time-bomb ticking away in Britain. The surge in monetary growth in 1972 and 1973 had produced a rise in the broad money stock of more than 60 per cent in two years. But the dangers of this were not fully recognized within the Treasury and the Bank of England.

The OPEC Shock

On 6 October 1973, perhaps the most important day in the post-war history of the world economy, Egyptian forces crossed the Suez Canal, striking into

Israel on the Jewish Day of Atonement, Yom Kippur. To intensify the pressure on Israel's Western backers, and in particular the United States in this situation, the Arab-dominated Organization of Petroleum Exporting Countries embarked on a policy of simultaneously squeezing the supply and raising the price of crude oil.

OPEC, set up in Baghdad in 1960, had had little influence on oil prices in the first ten years of its existence. During the 1960s the posted price of Saudi Arabian Light crude oil remained unwaveringly at $1.80 a barrel, and declined in real terms as a result of creeping world inflation. By 1973, the price had risen to $2.59 a barrel, but there were sharper price rises for other commodities.

On 16 October 1973, ten days after the start of the Yom Kippur war, the OPEC cartel made up for its relative ineffectiveness on prices. The posted price of Saudi Arabian Light was raised to $5.11 a barrel. The following day, a 5 per cent a month cumulative cutback in oil production was announced.

In the run-up to a Christmas of tremendous uncertainty for the West, OPEC first threatened a 25 per cent minimum cut in oil production, before deciding to use the price weapon, with devastating effect, once more. Saudi Light oil was raised to $11.65 a barrel from the beginning of 1974, and the cutback in output by the Arab oil producers was limited to 15 per cent.

In three months, the dollar price of crude oil had risen by nearly 350 per cent, to something rather more than four times its previous level. The result was a sudden and major shift of economic power and wealth from the oil consumers to the oil producers. OPEC's combined current account surplus increased from $1 billion in 1973 to $61 billion in 1974. The improvement, of $60 billion, was matched by a deterioration of a little over $30 billion for the Western industrialized countries, and just under $30 billion for the non-oil developing countries.

The oil bill of the Western industrialized countries increased by an annual $60–70 billion as a result of the price rise, or roughly 1.5 per cent of a combined gross national product which included major oil producers such as the United States and Canada. The additional burden on countries like Germany, Japan and, in those pre-North Sea oil days, Britain, was far greater.

Some of the rise, it is true, was immediately offset by a strong rise in imports from the West into the OPEC countries. This subsequently reduced the OPEC surplus to an average of less than $40 billion a year in the 1975–7 period. But no less worrying than the new trade imbalances were the complications that would be created by this oil money sloshing around the international monetary system, and the pressing need to develop mechanisms for recycling it and neutralizing its inflationary effects.

By 1974, the rise in oil prices outstripped the increases for other commodities.

But these were still, by any standard, dramatic. Non-oil commodity prices in 1973 were more than double their 1971 level. Food prices in 1974 had nearly trebled compared with their level three years earlier.

The monetarist explanation for these sharp increases was quite straight-forward. They were the result of allowing too much money into the system, set against the real constraints, determined by harvests, mining capacity and long lead times for investment, on commodity production. In this situation, commodity prices could confidently be expected to rise. Oil was slightly differ-ent, and there was no sterner critic of OPEC's use or abuse of monopoly power than Friedman, this time wearing his free-market hat. But, while the oil price rise was certainly exaggerated by the tactics of the OPEC cartel, a substantial increase in the price of oil, as in other commodities, was clearly due.

No less certain was the correct policy response, in the eyes of monetarists. Assuming stable velocity of circulation, the general price level in any country can only increase as a result of higher import prices if there is a prior expan-sion of the stock of money to permit it. If not, then the higher price of oil and other commodities would be offset by lower domestic prices. Thus a non-accommodating monetary policy was the right monetarist prescription for minimizing or neutralizing completely the inflationary effects of OPEC.

Monetarists recognized that, in practice, things were unlikely to be as clear-cut. The key relationship developed by Friedman was between the stock of money and national income, expressed in money terms, or the product of real output and the price level. Therefore, with a non-accommodating monetary policy and the (realistic) assumption that domestic producers could not or would not reduce their prices, there were bound to be effects on output. The question for policy-makers was how much pain they were prepared to allow for the economy in order to minimize the inflationary consequences of higher oil and commodity prices.

Set out in this way, the choices appear remarkably simple. But this framework of analysis was, in Britain at least, some way ahead of its time. The policy response that did emerge was an uneasy combination of belated concern for the money supply and full-blooded Keynesian reflation.

Wearing the Corset

In the last few months of the Heath administration, there was a marked tightening of both monetary and fiscal policy. Indeed, if David Laidler's 1974 evidence to the House of Commons Expenditure Committee can be taken as typical, the main criticism of policy was that it had shifted too abruptly from being excessively loose to unnecessarily tight.

During 1973, slowly becoming aware that it was presiding over a monetary boom of enormous proportions, the Bank of England began to set secret, internal money supply targets. The influence of these targets can be seen quite clearly in the Bank's conduct of policy towards the end of 1973. On 11 September it issued a notice to banks and building societies, declaring that: 'The banking system is close to being fully lent.'

Through the familiar device of moral suasion, banks were urged to limit lending in non-essential areas, including loans to individuals, and advances for property development and financial transactions. An interest rate limit of 9.5 per cent was set for deposits of less than £10,000, and the banks were required to employ tighter surveillance and control over what was described as the 'merry-go-round' of interest arbitrage – the technique of borrowing from the banks and re-lending in the money markets which swelled broad money growth.

When the effects of this package of measures did not seem to be working quickly enough, the Bank took further action on 13 November. Minimum lending rate (which had replaced the old bank rate) was raised from 11.25 to 13 per cent, and an extra 2 per cent of the banks' liabilities were called in as special deposits at the Bank of England.

Further stringency was to come. Accompanying Chancellor Barber's announcement on 17 December of £1,200 million of public spending cuts and a surcharge on hire-purchase controls and surtax was a new device designed to limit the growth in bank lending. The supplementary special deposits scheme, immediately christened 'the corset', introduced penalties for banks exceeding prescribed lending limits.

The corset, which in its first existence lasted until February 1975, set a limit of 8 per cent on the growth of the banks' interest-bearing liabilities from the end of 1973 to the middle of 1974, a period that was subsequently extended.

The banks, if they permitted growth to exceed that limit, were required to place non-interest-bearing deposits, of progressively larger amounts, at the Bank of England. The corset was clearly against the spirit of the 1971 Competition and Credit Control changes, but few – and least of all the banks – could deny its effectiveness.

This volley of measures to tighten both fiscal and monetary policy had a speedy impact on the growth of the money supply, or, at least, the broader measure of it which was the most watched. The growth rate of the M3 money measure, 28 per cent in both 1972 and 1973, slowed to less than 13 per cent in 1974 and under 8 per cent in 1975.

The record on narrow money was less impressive. The M1 measure slowed from a 15.4 per cent growth rate in 1972 to a rise of just over 5 per cent in 1973. But then it accelerated, rising by 11 per cent during 1974 and nearly 19 per cent in 1975. As in the 1960s, the money supply, rather than being controlled, was distorted by restrictions on the banks.

Even so, as was to be argued strongly later, an improved performance for one very important monetary aggregate was a step in the right direction, particularly in view of the broad money explosion that had gone before. But the Bank of England, having achieved a progress of sorts, was to find its resolve to pursue firm monetary policy sorely tested. In the latter days of the Heath–Barber period, the Bank had the advantage of a complementary tightening of fiscal policy. Under the new, expansionist-minded Labour government, this was far from the case.

Going It Alone

Labour, under Harold Wilson, won the February 1974 General Election by the narrowest of margins. Initially it appeared that Labour's four-seat majority over the Conservatives would not be enough to form a government. But Edward Heath, after exploring the possibility of a coalition with the Liberals, then led by Jeremy Thorpe, was finally forced to concede defeat.

Labour returned to power armed with a 'social contract' with the trade unions, designed to circumvent the industrial relations problems which had brought down Heath and which had dogged the previous Wilson government of 1964–70. The unions promised, but in the event manifestly failed to deliver, responsibility in pay bargaining, in return for government commitments to a fairer society and full employment.

Thus, despite a sharply rising inflation rate, which was to average almost 16 per cent in 1974, rising to over 24 per cent in 1975, Labour was required to act first on unemployment. The Barber boom had produced a near halving of unemployment, from close to a million early in 1972 to just over 500,000 late in 1973. But early in 1974 there were ominous signs that the jobless total was heading up again.

At this time, the National Institute of Economic and Social Research was by far the most influential voice in the British economic policy debate. Determinedly Keynesian in its outlook and approach, the views of the National Institute could justifiably be taken as a proxy for the sort of advice that the Chancellor of the Exchequer was receiving privately from his Treasury officials.

In February 1974, after the sharp rise in oil prices by OPEC, the National Institute offered the following advice: 'On balance a neutral budget might be best now, so long as there is the clear intention of taking reflationary action later in the year if unemployment continues to rise (as we think it probably will).'

The National Institute also allowed for the possibility of the introduction of import controls to insulate any reflationary action from outside pressures. In this, it picked up an important element in the policy debate which was energetically taken up by Kaldor, among Wilson's advisers, and by Tony Benn in the Labour Cabinet.

Import controls were resisted, but rarely could a policy prescription from outside have been taken up so precisely as that of the National Institute. The March 1974 Budget of Denis Healey was broadly neutral, raising taxes in order to boost public spending, including a large increase in state pensions. It was a notorious Budget, however, for among the tax increases was a lifting of the top rate of income tax on earned income to 83 per cent, and on earned and investment income to 98 per cent.

As it became clear that unemployment was on an upward trend, as the National Institute had predicted, policy switched from neutral to sharply expansionary. The Chancellor of the Exchequer, Denis Healey, became famous for his regular economic packages, soon dubbed 'mini-Budgets'. In 1974 and 1975 most of these packages injected extra public spending into the economy.

There were, however, notable exceptions. In July 1974, in what was described as an anti-inflationary measure, Healey reduced the standard rate of value added tax, the general tax on spending, from 10 to 8 per cent. The VAT reduction had an immediate, if short-lived, effect on the retail price index. But it was enough for Healey to claim, amid much ridicule, that he had succeeded in cutting the inflation rate to 8.4 per cent. He had, but only as measured by the annualized rate over the latest three months. Healey's claim came during the campaign for the second General Election of 1974, held in October, in which Labour was returned in a slightly stronger, but still highly vulnerable, parliamentary position.

The scale of the Healey expansion can be seen in the figures for public spending in this period. In the fiscal year 1974/5, public spending rose by no less than 35 per cent in cash terms, or nearly 13.5 per cent in real terms. In 1975/6 there was a further strong rise, of almost 25 per cent, in cash terms, although this almost exactly matched the inflation rate.

Joel Barnett, the Chief Secretary to the Treasury at this time, with direct responsibility for public expenditure, described in his book *Inside the Treasury* the reasoning behind the figures:

> The Chancellor had made the fundamental decision to react to the oil crisis in a different way from the Germans and Japanese, and indeed from many other countries. Instead of cutting expenditure to take account of the massive oil price increases of 1973, which in our case cut living standards by some 5 per cent, the Chancellor decided to maintain our expenditure plans and borrow to meet the deficit.

And borrow he did. The public sector borrowing requirement, the amount that the government has to borrow to bridge the gap between expenditure and tax revenues, increased sharply. The PSBR had been eliminated by the previous Labour Chancellor, Roy Jenkins, to the point of generating a surplus, or a net repayment of borrowing, in 1969/70. It had risen under Anthony Barber, reaching £4.5 billion in 1973/4. The first two years of the new Labour government pushed the PSBR up to £8 billion in 1974/5 and £10.6 billion in 1975/6.

Even non-monetarists could see the dangers inherent in such a sharp rise in borrowing. But monetarist analysis provided a ready explanation of why such a policy was bound to be damaging. The government could fully fund the PSBR by selling larger quantities of government stock (gilt-edged securities). But a larger public sector claim on the finite quantity of funds available in the City ran the clear risk of shutting out the private sector. This financial 'crowding out' would occur through higher interest rates, unless funds flowed in from abroad.

The second route was, for monetarists, even less palatable. The government could maintain its expenditure plans, without fully funding the PSBR, by allowing the money supply to increase – 'printing money'. This was the route to hyperinflation described in the 1950s by the Chicago economist Philip Cagan.

Most of the massive expansion of public spending in 1974 and 1975 was taken up in higher transfer payments – pensions and social security – and in public sector pay. Gross domestic product, after rising by more than 7 per cent in 1973, fell by 1.7 per cent in 1974 and a further 1.1 per cent in 1975. Unemployment rose steadily, breaking above one million in the second half of 1975.

The social contract, as originally framed, had turned out to be a lamentable failure. As a result of the Heath pay policy, higher oil prices fed directly into higher wages in the early months of 1974. From then on, wages never looked back. An unhappy combination of industrial unrest and fast rising wages, the British disease encapsulated, meant that the government had to resort to a statutory incomes policy in July 1975, with the agreement of the major trade unions.

By then, however, the damage had been done. Average earnings rose by nearly 18 per cent in 1974 and by 26.5 per cent in 1975. In both years, the increase in earnings comfortably outstripped the rise in prices. The consequence of big wage increases and declining output was that wages and salaries per unit of output, perhaps the best measure of Britain's ability to compete with other countries, rose by 21.5 per cent in 1974 and 30 per cent in 1975.

In every respect, Britain's attempt to reflate out of the oil crisis had failed. The decline in gross domestic product in Britain was larger, and lasted longer, than in countries which had adopted restrictive economic policies in response to OPEC.

In the United States, inflation rose to 11 per cent in 1974 but then fell back. In Germany, the inflation rate was held at 6 to 7 per cent. In Japan, there was one year of very high inflation, nearly 25 per cent in 1974, followed by a halving of the rate in 1975. In Britain, not only was inflation much higher in 1975 than in 1974, but there was great concern that it was spiralling out of control.

Every possible ingredient existed for a collapse of confidence in Britain as a viable economy, and in London as a haven for funds. The balance of payments was in bad shape. The initial impact of the oil price rise was to push the current account deficit up from less than £1 billion in 1973 to £3.3 billion in 1974. Britain, in common with other countries, enjoyed a surge in export orders to the oil-producing countries, but sharply deteriorating competitiveness ensured that the current account remained in large deficit, by £1.5 billion in 1975. Government borrowing was rising and was apparently out of control, and the secondary banking crisis pointed to fundamental weakness in the financial system.

The surprise was not that a sterling crisis occurred, but that it took so long.

IMF Monetarism

During 1975, Denis Healey embarked on a change of strategy for the economy. The growth in public expenditure, which appeared to be having a negligible effect on unemployment but was necessitating unpopular tax increases and a surge in public borrowing, was to be reined back. In its place, the private sector, and in particular manufacturing industry, was to be encouraged to take up the slack.

The first cuts in public expenditure, of £1.1 billion for the 1976/7 fiscal year, were announced in March 1975. A feature of public expenditure planning in Britain, as in other countries, is the long time lag between expenditure decisions being taken and their effects coming through. This was followed in November 1975, after unemployment had risen above one million, by demands from the Chancellor – presented forthrightly to an unsympathetic Cabinet – for further cuts, totalling £5 billion, in future years.

Cuts, that is reductions in planned programmes, of £1.6 billion were agreed for 1977/8. The debate over spending for the following year, which also took place at this time, was more problematical. According to Joel Barnett's account, Healey wanted cuts of £3.75 billion for that year, but was prepared to settle for £3 billion. Eventually, after much bitter wrangling and a certain amount of creative accounting, Healey's £3 billion was achieved, and both sets of cuts were incorporated in the public spending White Paper, published in February 1976.

The difficulty with the new strategy of attempting to hold public spending and stimulate private sector growth was that the massive increases in earnings and unit wage costs in 1974 and 1975 had left British industry badly uncompetitive at the prevailing exchange rate of a little over two dollars to the pound, early in 1976.

According to the International Monetary Fund's index of relative unit labour costs in manufacturing, British industry's competitiveness had deteriorated by about 7.5 per cent in 1974 and 6 per cent in 1975. In February 1976 the Permanent Secretary to the Treasury, Sir Douglas Wass, and the government's Chief Economic Adviser, Sir Bryan Hopkin, concluded that the pound needed to be pushed down to allow industry to compete.

Given the woeful state of the economy, and in particular the balance of payments, it may be thought that such a shove was not needed. But this was a time when the international financial system was awash with OPEC money. And much of it, through Britain's traditional links with the Middle East, was as naturally attracted to the City as a financial centre as were the oil sheikhs to London's clubs and casinos.

The first manifestation of the new exchange rate policy was on 4 March 1976, when the Bank of England sold sterling in the markets to stop the pound from rising. The reversal was quick and, in the manner of the foreign exchange markets under floating rates, very dramatic. Harold Wilson resigned the prime ministership on 16 March for reasons which to this day remain mysterious. His successor was James Callaghan who, as Chancellor of the Exchequer, had presided over the 1967 devaluation. To Callaghan, pleased as he was to be Prime Minister, it must have seemed like a recurring nightmare. For, almost immediately, he was faced with a sterling crisis.

The Treasury's attempt to achieve a controlled depreciation of the pound had reckoned without the killer instinct of the markets. Very soon an uncontrolled slide developed, with the pound dropping an average of 10 cents a month during the spring of 1976. Britain's official reserves had fallen since 1973 and, at less than $5 billion, were insufficient to support the pound.

In May, with the pound at $1.70, the Chancellor negotiated a stand-by credit of $5.3 billion, around $2 billion from the United States and the rest from the other major countries. The credit was for three months, renewable for a further three months, after which it would have to be repaid.

Another package of spending cuts amounting to £1 billion, to take effect in 1977/8, was agreed in July, but this was not enough to satisfy the foreign exchange dealers, by now casting a critical eye over every aspect of the British economy. The markets were similarly unimpressed with the first direct policy reference, under Healey's chancellorship, to the money supply. Included in the July package was a forecast that money supply growth in 1976/7 would be 'about 12 per cent'.

The pound remained weak, falling to a new low of just above $1.60 early in October, at a time when the temporary stand-by arrangements were drawing to a close. It was clear that a longer-term arrangement was needed, and this was achieved with a loan of $3.9 billion from the IMF. From that point the pound never looked back, apart from one flurry at the end of October following a report in the *Sunday Times*, hotly denied by all concerned, that the IMF wanted the pound at $1.50. Immediately after the report, sterling fell sharply, almost to $1.50.

On one description, the stand-by credit of $5.3 billion was the bait, and the $3.9 billion loan the trap which forced the government into adopting harsh economic medicine. But it was by no means clear that the Prime Minister, James Callaghan, and his Chancellor, Denis Healey, were unwilling participants in the process.

Callaghan, in a passage in his speech to the Labour Party Conference in September 1976 (thought to have been drafted by his monetarist convert son-in-law Peter Jay), effectively sounded the death-knell for post-war Keynesian policies, and ushered in the new era of monetarism:

> We used to think that you could just spend your way out of a recession, and increase employment, by cutting taxes and boosting government spending. I tell you in all candour that that option no longer exists, and in so far as it ever did exist, it worked by injecting inflation into the economy. And each time that happened, the average level of unemployment has risen. Higher inflation, followed by higher unemployment. That is the history of the last twenty years.

It was a period of extraordinary overseas influence on British economic policy. An IMF team arrived in London that autumn to discuss the conditions attached to the $3.9 billion loan. The team was headed by a former Bank of England official, Alan Whittome. His deputy was David Finch, an Australian, and the Fund's managing director, Johannes Witteveen, was also heavily involved.

Irritation arose, however, over the role of the United States Treasury Secretary, William Simon, with the support of his Under-Secretary, Ed Yeo, and the chairman of the Federal Reserve Board, Arthur Burns. They were keen to pursue a 'hands-on' approach to British economic policy. Simon, who viewed Britain as something approaching a lost cause, made an unscheduled visit to London in November 1976 to help oversee matters.

The conditions insisted upon by the IMF and the Americans were set out in a Letter of Intent despatched by the British government on 15 December 1976. 'An essential element of the government's strategy will be a continuing and substantial reduction over the next few years in the share of resources required for the public sector,' it said. 'It is also essential to reduce the PSBR in order to create monetary conditions which will encourage investment and support sustained growth and the control of inflation.'

The specific measures were a reduction in the borrowing requirement from its 'unacceptably high' level (it turned out to be £8.5 billion in 1976/7, although it had been £10.6 billion in 1975/6) to £8.7 billion in 1977/8 and £8.6 billion in 1978/9. To help achieve these PSBR targets, public spending cuts of £1.5 billion in 1977/8 and £2 billion in 1978/9 were to be implemented. This was in addition to the cuts already announced, including the £1 billion for 1977/8 pushed through the Cabinet by Healey in the previous July.

The IMF had, as in 1968, insisted on targets for domestic credit expansion, a logical move in view of Britain's balance of payments difficulties. It was to be progressively reduced from £9 billion in 1976/7 to £7.7 billion in 1977/8 and £6 billion in 1978/9.

Alongside the targets for domestic credit expansion, the Letter of Intent said that it was expected that the increase in the sterling M3 measure of money would be between 9 and 13 per cent. Sterling M3 – notes and coins and all private sector sterling deposits – was to achieve a prominence and notoriety that could hardly have been foreseen late in 1976. The rather vague 'expectation' for sterling M3 growth was soon elevated to the status of a formal target. Monetarism had arrived in Britain.

The IMF Letter of Intent of December 1976 has, in the eyes of many, a lot to answer for. Disgruntled Labour Party supporters felt that the government was bounced unnecessarily into unpopular and unacceptable economic measures. The linking of monetary targets to public spending cuts produced a powerful image in the minds of the British people, and one which the Conservative government of 1979 found impossible to shake. Monetarism was not, in the popular view, an uncontroversial tool of economic policy designed to allow stable growth without accompanying inflation. It was, rather, a means of justifying austerity.

Certainly, apart from the public spending cuts, other painful measures were needed in 1976 to bring the money supply under control. The supplementary special deposits scheme – the corset – had been reintroduced in November and the Bank of England's minimum lending rate pushed up to a record 15 per cent level early in October, when pressure on the pound was at its greatest.

These measures were taken following a period of rapid growth in the money supply between the spring and autumn of 1976. They succeeded in producing a sharp slow-down in monetary growth, to the extent that sterling M3 grew by just 7 per cent in 1976/7 – below the bottom end of the 9 to 13 per cent target range. Growth in narrow money, as might be expected with the corset in operation, was higher; the increase was 9 per cent. But the gap between broad and narrow money growth was much smaller than in 1974 and 1975.

The start of IMF monetarism in Britain coincided with a period of stronger growth for the world economy, as the effects of the first oil price shock became more muted. Growth in the Western industrialized countries exceeded 5 per cent in 1976 and was almost 4 per cent in 1977.

Britain's particular problems, and the greater depth of her post-OPEC recession, did not allow quite so much buoyancy in the economy. Even so, there was growth of nearly 3 per cent in both 1976 and 1977, not enough to reduce unemployment, but sufficient to slow its rise. After rising by around 500,000 during 1975, the jobless total increased by 170,000 in 1976 and about 100,000 in 1977. In 1978, unemployment actually fell.

In other respects, the economy was showing marked signs of improvement. The current account of the balance of payments narrowed to a deficit of less than £1 billion in 1976 and was virtually in balance in 1977. The inflation rate, nearly 25 per cent in 1975, fell to around 16 per cent in 1976 and 1977. Average earnings, up by 26.5 per cent in 1975, rose by 15 per cent in 1976 and 10 per cent in 1977.

This raises one of the difficulties in assessing the success of IMF monetarism. Throughout the period from 1976 to 1979, monetary targeting went alongside a formal incomes policy. And the incomes policy, introduced as a flat limit of £6 a week in pay increases in July 1975, preceded the monetary targets. Prices and incomes controls proceeded to a 5 per cent norm for pay rises in 1976, with minimum and maximum increases set at £2.50 and £4 a week respectively.

The incomes policy became looser, it is true, as the decade progressed. In 1977, for example, it was not much more than an agreement with the Trades Unions Congress that there should be only one pay rise per twelve-month period, and that percentage pay increases should be kept in single figures.

But the existence of an incomes policy during the period provided both succour and irritation for the two main schools of economic policy thinking – the *arriviste* monetarists and the Keynesians. The Keynesians could point to deflationary fiscal measures and incomes policy as the clear explanation for lower inflation. The monetarists, while unhappy that monetary targets were not permitted a freer run, were nevertheless in little doubt that control over the money supply was responsible for bringing about a sharp reduction in the inflation rate.

The almost immediate improvement in Britain's economic performance following the IMF crisis of the autumn of 1976, however it was viewed, produced problems of a rather different sort for the Chancellor of the Exchequer. Confidence in the pound had returned, because of the economic measures imposed by the IMF; a feeling that sterling's 1976 fall had been overdone; and the promise of North Sea oil, which would transform Britain's economy and, in particular, her balance of payments.

So, from the low point of $1.50 reached in October 1976, the pound began to recover. By early 1977, it had risen to just above $1.70, and the alarm bells began to ring in the Treasury. The extra cuts in public expenditure insisted upon as conditions for the IMF loan meant, more than ever, that the private sector had to fill the growth gap. But the pound's strong recovery was hitting industry's ability to compete.

Despite having had its fingers burned when attempting a similar exercise a year earlier, the Treasury instructed the Bank of England to hold the pound down by intervening in the foreign exchange markets. Sterling, as was soon very clear to foreign exchange dealers, had a practical upper limit of between $1.70 and $1.75, above which the Bank would not allow it to rise.

There was an unprecedented reduction in interest rates in Britain. Between October 1976 and October 1977, minimum lending rate was run down from 15 to 5 per cent. In addition, by selling pounds to hold down the exchange rate the Bank of England took on large quantities of foreign currency, mainly dollars. The official reserves showed a five-fold rise during 1977, from $4.1 billion to $20.6 billion.

It is not clear when the Treasury realized that holding down the pound in this way was in sharp conflict with the aim of meeting monetary targets. The kindest interpretation is that the upward pressure on the pound was expected to be short-lived, and that foreign money would be diverted elsewhere once it became clear that it was officially not welcome. However, unlike the situation in 1976, the foreign exchange markets did not respond by deserting sterling, and the pound continued to attract capital from abroad like bees around a honey-pot.

The Bank of England, having held the mob at the gates for most of 1977, finally conceded defeat at the end of October. A Treasury announcement on 31 October confirmed the shift in policy. 'A continuance of foreign inflows on a large scale could endanger continued adherence to the domestic monetary targets,' it said. The pound was allowed to find its own level, which it quickly did, rising to more than $1.90 by the end of the year.

Nevertheless, the damage had already been done as far as the sterling M3 target, maintained at 9 to 13 per cent in 1977/8, was concerned. Sterling M3 grew by 16 per cent over the fiscal year, an end-year surge in public borrowing adding to the expansionary effects of restraining the pound. The first two years of monetary targeting, whatever else they proved, showed that accuracy in hitting targets was, in practice, hard to achieve. An undershoot in 1976/7 was followed by an overshoot in 1977/8. It was small comfort that, taking the two years together, sterling M3 was just within its target range.

The record on the IMF's preferred money measure, domestic credit expansion, was rather better. Domestic credit expansion in 1976/7 was £4.9 billion, against a target of £9 billion. In 1977/8, the IMF target of £7.7 billion was again comfortably met, with an actual figure of £3.8 billion.

Callaghan's Error

Two years after telling the Labour Party Conference that Keynesian demand management was dead, in 1978 the Prime Minister, James Callaghan, could look with some satisfaction on the state of the economy. The rate of inflation was coming down sharply; at just over 8 per cent in 1978, it was half its 1977 rate. Unemployment had begun to fall, dropping by 100,000 during 1978, from a level of almost 1.5 million at the end of 1977.

Public sector borrowing, even more than the money supply, had been brought under control. In 1977/8, the PSBR was £5.6 billion, more than £3 billion below the Letter of Intent target. As a result, the Chancellor, with one eye on the General Election widely expected in the autumn of 1978, was able to announce tax cuts of £2 billion and extra public spending of more than £500 million in April 1978.

It was then that Denis Healey learned an important lesson. If you have monetary targets, then you also have an important body of outsiders – in the City of London – to monitor them. Despite the money supply overshoot in 1977/8, a lower target, of 8 to 12 per cent, was set in April 1978.

The City, quite simply, did not believe it. The tax cuts and public spending boost were seen as the start of a return to the bad old days of 1974 and 1975. Two years of good behaviour following the intervention of the IMF had left analysts unconvinced that the expansionist leopard had changed its spots.

In such circumstances, there is an important veto that the City can exercise – it can refuse to buy government stock. A buyers' 'strike' for gilt-edged securities is rare, but one began to emerge following the 1978 Budget, when a major inconsistency was detected between the government's fiscal and monetary policies.

The Bank of England warned the Treasury that something had to be done, and the City's pound of flesh came in the form of a June economic package, another mini-Budget. It included a further raising of minimum lending rate, to 10 per cent – double its level eight months earlier; and an increase in the national insurance surcharge paid by employers. The corset, which had been removed the previous August, was put back on.

Monetary targets undoubtedly limited Healey's freedom of action. The attempt to boost the economy in anticipation of a General Election was spotted at an early stage in the City and effectively nipped in the bud. When the 8 to 12 per cent target for sterling M3 was reaffirmed in the Chancellor's autumn statement in November, it was accompanied by a further rise in minimum lending rate, to 12.5 per cent. Over the winter, the rate was pushed up to 14 per cent and was still high, at 12 per cent, by the time the General Election finally took place in May 1979.

Healey and Callaghan, having embraced monetary targets in 1976, were very reluctant monetarists indeed by 1979. There was little comfort for them in the fact that sterling M3, while accelerating towards the end of the year, grew by just over 11 per cent in 1978/9, within the target range.

There was a little slippage on the other monetary target, for domestic credit expansion. The actual increase in 1978/9 was £7.3 billion, against a £6 billion IMF target. If there was a pre-election binge it was on the fiscal side, with a 6 per cent real increase in public spending in 1978/9. The PSBR rose to £9.2 billion, from £5.6 billion in 1977/8.

But even on public spending, the government's scope was limited. There had to be a firm attempt to hold the line on public sector pay, an attempt which, more than anything else, contributed to the downfall of James Callaghan.

In the summer of 1978, the overwhelming body of opinion in the country, and indeed in the Labour Party, expected an October election. Labour's pact with the Liberal Party was breaking up, and there were clear signs that the unions, after three years of pay policy, had had enough. The Prime Minister's pleas to the Trades Union Congress to agree on a 5 per cent pay limit were falling on stony ground. Despite all this, Labour's position looked a strong one – inflation had fallen sharply, tax cuts were in place, and unemployment was falling.

Callaghan broadcast to the nation on 7 September. Everyone expected a General Election the following month. But it was not to be. The Prime Minister, in a teasing address, kept the punch line until the very last. There was to be no election that year. Apparently influenced by private Labour Party polls suggesting that there was no guarantee of a clear parliamentary majority, Callaghan had decided to delay until near the end of the maximum parliamentary term – in theory an election did not have to take place until October 1979.

It was a decision he was soon to regret. Ford workers led the break-out from the straitjacket of pay policy, striking before settling for a 15 per cent rise. There followed a series of strikes by dockers, lorry-drivers, water workers and even civil servants. But most damaging of all, and most strongly associated with the 'winter of discontent' of 1978/9, were the strikes by refuse collectors and the low-paid ancillary workers in hospitals. Rubbish piled up in the streets and even sick children could not obtain medical attention, according to Fleet Street folklore.

When Callaghan finally called a General Election for 3 May 1979, on the issue of Scottish devolution, it was as a bitter and demoralized man. He felt badly let down by the unions. He had never fought an election as Labour Party leader. His opponent, Margaret Thatcher, was, similarly, in the ring for the first time as Conservative Party leader. But there was little doubt about who had more stomach for the fight.

6

THATCHER'S CHOICE

Milton Friedman must be credited with the intellectual revolution of monetarism, but Margaret Thatcher was, more than anyone, responsible for turning it into a potent political idea. This is not to say she was the first to put monetarist ideas into practice; indeed, she was beaten to it in Britain by James Callaghan. But no other politician, even in countries with a much longer tradition of sound money, had invested so much political capital in this particular economic philosophy.

When Edward Heath lost the second of the 1974 General Elections in October, it quickly became clear that he had to go as Conservative Party leader. But Margaret Thatcher's name was on few lips as a possible successor. She had been an unpopular Education minister in the Heath government and, at the time when the leadership challenge came up, was a junior Treasury spokeswoman. As well as her obvious inexperience, the idea of the Conservative Party electing a woman as leader was simply too far-fetched to be worthy of consideration.

A gap opened up, however, as potential leaders on the right of the party committed political hara-kiri. Enoch Powell, long the voice of monetarism in Parliament, had resigned in February 1974 in protest at what he considered to be a sham General Election. What is more, he committed an act of treachery by urging his Wolverhampton constituents to vote Labour, which meant that he could never be taken back within the party ranks.

The mantle was taken up, between the two elections of 1974, by Sir Keith Joseph. Under Heath he had been, by nature of his position, a high-spending Secretary of State for Health and Social Security. Soon after the February 1974 election defeat he changed from being an unquestioning Heathite, becoming a powerful challenger to Heath's leadership. Later, he was to write: 'It was only in April 1974 that I was converted to Conservatism. I had thought that I was a Conservative but I can see now that I was not really one at all.'

Joseph set up the Centre for Policy Studies, intended to serve as a 'think tank' for the whole of the party but soon emerging as a body which developed only the ideas of its right wing. Thatcher was his vice-chairman.

Having made it known that he would stand against Heath in any leadership election, Joseph set about making his manifesto public. At Preston in September 1974, against the Heath line, he set out his monetarist principles, apparently newly discovered. 'Our inflation,' he said, 'has been the result of the creation of new money – and the consequent deficit financing – out of proportion to the additional goods and services available. When the money supply grows too quickly, inflation results. This has been known for centuries.' Attempts to control pay directly would not solve the problem. 'Incomes policy alone as a way to abate inflation caused by excessive money supply is like trying to stop water coming out of a leaky hose without turning off the tap; if you stop one hole, it will find two others.'

The economic battleground for the leadership contest had now been mapped out. Heath's interventionism, with a statutory prices and incomes policy, would have to stand up and fight against monetarism and free market economics.

But it was Thatcher, not Joseph, who was to carry the challenge. Shortly after the second election defeat of 1974, Joseph made a speech on social policy at Edgbaston. It included an ill-judged passage in which he appeared to suggest that the lower classes should be encouraged to adopt more effective contraception. Joseph, feeling misunderstood then as he was to feel on many occasions later, was shaken by the furore the speech created. This, together with family difficulties, led him to withdraw his challenge. But he was pleased for Thatcher to go forward as his champion.

With most of the Shadow Cabinet unwilling to issue a direct challenge to Heath, Thatcher's short campaign for the leadership quickly gathered momentum. Early in 1975, a first ballot was held and she defeated both Heath and Hugh Fraser, the only other candidate. Several heavyweights came in for the second ballot – William Whitelaw, James Prior, Geoffrey Howe and John Peyton – but they were too late. Thatcher's defeat of Heath had turned her from an unlikely challenger into a potential leader overnight. On 11 February she was elected leader: the first woman to lead a major political party in Britain.

Thatcher's spirited advocacy of monetarism is generally assumed to have begun at that point, and to have developed in the hot-house atmosphere of opposition politics. There are indications, however, that her monetarist thinking went back somewhat further than that. In October 1968, at the Conservative Party Conference in Blackpool, she made a speech on behalf of the Conservative Political Centre. It contained the following passage:

> We now put so much emphasis on the control of incomes that we have too little regard for the essential role of government, which is the control of money supply and management of demand. Greater attention to this role and less to the outward detailed

control would have achieved more for the economy. It would mean, of course, that the government had to exercise itself some of the disciplines on expenditure it is so anxious to impose on others. It would mean that expenditure in the vast public sector would not have to be greater than the amount which would be financed out of taxation plus genuine saving. For a number of years some expenditure has been financed by what amounts to printing money.

There were important differences. The later Thatcher would never allow that government had a role to play in the management of demand. But both the money supply and control of public borrowing were present in that speech. Her regular contacts with monetarist economists from the mid 1970s onwards were to provide the future Prime Minister with more insight into how to put these sound money ideas into practice.

Monetarist Advice

The Conservative Party after February 1975 was a natural magnet for monetarists seeking to bring their influence to bear on policy. Advice there was in plenty, but if Margaret Thatcher did have a 'kitchen Cabinet' of monetarists, it was one which changed personnel frequently.

Sir Alan Walters had met Thatcher at Institute of Economic Affairs lunches well before she became leader. He was a major influence. His Leicester bluntness appealed to Thatcher's Grantham common-sense, and he had a ready explanation for the failure of post-war 'fiscalist' policies. He had established his monetarist credentials both through academic work and, on a more public stage, as one of the Economic Radicals in November 1972. But the squeeze on public expenditure imposed by the IMF was starting to affect higher education, and for many British academics, in the mid 1970s, the grass looked greener elsewhere. Walters left the London School of Economics for the Johns Hopkins University in Baltimore in 1976 and, until his return as Thatcher's personal economic adviser in 1981, much of his advice had to be proffered from a long distance.

David Laidler and Michael Parkin, whose work at the Manchester Inflation Workshop was so important in the development of British monetarism, were also tempted away in 1976, to the University of Western Ontario.

But one fairly frequent visitor to Britain, often through the good offices of the Institute of Economic Affairs, was Milton Friedman. He was impressed, on the first of numerous meetings, with Margaret Thatcher's economic understanding. 'She recognized very clearly the relationship between monetary policy on the one hand and inflation on the other,' he said.

Brian Griffiths, Professor of Economics at the City University and later head of the Downing Street policy unit, was on hand. He advised the party's

Economic Reconstruction Group, chaired by Sir Geoffrey Howe, which in 1977 put together 'The Right Approach to the Economy'. It was a document which contained all the elements of Thatcherite economics, as presented to the electorate in 1979 – monetarism, public expenditure control, trade union reform, and improved 'supply-side' incentives through the tax system.

Mrs Thatcher did not confine her economic education to strict monetarism. In the mid 1970s two Oxford economists, Robert Bacon and Walter Eltis, wrote a book called *Britain's Economic Problem: Too Few Producers*. The book, published in 1976, was developed from a series of articles in the *Sunday Times* in 1974 and 1975. It was immaculately timed, coinciding with the publication of official figures suggesting that public expenditure was equivalent to 60 per cent of gross domestic product. The figures, which appeared in the 1976 public expenditure White Paper, were wrong, involving several elements of double counting. But, together with the Bacon and Eltis thesis, they fuelled widespread fears that Britain was being submerged by big government.

Bacon and Eltis drew a distinction between marketed and non-marketed output, the former mainly provided by the private sector, the latter by the public sector.

Marketed output by its nature was subject to competitive pressures, which push the private sector towards greater productivity. The same disciplines, it was claimed, were not present in the non-marketed sector. Apart from confirming many of the Thatcher prejudices about the public sector, the book contained several elements of relevance to the monetarist debate.

The first was the 'crowding out' argument implicit in the Bacon and Eltis thesis. Too rapid growth in the public sector, it was suggested, crowds out the private sector either by discouraging investment, as government borrowing pushes up interest rates, or by claiming scarce resources, for example skilled labour.

Bacon and Eltis also stressed the damaging role of the unions in the labour market. Excessive union power had pushed up the natural rate of unemployment in Britain and, while prudent monetary policies could ensure low inflation at the natural rate, other actions, and in particular trade union reform, would be required to reduce unemployment by cutting the natural rate.

A third and perhaps most relevant implication of Bacon and Eltis's work was that monetarism, without accompanying controls on the public sector, would bear down disproportionately on the private sector. Theories of the demand for money, including that of Friedman in his restatement of the quantity theory, are concerned with the private sector's demand for money. The public sector to all intents and purposes is assumed to have no money requirements. Thus, according to the monetarist economist Tim Congdon, the demand for money may bear a stable relationship to the income associated with marketed output, and not national income as a whole. It follows that the true monetarist relationship may be between the money supply and the marketed proportion of national income, but that control of the money supply will have little influence on the non-marketed public sector.

Therefore, while monetarist theory appeared to be neutral regarding the size of the public sector, monetarist practice, it seemed, required the sort of control over public expenditure imposed on Britain by the IMF in 1976.

Another influence was Patrick Minford, who emerged in 1976 from the Keynesian stronghold of the National Institute, having previously worked at the Treasury. He had become a passionate monetarist, with a certainty of view which appealed to Thatcher. Minford developed, as Professor of Applied Economics at Liverpool, lines of theoretical and empirical support, admittedly often very controversial ones, for a whole range of Thatcherite economic ideas. These included the economic need for trade union reform; the desirability of reducing state benefits; and the bankruptcy of Keynesian ideas about the effectiveness of fiscal policy. He combined monetarism and supply-side economics.

The New Wave

In 1976, Minford became the prime British exponent of an important second wave of monetarism, which offered even fewer concessions to the Keynesian position than did Friedman. This second wave, the new classical or rational expectations approach, offered a direct and express route from excessive monetary growth to inflation. The new classical economist did not allow that fiscal expansion could have even short-term output-boosting effects. Rather, the consequences of any such expansion would be quickly dissipated in higher prices.

Like Friedman's monetarism, the new wave was developed in the United States. In the early 1960s, John Muth had examined the behaviour of investors in financial markets and had come up with his efficient market hypothesis. The essence of this was that, in a financial market where transaction costs are low, investors act rationally on the basis of the information available to them.

Investors' behaviour is determined by their expectation of what the market is going to do, and by avoiding errors that could be spotted in advance. Thus, in a mature market, expectations are rational and actual behaviour is determined by such expectations. Markets therefore operate efficiently; people do not systematically make the same mistakes.

The concept of rational expectations did not necessarily carry a bias in favour of either Keynesian or monetarist viewpoints. Indeed, it has been applied in many Keynesian economic models. But, as applied by the new classical economists in the 1970s, it appeared to offer a devastating indictment of Keynesian demand management.

The pioneers in the United States were Robert Lucas, Thomas Sargent and Neil Wallace. They applied the rational expectations approach, not just to financial markets, but to the whole economy. The key to this was in Friedman's analysis of the Phillips curve.

In Friedman's analysis, there was only a trade-off between unemployment and unanticipated inflation. Starting from a position with inflation at 2 per cent and unemployment at 3 per cent, a fiscal and monetary expansion could temporarily reduce unemployment. However, when people begin to realize that the expansion is resulting in inflation of 4 per cent, they demand higher wages and unemployment rises once more. The same thing can happen again, as long as the government is prepared to live with higher inflation. But again, after a time behaviour adapts to the even higher inflation, and unemployment returns to its starting point.

The new classical economists replaced the 'adaptive' expectations assumption implicit in Friedman's analysis with one of rational expectations. By doing this, they dispensed with even the short-term trade-off between inflation and unemployment. Lucas and the other new classical economists argued that the adaptive expectations approach would be subject to a learning curve, probably of very short duration. Economic agents would quickly develop efficient methods of seeing through the short-term real effects of expansionary fiscal policies.

Individuals would, in effect, develop methods of forecasting the inflationary consequences of government action. For example, on the day after the Chancellor of the Exchequer had announced a major budgetary boost to the economy, unions would give notice to employers that they would be seeking higher wages to compensate for the price rises that were bound to result. Because of this, employers would be reluctant, either to take on extra workers, or to increase output. Instead, the whole of the budgetary boost would come through speedily, or instantaneously, in higher prices.

Going back to the Phillips curve analysis, the new classical approach implied no trade-off, either in the short term or the long term, between inflation and unemployment. Friedman's long-run vertical Phillips curve also existed in the short run.

Taken at face value, the new classical approach seems far-fetched. It requires that individuals can immediately see the inflationary effects of policy when its perpetrators, governments, with more sophisticated forecasting models at their disposal, could not. The new classicists allowed, however, that it was still possible for unanticipated inflation to take people by surprise and generate real effects. What it said was that governments could not fool the people indefinitely.

And the new wave, or Monetarism Mark II, emerged at a time when the financial markets did appear to be adopting a rational expectations approach to economic policy. It was the case that financial market economists provided instantaneous estimates of the inflationary consequences of any government action. In wage bargaining behaviour, in addition, there was increasing evidence that unions were no longer prey to the 'money illusion'. Rather, they were taking account of future inflation in framing pay claims.

The policy prescription of the new classical economists, albeit with even fewer caveats, was the same as that of Friedman. Governments should eschew discretionary monetary and fiscal policies and adopt fixed rules, month in, month out, for the growth of the money supply. The difference was that, under Monetarism Mark I, there could be short-term electoral advantages in expanding the economy – taking the credit for stronger growth now and dealing with the inflationary consequences after the election. In Monetarism Mark II, such options no longer existed.

Keynesians did not like Friedman's version of monetarism, and they were even less happy with Monetarism Mark II. James Tobin pointed out what he thought to be the great contradiction of the new classical economics. He said that it regarded inflation as the target of policy, the evil to be eliminated by means of tight monetary rules, but there was nothing in the new classical approach to say why inflation had to be driven out of the system. If all inflation is anticipated by all economic agents, and they all have the power to ensure that they are compensated for it as it happens, then inflation looks to be fairly harmless.

The challenge was a valid one, particularly in the framework of the simple, closed-economy models employed by the new classical economists. But old and new monetarists alike could provide a ready answer for why excess monetary growth and inflation were harmful in an open economy subject to the pressures of both foreign trade and capital movements. The international monetarism of the London Business School provided a formal framework for this.

The London Business School

The London Business School was established in 1965 as one of two centres of excellence for management education in Britain, the other being Manchester.

Its first Professor of Economics was James Ball, and one of his first decisions was the appointment of Terence Burns, newly graduated in economics from Manchester, in a research capacity. It was not clear from the outside what, if any, research role in economics the London Business School could be expected to take on. Its economics staff was tiny in number and looked on the face of it to have plenty to do in maintaining the teaching of economics in management courses, let alone developing research ideas.

But Jim Ball had other ideas. Keenly interested in economic forecasting and policy, he was determined to pursue those interests at the School. And in Terry Burns he had found an ideal foil. The first step was to develop a simple Keynesian model and to present regular forecasts for the British economy, in the pages of the *Sunday Times*. This was started towards the end of the 1960s, when economic forecasts carried more mystique and were held in greater trust than was to be the case later.

The economic forecasts put the London Business School on the map. To this day, the School is probably better known among the general public for its economic forecasting activities, formalized in the creation of a Centre for Economic Forecasting in 1976 (with Burns as the first director), than for its mainstream role of management education.

In the mid 1970s, when Margaret Thatcher was leader of the Opposition, Ball and Burns began to develop an alternative framework for the British economy to the Keynesian consensus in which they had been brought up.

The impetus for the London Business School's international monetarist approach came from two main sources. The first was the monetary approach to the balance of payments, developed by Jacob Frenkel and Harry Johnson. The second was the Keynesian New Cambridge theory (as quite distinct from the new classical approach described above) of Wynne Godley and Francis Cripps.

The New Cambridge approach developed during the first half of the 1970s and was seen as an attempt both to widen Keynesianism and to bring it into line with what was actually happening in the world. It focused on the financial balances of the three sectors of the economy – the private sector, the public sector and the overseas sector. There is a simple accounting identity, whereby the surplus or deficit of the overseas sector, the balance of payments, has to equal the sum of the surpluses or deficits of the private and public sectors combined.

Professor Godley and his colleagues found that the private sector was always in steady and predictable surplus, so that the deficit of the public sector, less this surplus, would be exactly reflected in the balance of payments. As initially framed, New Cambridge offered policy-makers a check for the important policy goal of balance of payments equilibrium. But as later developed, particularly when the assumption of a steady private-sector financial surplus broke down, its chief policy prescription became reflation behind a wall of import controls, as advocated by Kaldor when he was advising Harold Wilson in 1974 and 1975.

Burns, now joined by Alan Budd, was attracted by the New Cambridge concept of linking domestic policy to the external account. But his extensive work on financial flows suggested that the rate of growth of the money supply was of more direct relevance than the government deficit. The London Business School's international monetarist approach thus took the increase in the stock of money in Britain and set it against some measure of the rise in the world's money stock. The old doctrine of purchasing power parity implied that if one country had a higher inflation rate than another, the high-inflation country's currency would fall. The international monetarist approach said that such adjustment would occur earlier, as a result of differences in relative rates of monetary growth.

The London Business School's innovation was to solve the problem of how, in an open economy like that of Britain, changes in the money supply feed through to higher prices. Under the Burns, Ball and Budd approach, the transmission mechanism was the exchange rate. When the authorities in Britain allowed the money supply to rise sharply, relative to that in other countries, the resulting fall in the pound would lead to higher import prices and, after a lag, to higher inflation.

Although clearly a departure from Friedmanite monetarism, the London Business School analysis was very influential in Britain. The decision of the Chancellor of the Exchequer, Denis Healey, to stop trying to hold the pound down in October 1977 is generally attributed to the stern warnings from the London Business School of the consequences of doing so.

Burns and Budd also made their mark on policy with an article, published in the same year, advocating a medium-term financial plan.* 'In addition to an annual budget which contains a detailed description of components of tax revenue and expenditure,' they said, 'there should be a medium-term outline budget or financial plan which would contain estimates of tax receipts, expenditures and the borrowing requirement on the basis of existing policies with a set of targets for monetary aggregates, domestic credit expansion and reserve changes.'

It was, in essence, David Laidler's gradualist approach to monetarism, with the addition of the external sector. But Ball and Burns provided a practical example of how such a plan could be formulated and applied to the British economy in 1977. Their proposal was taken up by the Conservative authors of 'The Right Approach to the Economy', although there was some uneasiness with its description as a plan. In the minds of the *cognoscenti*, the word 'plan' carried the unhappy connotations of Labour's failed attempt to introduce full-scale national economic planning in 1965.

So when the proposal was put into practice three years later in March 1980, it was a medium-term financial strategy, setting out a programme of steady reductions in both the money supply and public sector borrowing over a four-

* 'How Much Reflation?', London Business School *Economic Outlook*, October 1977.

year period. By this time Burns was on hand to supervise it, having been lured away from the London Business School to become the government's Chief Economic Adviser. The post of Chief Economic Adviser, held by Burns, is distinct from that of personal economic adviser to the Prime Minister, taken up by Alan Walters in 1981. The Chief Economic Adviser is head of the Government Economic Service, is located in the Treasury, and has responsibility both for policy advice to the Chancellor of the Exchequer and for official economic forecasting. Often, as we shall see, the two advisers could differ on policy.

The London Business School was not and is not party political. Its advice and forecasts are available to policy-makers of all parties. But its emergence as an important centre of monetarist thinking, at a time when the Conservative Party under Margaret Thatcher was moving strongly in that direction, was a key element in the rise of monetarism in Britain. It offered a counter-weight to the Keynesian orthodoxy of the National Institute and Treasury, and served, perhaps more than any organization, to make monetarism respectable in Britain.

The City

The City of London, unlike the London Business School, has definite political preferences. Conservative governments are seen as more financially responsible and more likely to provide an environment favourable to the financial markets. Hence the City's dismay over the financial irresponsibility of the Heath/Barber boom, and hence the successful attempt by the financial markets to stamp down upon Denis Healey's attempt to reflate the economy too sharply in 1978.

The City, because it is in the business of moving and making money, was always likely to be more sympathetic to the notion that money matters in economic policy. The Bank of England shifted towards monetarism several years before the Treasury, and occasionally, in the 1980s, appeared to act as the Treasury's monetarist conscience.

During the 1970s, circulars written by stockbrokers' economists became steadily more monetarist in tone. Written primarily for institutional clients, they were also available to journalists, and were studied closely in the Bank of England and the Treasury. Their influence could be very considerable.

The prime area of concern for City economists is the market for government bonds, usually known as the gilt-edged market – because stock certificates traditionally had a gold border. A small rise or fall in interest rates, or a shift in the size of the public sector borrowing requirement, can have major effects on this market. But City economists also influence the equity and foreign exchange markets. The judgement on policy by City economists can mean the difference between success and failure in the government's funding efforts, and a rise or a fall for sterling and share prices.

Gordon Pepper and Tim Congdon stood out among City monetarists in the 1970s. Gordon Pepper, a Cambridge economics graduate, introduced the clients of his firm, W. Greenwell & Co., to monetarism long before it became fashionable. He has described his conversion to monetarism:

> Our researches into the money supply ... started in earnest in August 1968, partially inspired by meeting Beryl Sprinkel of Harris Trust & Savings Bank of Chicago, one of the most vocal of US monetarists.
>
> We were particularly impressed by his record of accurate forecasts, which he had documented. As a result we had had several months' progress by the time the IMF delegation arrived in the UK on 15 October 1968, after which the money supply became topical. Our first money supply note was circulated three days later and the second on 5 November 1968.

Pepper began to use a monetarist framework for forecasting the British economy in 1969 and quickly claimed a forecasting record superior to that of Keynesian models. In 1972, after research conducted with his colleague Robert Thomas, he concluded that: 'There is considerable empirical evidence in the UK that the money supply alters prior to a change in economic activity, but that the lag is long and variable. In general, the pattern appears to be very similar to that in the US.' He undoubtedly influenced Bank of England thinking in the 1970s, as the monetarist chorus in the City grew louder.

Tim Congdon worked as economics correspondent for *The Times* when Peter Jay was economics editor. In 1976, he left to work in the City for the stockbroking firm of L. Messel & Co. Two years later he wrote: 'The City has become the spiritual centre of British monetarism – particularly after the emigration of some academic monetarists, such as Laidler and Parkin, associated with Manchester University, in 1976. This outcome is not perhaps all that surprising since the City, far more than any other industry, is concerned that monetary policy be conducted on the right lines.'

As a former journalist, Congdon had the means of obtaining access to a far wider audience than most City economists. He continued to write for *The Times*, as well as for other publications such as the *Spectator* and the *Banker*.

It would be wrong to describe the City in the 1970s as completely won over to monetarism. Some City economists remained determinedly Keynesian, but the conversion rate of economists to monetarism was much faster in the City than elsewhere. And stockbroking firms without a resident monetarist could always draw on help from outside. Alan Walters, for example, wrote circulars for the now defunct firm of Joseph Sebag.

Selling Monetarism

In Britain during Margaret Thatcher's period as leader of the Opposition, it was possible to get the impression that the monetarists had all the answers. But, while many Keynesians had gone to ground, there was no shortage of intellectual opposition to monetarism, if one cared to look for it. The National Institute, for example, accurately predicted most of the problems and consequences of monetarism if applied, as the Conservatives appeared to be determined to apply it, to the British economy. But it was hard to run against the tide of fashion. The late Patrick Hutber, a vigorously pro-Thatcher financial commentator, described the National Institute's Economic Review as 'the Comic Cuts of economic forecasting'.

Having convinced themselves that they held the key, the Conservatives had to convince the electorate, and not least that what they were offering was different from Labour's monetary targeting. Two things assisted them in this task. The first was that James Callaghan and Denis Healey, having initially embraced monetary targets enthusiastically, were straining to break free from the monetarist yoke. The targets, it was argued strongly in the Labour Party, were imposing an unacceptable constraint on the government's freedom of action, particularly in fiscal policy.

Secondly, the monetarism of 1976 to 1979 was backed up by incomes policy, and this was becoming increasingly unpopular, not least in Labour's traditional area of support, the trade union movement. When the unions set in train the 'winter of discontent' of 1978/9 to break Labour's pay policy, they knew that they risked allowing in a Conservative government, albeit one that promised far-reaching trade union reforms.

The Conservative manifesto of 1979 went into some detail on the evils of inflation. Under Labour, it said, prices had risen faster than in any peacetime period 'in the three centuries in which records had been kept'. Labour had achieved a temporary reduction in the inflation rate, but it was now accelerating again: 'Inflation on this scale has come near to destroying our political and social stability.' Fortunately, the document went on, the remedy was at hand:

> To master inflation, proper monetary discipline is essential, with publicly stated targets for the rate of growth of the money supply. At the same time, a gradual reduction in the size of the Government's borrowing requirement is also vital. This Government's price controls have done nothing to prevent inflation, as is proved by the doubling of prices since they came to power. All the controls have achieved is a loss of jobs and a reduction in consumer choice.

The selling of monetarism, and the more general task of selling Margaret Thatcher as Prime Minister, was highly successful. Only a tiny minority of voters actually look at party manifestos but, through election broadcasts, political speeches and sympathetic newspaper coverage, the impression was conveyed of an economic policy package that was easy to understand and steeped in common-sense. In case anyone doubted this, Conservatives could point to the fact that Labour had also been persuaded of the wisdom of monetary targets, if unwillingly. The difference was that Conservatives understood such things better and would not require the unnecessary prop of prices and incomes policies.

In all this, two things were either not foreseen or intentionally played down. The first was that the monetarist route to the defeat of inflation would involve pain for the economy. The second was that saying you intend to control the money supply is one thing, but achieving such control may prove impossible. The stream of advice received by Mrs Thatcher and her colleagues could all be conveniently lumped under the general heading of 'monetarist'. The difficulty was that this catch-all description included several different schools of monetarism, all seeking to put forward their particular view of the world.

Thus there was the relatively straightforward quantity theory monetarism of Friedman and Alan Walters. There was the more eclectic international monetarism of the London Business School. There were the forthright advocates of monetary base control, an approach which implied acceptance of greater volatility of interest rates, such as Gordon Pepper and Brian Griffiths. And there was the rational expectations, new classical approach of Patrick Minford.

The distinctions were blurred. Friedman and Walters, and for that matter Minford, clearly favoured the monetary base – notes and coins held by the public and the banks, together with bankers' balances at the Bank of England – as the appropriate measure of money to target and control. There were, however, important differences of emphasis. And, having discovered a group of politicians actively interested in putting monetarism into practice, there was a clear reluctance among monetarists to blind them with too much science.

The advice was not necessarily consistent and, because it emanated from competitive viewpoints, it emphasized the painless aspects of monetarism. Any monetarist who sat down with the prospective Prime Minister and told her candidly that one of the consequences of the recommended policy would be unemployment of 3.5 million might not have been invited back.

To be fair, the playing-down of the pain probably arose less from deliberate concealment than genuine unawareness. As David Laidler wrote in 1985:[*]

> The successful critic of policy runs the danger of attracting an invitation to do better himself. Such was the fate of British monetarists when Mrs Thatcher came to

[*] *Oxford Review of Economic Policy*, Spring 1985.

power and for them (or us if I am still regarded as a member of the group) the experience has been chastening. Though some of us did expect the implementation of a monetary strategy designed finally to bring the great inflation of the 1970s to an end to have significant adverse effects, none of us expected the deep and prolonged depression that ensued.

The second difficulty, that of actually controlling the money supply, could have been foreseen. With the benefit of hindsight, it is clear that the Conservatives should have undertaken a great deal more preparatory work on the details of monetary policy, and the practicalities of monetary control. Such details, however, were not the natural preserve of the party leader, who was making the running on monetarism. The difficulty for a party in opposition is that it has no expert civil servants or central bank officials to hand to undertake such work, although Conservative supporters in the City could have been brought in to help more.

As it was, there was much complacency among Conservatives about this key aspect of monetarism. When elected in May 1979, the new government accepted the broad money measure inherited from Labour as the basis for monetary policy. At the same time, it undertook a number of bold steps which effectively threw a spanner into the works of monetary control.

7

TRIAL AND ERROR, 1979–82

Margaret Thatcher swept into office on 3 May 1979, with a bigger swing of support in her favour than any party leader had experienced since Labour's Clement Attlee in 1945. The Conservative campaign, a mixture of skill and good fortune, had worked unexpectedly well, providing her with the mandate to embark on radical changes in policy.

The Conservatives won 339 seats in the House of Commons, a majority of 70 seats over Labour and of 43 over all other parties combined. There was no question, or so it seemed, of the sort of fudge and compromise that Labour, with its narrow parliamentary majority in the period 1974–9, had been forced into. The May 1979 election also brought into the House of Commons a new generation of Conservative Members of Parliament, supportive of Thatcher's leadership and, initially at least, unlikely to rock the political boat.

It is a claim of all governments that they inherited virtually insurmountable problems from their predecessors, and it was one used frequently by the Conservatives following their 1979 election victory. The rate of inflation in May 1979 was 10.3 per cent, but there was evidence that it was accelerating. In the six months before the election, prices were rising at an annualized rate of nearly 14 per cent. More importantly, after four years of incomes policy, wage pressures were breaking out everywhere. In an attempt to bring an end to the industrial unrest of the 'winter of discontent', Labour had established a Comparability Commission for public sector pay, under the chairmanship of Professor Hugh Clegg.

The body could hardly have been more out of step with the new Conservative economic philosophy. Not only did it imply acceptance of the principle of interference in the labour market, as far as public sector pay was concerned, but it also squared badly with the aim of reining back public expenditure. The decision was taken, however, to honour the recommendations of the Clegg Commission which, when they appeared soon after the election, were for public sector pay rises of 15 to 25 per cent.

The decision to honour Clegg was soon regretted. The promise was made 'in the heat of the pre-election period', according to Nigel Lawson later. There was also a view, incautiously expressed in some ministerial speeches, that wage rises were an irrelevance, as long as the money supply was under control. This view appears to have been based on an imperfect understanding, to say the least. Monetarists, it is true, argued that a failure of wages to adjust would be reflected mainly in a movement of the recorded rate of unemployment above the natural rate. But the specific example of public sector pay was rather different, because of the key role ascribed to the public sector borrowing requirement in the control of sterling M3, the government's chosen target monetary aggregate.

As it was, there was a rise in the relative pay of the public sector, within the context of a sharp overall increase in wages, freed from the shackles of incomes policy. Average earnings in 1978 were 13 per cent up on a year earlier, in 1979 the rate of increase accelerated to 15.5 per cent, and in 1980 to nearly 21 per cent.

Even without the additional problems created by Clegg, public spending was on a rising trend when the Conservatives took office. It had risen by 6 per cent in real terms in 1978/9 to a correctly defined 40 per cent plus of gross domestic product. Labour's plans were for a real rise in spending of around 10 per cent between 1978/9 and 1982/3, so 'cuts' were needed just to hold the level of spending steady.

However, Thatcher did not inherit a monetary time-bomb of the type bequeathed to Labour by Edward Heath in 1974. Growth in sterling M3 in the twelve months to April 1979 was a little over 11 per cent, albeit partly held down by the corset controls on the banks. But the rise in M1, of 14.5 per cent, was by no means disastrous.

And there was an important bonus for the Conservatives. North Sea oil production had commenced in 1976 and, by 1979, was rising strongly. It was clear that among the spoils of victory in the 1979 General Election would, from the early 1980s, be oil self-sufficiency. This, removing the balance of payments constraint which had dogged successive British governments since 1945, and providing a substantial and sustained revenue boost for the Exchequer, gave the new government considerable room for manoeuvre.

The June 1979 Budget

After all the talk in opposition about what was going to be done to the economy, the Conservatives had just six weeks, once elected, to put together their first package of measures. Margaret Thatcher's first Chancellor of the Exchequer, Geoffrey Howe, presented his first Budget on 12 June 1979. It contained many of the elements signposted in the manifesto and 'The Right Approach to the Economy'. The main surprise was that so much was attempted in a single announcement.

Monetary policy was tightened. A target for sterling M3 of 7 to 11 per cent, at an annual rate, was set for the remainder of the 1979/80 fiscal year, and minimum lending rate was raised from 12 to 14 per cent. The 1978/9 sterling M3 target under Labour had been 8 to 12 per cent.

Public expenditure cuts, compared with Labour's plans, of £1.5 billion for 1979/80 were announced. In addition, £1 billion was to be raised from the sale of state assets, which counts as negative public spending, mainly from the disposal of part of the government's shareholding in British Petroleum.

The most controversial aspect of the Budget was, however, the Chancellor's tax measures. Even with the public expenditure cuts, Treasury calculations showed that there was little room for the substantial cuts in income tax promised by the Conservatives. The solution was, in part, to claw back in higher taxes on spending what was given away in lower taxes on income. Such a shift from direct to indirect tax was 'the only way that we can restore incentives and make it more worthwhile to work', according to Howe. The basic rate of income tax was reduced from 33 to 30 per cent, and all the higher rates were cut, the top rate of tax on earned income coming down from 83 to 60 per cent. Personal allowances against income tax were also raised, by more than 18 per cent. The cost in the 1979/80 fiscal year of these measures was estimated to be £3.5 billion, the full-year cost £4.5 billion.

Labour had warned during the election campaign that the Conservatives, if elected, would double the rate of value added tax. The charge was denied; indeed, it was nailed as one of Labour's twelve 'lies' about the Conservatives in the *Daily Mail*. But VAT was all but doubled in the June 1979 Budget. VAT on most non-food items had been levied at a standard rate of 8 per cent since July 1974; there was a higher rate of 12.5 per cent for so-called 'luxury items'.

Howe introduced a new unified VAT rate of 15 per cent, to raise £2 billion extra revenue in 1979/80 and £4.2 billion in a full year, but added 3.5 per cent to the retail price index in the process. Keynesians were bemused. Monetarists such as those at the London Business School, who had emphasized gradualism as a means of steadily reducing inflationary expectations, took the view – albeit politely – that the government had shot itself in the foot.

But other monetarists argued that, just as the 1974 reduction in VAT could not be regarded as an anti-inflationary measure, so the 1979 rise would not add to inflationary pressures. Alan Walters wrote later:

> It is difficult to see why such an obvious step-increase in certain prices, combined with downward pressure on the prices of excluded commodities, should lead to expectations of higher inflation (if, by inflation, we mean the persistent increase of

prices year after year). Rationality would suggest expectations of lower price increases in future years. Price increases remove inflationary pressure; they do not add to it.

Even if one accepts this argument, which many people would not, it rested on the assumption that the VAT increase was a once-for-all measure. And this was by no means clear at the time. The shift from direct to indirect taxation was presented as a continuing process.

There is another reason why the VAT increase is seen as an early and fundamental error of the Thatcher years. The June 1979 Budget was presented in an atmosphere, not of stable inflationary expectations, but of sharply rising expectations. The VAT increase added fuel to an already roaring fire. As well as the free-for-all of unfettered collective bargaining and the prospect of large pay rises in the public sector, there was a second major rise in oil prices.

OPEC II

After the first oil crisis of 1973/4, the world economy had to adjust to higher oil prices but not to further major price increases. The posted price of Saudi Arabian Light crude rose by about $2 a barrel between the middle of 1974 and the middle of 1978, to $13.66 a barrel. But in a time of fairly rapid world inflation, this implied a real price cut of around 15 per cent.

In the winter of 1978/9, all this changed dramatically. The trigger was the Iranian revolution late in 1978, when Islamic fundamentalists, under the leadership of the Ayatollah Khomeini, overthrew the Shah of Iran. Iran's 5 million barrels a day of oil production – she was the second largest OPEC producer – was suspended for ten weeks from 27 December 1978, before resuming at the much lower level of 2 million barrels a day.

There were other factors. Energy conservation measures had been introduced in all the major industrialized countries after the 1973/4 price rise, but had not gone far enough to reduce significantly the West's dependence on OPEC. The 1974/5 recession had given way to world recovery, and higher oil consumption. And the winter of 1978/9 was a harsh one in both Europe and the United States, automatically increasing oil demand.

This combination of events pushed up the price of oil sharply. The spot price of Saudi Light crude rose from $12.98 to $35.40 a barrel between October 1978 and June 1979. The spot market, where marginal, non-contract oil is sold, reflects the supply/demand situation far more quickly than official prices. Some crudes, including those of Nigeria and those produced in the North Sea, rose to more than $40 a barrel. Official OPEC prices, thanks to the restraining influence of Saudi Arabia, were held down. Even so, the official price of Saudi Light, OPEC's 'marker' crude, rose to $18 a barrel by June 1979 and $28 a barrel in May 1980.

The second oil price rise was both damaging and convenient for the Thatcher government. There was no substantial disagreement among the Western economies about the correct response to the oil price rise, unlike the situation in 1973/4. Thus there was an international seal of approval on the fiscal and monetary tightening embarked upon by the Conservatives which, without OPEC II, there might not have been. At the Bonn economic summit in 1978, Germany had been persuaded, temporarily, to reflate to promote stronger world growth.

The oil price rise also provided a ready explanation for the strength of sterling, by then regarded as a petrocurrency. A strong currency was useful, indeed indispensable, for a government which put the defeat of inflation at the head of its list of priorities. And it was so much better, when industry started complaining loudly, if the pound's rise could be blamed on factors outside the government's control.

Sterling's remarkable rise – it soared from a little over $2 when the Conservatives took office to $2.45 towards the end of 1980 – looked like a straightforward function of the oil price. The pound also rose against the traditionally strong currencies of Britain's major industrial competitors. It appreciated by more than 20 per cent against the Japanese yen and the German mark.

The Slump and the Medium-Term Financial Strategy

The bald facts of the 1979–81 recession are that Britain's gross domestic product fell by 2.2 per cent in 1980 and 1.6 per cent in 1981. But these figures conceal the severity of the recession and, in particular, its uneven impact. Between the second quarter of 1979, when the Conservatives took office, and the first quarter of 1981, industrial production fell by 12.8 per cent.

Manufacturing output, which did not include the booming North Sea sector, fell by 17.5 per cent over the same period. The Conservatives had inherited an unemployment total of just over 1.2 million. By the end of 1980, the total, including school-leavers, was above 2 million; by the autumn of 1982 it was through the 3 million barrier. For parts of the country there was economic devastation on a scale not seen since the 1930s. Factory closures and redundancies became an everyday occurrence. The West Midlands, on official figures, was second only to the South-East in gross domestic product per head in the mid 1970s. In the early 1980s, following the collapse of its manufacturing industry, it became the poorest region in England.

Following the bleak winter of 1980/81, with unemployment rising by more than 100,000 a month, the summer of 1981 was characterized by widespread rioting in Britain's inner cities. The cause of the riots remains a subject of some debate, but few would deny that unemployment played a part.

The recession was not the only problem facing a government just a few months into its attempt to pursue monetarism to its logical conclusion: the elimination of inflation. Within a year of the election, in May 1980, the rate of inflation had more than doubled, to nearly 22 per cent. The criticisms of Labour's economic management, which had allowed inflation to rise to more than 25 per cent during 1975, began to look a little hollow.

Inflation in the spring and summer of 1980 did, of course, reflect the special factors of the sharp rise in oil prices and the increase in VAT in the June 1979 Budget. Even so, inflation was clearly on a rising trend, from just over 8 per cent in 1978, to 13 per cent in 1979 and 18 per cent in 1980. Average earnings rose by 15.6 per cent in 1979 and almost 19 per cent in 1980. Creating a vicious circle of industrial decline, wages and salaries per unit of output rose by 21 per cent in 1980.

Sir Geoffrey Howe's attempt to control government borrowing was running into serious difficulties. The public sector borrowing requirement was £10 billion in 1979/80, boosted by, among other things, higher unemployment-related outlays on benefits. The target, set in June 1979, had been £8.25 billion.

There was one crumb of comfort, however, and an important one. The annualized growth of sterling M3 in the ten months from June 1979 was 10 per cent, within the 7 to 11 per cent target range.

Whether it was this latter sign of success amid all the other indications of policy failure, or a dogged determination not to repeat the Heath U-turn of 1972, Thatcher sided completely with her Treasury ministers when they demanded that the monetarist experiment be given its head. And so, in the difficult circumstances of March 1980, the medium-term financial strategy was launched. John Biffen, the Chief Secretary to the Treasury, and a man given to outbursts of occasionally embarrassing honesty, warned of 'three years of unparalleled austerity'. But he and the other Treasury ministers, and not least the Financial Secretary Nigel Lawson, were convinced that the pain was worth it.

The energetic Lawson, along with Terry Burns, the Chief Economic Adviser, and Peter Middleton, then deputy secretary but later Permanent Secretary to the Treasury, were the architects of the medium-term financial strategy (MTFS). The MTFS, embodying the gradualist approach of reducing inflation through steadily declining monetary growth, was launched by their political master, Chancellor Sir Geoffrey Howe, on 26 March 1980. The intention was clearly set out:

Control of the money supply will over a period of years reduce the rate of inflation. The speed with which inflation falls will depend crucially on expectations both within the United Kingdom and overseas. It is to provide a firm basis for those expectations that the Government has announced its firm commitment to a progressive reduction in money supply growth. Public expenditure plans and tax policies and interest rates will be adjusted as necessary in order to achieve the objective.

The target range for sterling M3 was maintained as 7 to 11 per cent for 1980/81 and then reduced to 6 to 10 per cent for 1981/2, 5 to 9 per cent for 1982/3 and 4 to 8 per cent for 1983/4. The public sector borrowing requirement was, similarly, to be steadily reduced over the period, from 4.75 per cent of gross domestic product in 1979/80, to 3.75 per cent in 1980/81, 3 per cent in 1981/2, 2.25 per cent in 1982/3 and 1.5 per cent in 1983/4. The main mechanism for achieving this was to be a reduction in public expenditure. The volume of spending was to be reduced by 4 per cent by 1983/4, overturning Labour's plans for a 10 per cent real increase by 1982/3.

The MTFS also included something which no government had attempted before, projections of future tax cuts, which proved irresistible to journalists. The strategy included figures for 'implied fiscal adjustments' in future years. In the March 1980 version, there were to be no net reductions in tax, apart from the normal indexation of personal tax allowances, in 1980 or 1981. But there were implied fiscal adjustments, or tax cuts, of £2.5 billion in 1982/3 and £3.5 billion in 1983/4.

The March 1980 Financial Statement and Budget Report was a remarkable document. As well as setting out the MTFS, it made no attempt to conceal the depressing short-term outlook for the economy. The Treasury forecast was for a 2.5 per cent fall in gross domestic product in 1980, followed by a further drop, of 1.5 per cent compared with the corresponding period of 1980, in the first half of 1981.

The Treasury, normally very cautious about committing itself to an unemployment forecast, conceded that there would be a rise. 'The implication of this forecast is for a further decline in employment and an increase in unemployment,' the Financial Statement said. 'The duration and scale of the rise in unemployment depends a great deal on how quickly the rate of inflation comes down.'

The 1980 Budget itself, despite the gloomy economic prospect, raised the overall level of taxation and reduced public spending, with the aim of achieving a public sector borrowing target of £8.5 billion. Tax increases and public spending reductions totalled £800 million. It was proof positive that the old ways, of a fiscal expansion out of recession, were no more. A year later, the 1981 Budget was to provide an even more dramatic demonstration of this.

The authors of the MTFS were well aware of the possible upsets that lay ahead on the four-year road mapped out. The assumptions on economic growth were deliberately cautious – an average of 1 per cent a year from 1980 onwards. There were, it was admitted, uncertainties over the world economy, over oil and other commodity prices, and over how quickly earnings would respond to lower inflation. There was also the major unknown of what the supply response of the British economy would be to lower inflation, and the promise of lower taxation. To keep public sector borrowing on a path consistent with a steady reduction in the growth of the money supply could involve some hard decisions.

However, through all these potential minefields the government would follow a single and powerful star. 'There would be no question,' it was said, 'of departing from the money supply policy, which is essential to the success of any anti-inflationary strategy.'

In the first three years the monetary targets were badly missed. Only in 1983/4 did monetary growth slow to within sight of the original 1980 target.

Table 1 The Medium-Term Financial Strategy (March 1980)

	1980/81	1981/2	1982/3	1983/4
Sterling M3 (per cent increase)				
Target	7–11	6–10	5–9	4–8
Actual	17.9	13.6	11. 7	8.2
Public Sector Borrowing Requirement				
(as per cent of gross domestic product)				
Target	3.75	3	2.25	1.5
Actual	5.4	3.3	3.1	3.2

Source: Financial Statement and Budget Report, 1980; *Financial Statistics*, HMSO

Even so, in every case the original monetary and fiscal targets were overshot. One school of thought has it that the severity of the 1979–81 recession was partly due to the fact that businessmen took the government at face value in its determination to beat inflation and, anticipating the consequent downturn, ran down their stocks and cut investment plans. Workers, on the other hand, did not believe it, wages were slow to adjust, and so the unemployment effects were particularly harsh. Looking at the government's record against its targets in the medium term, it is hard to know who had the better judgement.

The Great Monetary Control Debate

The Chancellor of the Exchequer, Sir Geoffrey Howe, was nothing if not bold. His June 1979 Budget had shocked, but he sprang another surprise on 23 October 1979 by announcing that, from midnight, all remaining exchange controls would be abolished. From that day on the controls, most notably on overseas investment by British institutions, were no more. The pound, it was thought, had lost its traditional prop and would quickly collapse. But it was not to be; investment outflows by institutions using their new-found freedom – overseas assets rose from £11 billion at the end of 1979 to £80 billion at the end of 1985 – were more than offset, initially, by capital inflows into Britain.

There was, however, an important monetary policy consequence of the removal of exchange controls. From 24 October 1979, the banking corset became redundant. Banks could by-pass the corset controls by lending to British customers from overseas subsidiaries. The corset, it was clear, had to go. The Chancellor announced its impending demise in his March 1980 Budget speech, and it was removed in June of that year.

The Bank of England had warned that the removal of the corset controls on lending would result in a one-off boost to sterling M3, as lending outside the broad money aggregate was brought back inside it. The Bank's best guess was that there would be a 3 per cent rise in sterling M3 as a result. This sort of figure, as a result of Bank guidance, was also generally the view of the financial markets. And so, when sterling M3 rose by 5 per cent in the July banking month alone, and by nearly 3 per cent in August, it was an early and substantial blow to the medium-term financial strategy.

There was, in any case, widespread dissatisfaction, inside and outside government, with existing methods of monetary control. Howe's first-year success in keeping sterling M3 within its target range had been achieved at considerable cost. Minimum lending rate had been pushed to a record 17 per cent in November 1979, where it was to remain for eight months. Even then, the money supply had only been kept within its target temporarily.

Bank of England and Treasury officials were instructed to put together proposals for changing the methods of monetary control, with a view to moving away from excessive reliance on high interest rates. High interest rates, far from acting as a brake on bank lending, appeared to add to the amount of distress borrowing undertaken by companies. Monetarists such as Brian Griffiths and Gordon Pepper urged the adoption of control of the monetary base – cash plus bankers' balances at the central bank: monetary control proper, albeit at the expense of a loss of central bank control over interest rates.

The Bank of England, is was clear from an early stage, was unwilling to cede control over interest rates, and move towards a monetary base system. In this it had important support within the Treasury, from the Chief Economic Adviser, Terry Burns, and from ministers, in particular Nigel Lawson. They saw sterling M3 as a highly appropriate monetary target for Britain, encapsulating, in a single aggregate, monetary control and a limitation on public borrowing. Burns, however, disagreed with his ministers on the need for a rigid, year-by-year reduction in the public sector borrowing requirement, arguing that it should be allowed to vary over the economic cycle.

A Green Paper, or consultative document, on monetary control was published in March 1980. It proposed technical changes in monetary control methods but stopped well short of a move towards a monetary base system. Both the analysis and recommendations infuriated a number of monetarists.

Milton Friedman, in evidence to the Treasury and Civil Service Committee, an all-party committee of Members of Parliament which in 1980 conducted its own investigation into monetary policy, was the most colourful. Referring to the Green Paper, he said: 'I could hardly believe my eyes when I read, in the first paragraph of the summary chapter, "The principal means of controlling the money supply must be fiscal policy – both public expenditure and tax policy – and interest rates." Interpreted literally, this sentence is simply wrong. Only a Rip Van Winkle, who had not read any of the flood of literature during the past decade and more on the money supply process, could possibly have written that sentence. Direct control of the monetary base is an alternative to fiscal policy and interest rates as a means of controlling monetary growth.'

Friedman was associated with the view, popular among monetarists outside government at this time, that some sort of conspiracy was under way between the Keynesian officials at the Treasury and the traditionalists at the Bank of England to sabotage the government's economic strategy. This was one factor which led Margaret Thatcher to call in independent economic advice in the form of Alan Walters – advice for which he was later to receive a knighthood.

The consultation process on the monetary control Green Paper produced a good old-fashioned British compromise. Sterling M3 was to remain the guiding light of policy but changes in methods 'consistent with the eventual adoption of a monetary base system' were also introduced.

Among these changes, introduced on 20 August 1981, was the abolition of the reserve asset ratio for the banks, introduced under the Competition and Credit Control changes of the early 1970s. There was a widening of the monetary sector to take in, as well as banks and licensed deposit-takers, the National Girobank, the Trustee Savings Banks, the banking department of the Bank of England itself and certain Isle of Man and Channel Islands banks. The requirement that the clearing banks alone should retain 1.5 per cent of their eligible liabilities at the Bank of England, in non-interest-bearing accounts, was removed. In future there would be the more equitable requirement that the new wider list of banks and licensed deposit-takers should hold 0.5 per cent of eligible liabilities at the Bank.

Perhaps most importantly, in a move which contained a hint, but no more, of a response to the criticism by Friedman and others, the Bank was to give up part of its role in setting interest rate. Minimum lending rate was suspended 'to allow market factors a greater role in determining the structure of short-term interest rates, and permit greater flexibility in these interest rates'.

The Bank would instead switch to dealing in money market bills, operating within an unpublished interest rate band, thus allowing the markets considerable leeway in setting rates. But any pretence that this constituted a 'hands-off' approach to interest rates by the authorities was short-lived. Within a few weeks of the August 1981 changes, the pound, by now experiencing a sharp reversal of its earlier strength, was falling fast. The Bank was obliged to force a rise in interest rates, which it did through its dealing operations in the money markets. Clearing bank base rates rose from 12 to 14 per cent in mid September, and further – to 16 per cent – in early October. The money markets quickly became adept at reading the Bank of England's intentions. Central bank control over interest rates was as firm as it had ever been.

Monetary Policy – Tight or Loose?

During this period, when monetary policy was under the microscope to an unprecedented degree, another important dispute occurred. Was it possible that the performance of sterling M3, which pointed to very loose monetary policy, was misleading? After all, during 1980 and the early part of 1981 the exchange rate was very strong, narrow money was growing only slowly, and industry was collapsing under the weight of high interest rates and the pound's strength.

It was a question to which Alan Walters, newly summoned from the United States to be the Prime Minister's personal economic adviser, addressed himself. The Centre for Policy Studies, the body set up in the mid 1970s by Sir Keith Joseph and Margaret Thatcher had, at Walters's suggestion, commissioned Jürg Niehans, the monetarist Professor of Economics from Bern University in Switzerland, to conduct an investigation into monetary conditions in Britain and, in particular, the strength of sterling.

The study's verdict was that the evidence pointed overwhelmingly to the conclusion that monetary policy in 1979/80 was far too tight, and that the popular explanation for the pound's strength, North Sea oil, only accounted for about 20 per cent of its rise. 'UK monetary policy not only seems to have rejected any concession to gradualism, but also refused to make any allowance for real growth,' he concluded. 'It thus appears to have been more abrupt than even the most ardent monetarists advocated. This was a policy shift with few historic precedents.'

Niehans advocated, as well as an easing of monetary policy, massive intervention in the foreign exchanges to drive the pound down from its $2.40-plus heights. Walters, when he arrived at Downing Street in January 1981, could not concur with all of Niehans's recommendations, but he agreed with the analysis. 'Before I came to No. 10,' he has recalled in his book, *Britain's Economic Renaissance*,

> I had already given a seminar and briefing in the United States in October and November when I argued that monetary policy was, if anything, too tight in 1979/80 and not too loose as indicated by sterling M3. The appreciation of sterling and all events other than the broad aggregates seemed to me to corroborate this view ... Subsequently, this view emerged from the study by Jürg Niehans which was commissioned by the Centre for Policy Studies.

These views, quickly available to Thatcher, clearly put the Treasury, and the government as a whole, in a difficult and embarrassing position. For eighteen months, it appeared, policy had been woefully misdirected. It had all been a dreadful mistake, and the consequences were there to see in factory closures and rapidly lengthening dole queues. It was small wonder that the initial response of Treasury ministers was to challenge the Niehans/Walters conclusions.

Nigel Lawson, the Financial Secretary, addressing the Zurich Society of Economics,* offered the following assessment:

> Certainly the evidence of the main financial indicators which generally speaking reflect monetary conditions – the strong exchange rate, high interest rates, the tight corporate liquidity position and decelerating inflation – would appear to confirm the message of the narrow money figures: namely that monetary policy has indeed been tight. Unfortunately it is not quite as simple as that. For the purpose of setting the annual target for monetary growth ... we have ... chosen broad money as the most useful guide.

After reminding his audience that the Heath government had been misled into thinking that monetary policy was not lax by low rates of narrow money growth, Lawson argued that the real question was whether monetary policy was too loose, as indicated by the pace of broad money growth. 'The conclusion I draw from all this,' he said,

> is that monetary conditions in the UK have not been inflationary so far, but that it is essential from now on to secure a lower rate of growth of broad money, and indeed, over the three remaining years of the medium-term financial strategy, it might well be prudent to claw back at least some of the excess growth that has already occurred.

And so the battle lines were drawn, Walters in Downing Street urging a monetary relaxation, based on narrow money growth and the other signs of tightness, and the Treasury ministers and their senior officials, their reputations

---

* 'Thatcherism in Practice: A Progress Report', delivered to the Zurich Society of Economics on 14 January 1981.

and the credibility of the medium-term financial strategy resting upon sterling M3, urging more of the same tightness for the next three years.

The message from narrow money, M1, referred to in Lawson's speech, was that it appeared to be very tightly under control. The high-interest regime actually produced a 1 per cent decline in M1 in the first quarter of 1980, followed by small rises in the subsequent three quarters.

The Treasury was on solid ground in arguing that the growth of M1 in this period seriously understated the true increase in the stock of money. Whatever other effects record interest rates were having on the economy, they were clearly rendering the holding of money in non-interest-bearing accounts unattractive – and 80 per cent of M1, which comprises notes and coin plus sterling sight deposits, was non-interest-bearing.

Nevertheless, it was clear that a route had to be found which steered a course between the two views. In fact, and perhaps not entirely intentionally, a shift in policy had already begun several weeks before Lawson's Zurich address and Walters's first day in Downing Street.

In the autumn of 1980, with the pound heading towards $2.50, the government came under intense pressure from industry to do something about the soaring pound and punitively high interest rates. Sir Terence Beckett, the recently appointed Director General of the Confederation of British Industry, promised, at the employers' organization's annual conference, a 'bare knuckle fight' with the government. The Chairman of I C I, Sir Maurice Hodgson, took the unprecedented step of warning the Prime Minister that his company, then regarded as the bellwether of British industry, was to announce a third-quarter loss. The result was that, in spite of continued above-target sterling M3 growth – by November the official target could only have been achieved by a decline in the broad money stock over the remaining months of the financial year – interest rates were reduced. On 24 November, the Bank of England reduced its minimum lending rate from 16 to 14 per cent.

The Budget of March 1981, generally taken to be the most dramatic demonstration of the fact that Keynesianism was no more, was also the starting-point for a further, and more substantial, monetary relaxation.

The Hair-shirt Budget

There have been several occasions in the post-war period when British Chancellors of the Exchequer have imposed severe fiscal squeezes on the economy. Roy Jenkins's 1968 Budget stands out, as do the various measures introduced by Denis Healey in 1976. The March 1981 Budget was not imposed from outside. But it is notable, when set against the economic conditions under which it was introduced, as the harshest of them all.

Fig. 2 The monetary squeeze

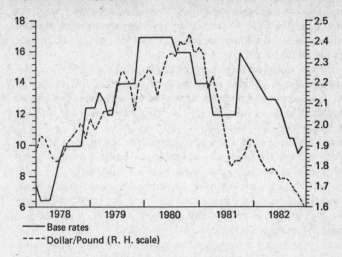

— Base rates
---- Dollar/Pound (R. H. scale)

There are any number of ways of assessing the stance of fiscal policy, all of them open to objections of one sort or another. But all show that the 1981 Budget produced a dramatic tightening of fiscal policy. On one estimate, by Professor Marcus Miller, the government's structural balance – the fiscal deficit adjusted to take account of the economic cycle – moved from a deficit equivalent to 4.4 per cent of gross domestic product in 1979 to a surplus of 2.6 per cent of GDP in 1982.

A fiscal tightening equivalent to 7 per cent of gross domestic product was unprecedented. The 1981 Budget was introduced at the trough of the cycle, after an eighteen-month period when manufacturing output had plummeted by 17.5 per cent and unemployment had broken through 2 million and was rising by 100,000 a month. The Treasury and some outside economists had detected signs of a bottoming-out for the economy, but such evidence was highly tentative. The fiscal hair-shirt was being worn at a time when all previous post-war governments would have regarded it as their duty to provide a budgetary boost to a badly depressed economy.

A demonstration of how extreme the Budget was regarded was provided by an outburst of Keynesian indignation. Frank Hahn and Robert Neild, two of Britain's most distinguished Professors of Economics, circulated a statement of protest from Cambridge to economics departments around the country. It attracted 364 signatures, including those of four former Chief Economic Advisers to the government.

The statement, published at the end of March 1981, and sent to Downing Street and the Treasury, concluded that: 'Present policies will deepen the depression, erode the industrial base of our economy, and threaten its social and political stability.' It attracted a great deal of interest and a certain amount of government-inspired ridicule.

The statement was interesting in two respects. It showed that, long after the monetarist counter-revolution, large numbers of economists in Britain remained, to all intents and purposes, untouched by it. Perhaps more significantly, it illustrated the fact that the shift in policy taking place had not been picked up, even by the professionals.

The fiscal tightening of 1981 was accompanied by a relaxation of monetary policy. And this was the principal outcome of the debate conducted in the winter of 1980/81 on whether or not monetary policy was too tight. Treasury ministers and officials, while defending the existing monetary policy stance and the appropriateness of the broad money, sterling M3 target, could agree with Alan Walters, and others who took the opposing view, on one thing at least. Fiscal policy was not under control.

At the time the March 1981 Budget was being prepared, the public sector borrowing requirement for 1980/81 appeared to be heading for around £13.5 billion, a full £5 billion above target. The eventual out-turn was £12.7 billion, still well above target. The combination of, as it appeared, relatively tight monetary policy and relatively loose fiscal policy could be expected to produce high interest rates and, as a result, a strong exchange rate. These were the very conditions that were being experienced in Britain at the time.

So, while the Treasury could not be persuaded to shift the focus of policy visibly from sterling M3, a tilting of the fiscal/monetary mix was in order. Thus the austere 1981 Budget was essentially a smokescreen for a relaxation of monetary policy.

The Budget itself aimed to reduce the PSBR to £10.5 billion in 1981/2, mainly through higher taxation. Excise duties were raised by £2.4 billion, adding 2 per cent to the retail price index. There was a supplementary petroleum duty designed to milk a greater proportion of North Sea profits and a one-off 'windfall' tax on the banks, to bring in £400 million.

But most notable was the fact that Howe broke with what had become a requirement for Chancellors since the mid 1970s, and which Nigel Lawson, while in opposition, had been instrumental in making so – the raising of personal tax allowances and thresholds in line with inflation. The Budget left allowances unchanged which, with inflation at 13 per cent, implied an increase of £1.9 billion in income tax. Less than two years after the Chancellor had made such a play of reducing income tax this was hard to swallow, for Conservative supporters and opponents alike.

The Budget would have been tighter still had Walters, with the support of Sir John Hoskyns, head of the Prime Minister's policy unit, had his way. They were arguing for a package which would have reduced the PSBR to well under £10 billion, although Walters later accepted that £10.5 billion was the minimum that was politically acceptable at the time.

The Budget kept to the letter of the medium-term financial strategy with a sterling M3 target of 6 to 10 per cent. But, contrary to Lawson's Zurich suggestion of January, no attempt was to be made to claw back the excess growth of 1980/81, when sterling M3 grew at double the rate implied by its target range. More importantly, despite that overshoot, minimum lending rate was reduced by two points to 12 per cent in the Budget.

The effects of the tilting of policy came through quickly. The pound, which averaged $2.30 in the first quarter of 1981, fell below $2.10 at the end of May, to $1.95 at the end of June, and to $1.85 in the last week of July. The rate of monetary growth accelerated. Sterling M3, which had risen by 2.2 per cent in the first quarter of 1981, grew by 4.2 per cent in the second and 4.8 per cent in the third quarter. Narrow money, M1, which had increased by less than 3 per cent in the twelve months to September 1980, rose by 12 per cent in the following twelve months.

It has been the experience of the floating exchange rate era that controlled currency movements are virtually impossible to achieve. So it proved in 1981.

Fig. 3 Volatile money

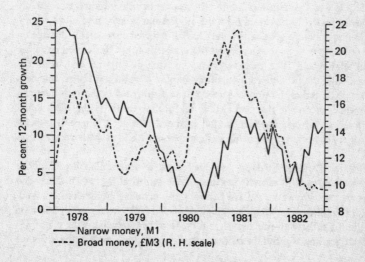

— Narrow money, M1
---- Broad money, £M3 (R. H. scale)

The foreign exchange markets, now seeing the British government as willing to tolerate a monetary overshoot and anxious to drive down the pound, regarded sterling as a straight sell. When the policy tilt of March 1981 was embarked upon, the Treasury and the Bank of England clearly had a reasonable idea of what size of fall in the exchange rate would steer the right course of boosting output without fostering too much extra inflation through higher import prices. Although exchange rate targets were never stated and, it is claimed, did not even feature as internal aims, it appears that the initial goal was to move the pound's average value, as measured by the sterling index, from a level of over 100 early in 1981, to about 90.

By the end of August, it appeared that this had been accomplished successfully. The pound had dropped further against a strong dollar, to about $1.75, but this was followed by a recovery. By the end of the month it was at $1.85 and the sterling index was just above 91.

Then, however, the pound was hit by a second wave of selling, driving it down both against a weaker dollar and other major currencies. By mid September it had dropped by a further 5 per cent and the inflation warning signals were flashing. The Bank of England forced interest rates up by two percentage points, from 12 to 14 per cent. But, in a market hungry for blood, this was not enough. A second, Bank of England-inspired raising of short-term interest rates from 14 to 16 per cent followed at the beginning of October and finally succeeded in steadying the sterling index around 90.

The game had very clearly changed. The monetary targets still existed but appeared to be subservient to the exchange rate in determining monetary policy. It was a pattern familiar to all post-war British governments, scarcely different under floating rates from the old Bretton Woods fixed rate system.

So was the monetarist experiment, having inflicted considerable damage on the economy with its misguided tightness, already over? Not according to the Bank of England. The exchange rate, the Bank of England said in its explanation of the two interest rises of the autumn of 1981, was indeed the main factor. 'The authorities were concerned that a further fall in the exchange rate, following the decline that had already taken place earlier in the year, would have serious adverse implications for inflation,' it said. 'A failure to respond rapidly to downward pressure on sterling appeared likely to accelerate sterling's fall.'

But the Bank of England also cited signs of accelerating broad money growth – admittedly sketchy because of the statistical fog which descended over the economy with the Civil Service strike of 1981 – in the decision. And, again according to the Bank, nothing had changed. 'Monetary policy had thus continued to have to pay regard to a range of considerations: the target aggregate, sterling M3, and the other monetary aggregates, as well as the exchange rate, the rate of inflation and developments in the economy affecting them,' it said.

It made sense, but was it monetarism? Certainly, it could hardly have been further away from Friedman's textbook version of monetarism, with fixed monetary rules and non-discretionary monetary policy. And certainly it was a long way from the vision provided by the Conservatives in 1979. Perhaps most damning of all, the Bank of England's claim of consistency in policy implied that the rise in the exchange rate which had wrought so much havoc was willingly tolerated.

Money GDP

By the autumn of 1981, Britain's monetarist experiment was in a mess. The attempt to control sterling M3 had run into enormous difficulties and these appeared to offer a classic demonstration of Goodhart's Law. This, coined by Professor Charles Goodhart, then chief monetary adviser to the Bank of England, is a sort of Murphy's Law of economic policy. It says that any monetary aggregate which the authorities try to control automatically becomes subject to distortions which render such control difficult in the extreme.

It was not clear, either in the financial markets or, it appears, within the government, precisely what weights were to be attached to the monetary targets, the exchange rate, and other factors. Fortunately, help was at hand.

Samuel Brittan, the principal economics commentator of the *Financial Times*, had begun to urge a change of emphasis. Policy was bogged down in the fine details of individual targets for the money supply and public sector borrowing, he said. The financial markets had an easy prey. Picking holes in policy was relatively easy, forcing the authorities into short-term actions which were not necessarily consistent with long-term objectives. The targets and the policy response were determined by what was happening on the MV side of the quantity theory equation, whereas the objectives were on the opposite, PY side, the path of gross domestic product in money terms. 'A stable growth of monetary demand (i.e. total spending or money GDP) is the most that can be achieved by fiscal, monetary or exchange rate policy,' he wrote. 'If money GDP can be kept on a stable path, a contribution will be made to avoiding fluctuations in output and employment as well as to securing price stability. If these modest goals can be achieved, the climate may also be improved for the long-term growth of output and employment.'

In other words, if money GDP is the prime target, it matters less if the targets for the intermediate money supply and borrowing targets are achieved to the last decimal point. There is a reduction in the tendency for policy to be held hostage by the financial markets.

However, money GDP targeting, which had earlier been advocated by the Nobel Prize-winning British economist Professor James Meade, was not welcomed, either in Downing Street or the Treasury. The monetarist objection was quite straightforward. Targeting money GDP was rather like having your cake and then deciding what the ingredients should be. If money GDP was found to be diverging from its growth path now, the correct response, if it was possible, was to go back twelve or eighteen months and change the course of the money supply. Money GDP was the product of earlier changes in the money stock.

Even setting aside this fundamental problem, the concept was attacked for its lack of practicality. Official figures for money GDP are produced on a quarterly basis, three or four months after the end of the quarter to which they apply. Policy would not necessarily be operating on last year's Bradshaw, but it would clearly be responding to something that was already history.

This objection has probably been overstated. Even though money GDP figures were not available in a timely fashion it was possible, from the regular monthly statistics for inflation, output and spending, to build up a reasonably accurate and up-to-date proxy path for money GDP.

It was not to be. The Treasury, out of the difficulties of the years 1979 to 1981, had accepted that a recasting of the medium-term financial strategy was necessary, but within the existing framework of policy. In Downing Street, Alan Walters, pleased to have brought narrow money into the policy equation, was most unwilling to flirt with money GDP targeting.

Money GDP entered the jargon of Treasury speech-writers and featured in the March 1982 Budget document. 'In judging the rate of monetary growth now appropriate,' it said, 'the government has taken account of the sharp deceleration in money GDP that has occurred.' But there were no money GDP targets.

According to Alan Walters, writing of 1982: 'There were suspicions that the government was really targeting the growth of nominal [money] GDP, which appeared to be declining in a steady course ... such suggestions were mistaken.'

Pragmatism was preferred.

8

UNWINDING THE POLICY

By the end of 1981, Britain's monetarist experiment appeared to have been an unmitigated disaster. Inflation, at nearly 12 per cent, was higher than when Mrs Thatcher took office, despite the worst recession since the 1930s. Unemployment rose by three-quarters of a million in 1981 alone, and was heading relentlessly towards three million. The attempt to relax monetary policy, which began formally with the March Budget, had been halted in the autumn by the financial markets.

The government was achieving a reputation for savage cuts in public spending without making any inroads into total expenditure. In its first three years, real public spending rose by nearly 6 per cent overall, and increased from 40.5 to 44 per cent of gross domestic product.

Public spending was proving to be a nightmare for successive Chief Secretaries to the Treasury – first John Biffen and then Leon Brittan. Despite clearing out much of the 'wet' opposition from within her Cabinet in a major reshuffle in September 1981 (the departures included those of Sir Ian Gilmour, Mark Carlisle and Lord Soames, while James Prior was sent away to Northern Ireland), the autumn spending round was bitterly fought.

Public spending was partly buoyed up by demand-led outlays on higher unemployment and social security benefits, and partly by election commitments to spend more in areas such as law and order and defence. Higher spending disposed of any spare resources for tax cuts, and continued to exert pressure on the targets for public sector borrowing, even though these were far higher than envisaged in the 1980 medium-term financial strategy.

In one of a number of 'catch 22s' emerging at this time, it appeared that reining back spending on the nationalized industries and local authorities had to involve higher charges and rates. These, while adding directly to the recorded rate of inflation, also gave a further turn to the vicious circle by adding to the pressure on industry to shed labour – pressure already intense because, following the pound's too sudden fall, bank base rates had been pushed back up to near-record levels in October 1981.

Margaret Thatcher's political star, riding so high in 1979, was now falling alarmingly. The very qualities of strength and resoluteness which had appealed to the electorate now began to smack of pig-headedness. Her harsh, unbending style had become a political liability. The Falklands war of the spring of 1982, which was to rescue the Prime Minister politically, was still some way off, and could not have been foreseen. In the meantime, early in 1982, Mrs Thatcher's standing appeared to rest on the state of the economy. The one could not improve without noticeable improvements in the other.

The first attempt at moving away from the rigidity of the government's initial approach had failed. It was the task assigned to Sir Geoffrey Howe and his Treasury team to convey, in the 1982 Budget, a multi-faceted message. This was that inflation was being defeated, and that there had been no let-up in the government's resolve to beat it; that a consistent policy line had been followed since 1979, despite indications to the contrary; and, perhaps most importantly, that there was now plenty of room for growth in the economy if people chose to look for it.

The Medium-Term Strategy, Mark II

March 1982 marked the official end of the attempt at simple monetarism in Britain – the idea that rules could be set for the growth of the money stock and that, come hell or high water, those rules should not be tampered with at the whim of politicians.

The actual end of 'punk monetarism', as Denis Healey, by then the chief thorn in Sir Geoffrey Howe's flesh on the Opposition front bench, described it, had come earlier. To some commentators, March 1982 represented the end of the monetarist experiment. That was premature. But it was the start of the official process of unwinding the policy, beginning with a pragmatic monetarism that was to give way to total pragmatism.

Two years of missed targets, for both the money supply and public sector borrowing, had made the medium-term financial strategy of March 1980 a laughing stock. A new and more accommodative version was devised for the March 1982 Budget. It was less a question of moving the goalposts than laying out a new pitch.

The re-writing of the MTFS in March 1982 was important in several respects. It denoted a recognition that the 1980 targets had been wildly optimistic. In places where the two versions overlapped, this was shown particularly clearly. The ranges for monetary growth in 1982/3 and 1983/4 were set three percentage points higher in the second version than the first. Similarly for the public sector borrowing requirement as a proportion of gross domestic product, the new targets were substantially more generous than the old.

The Treasury, having framed the original strategy in terms of a single target

Table 2 The Medium-Term Financial Strategy, Marks I and II

	1980/81	1981/2	1982/3	1983/4	1984/5
March 1980 ranges for monetary growth (£M3), per cent	7–11	6–10	5–9	4–8	—
March 1982 ranges for monetary growth (M1, £M3, PSL2), per cent	—	—	8–12	7–11	6–10
March 1980 PSBR/GDP, per cent	3.75	3	2.25	1.5	—
March 1982 PSBR/GDP, per cent	—	—	3.5	2.75	2

Source: Financial Statement and Budget Report, 1980 and 1982; *Financial Statistics*, HMSO

aggregate, sterling M3, now included additional money measures. Thus there was a narrow measure, M1, to satisfy the Downing Street critics of the over-reliance on sterling M3 in 1980/81, and there was an even broader measure, PSL (private sector liquidity) 2. This, which included building society deposits withdrawable on demand, could be expected to overcome one problem with sterling M3, that part of its excessive growth may simply have reflected changes in market share between banks and building societies. PSL2, a broader catch-all measure, would be neutral regarding such changes although not, until it was redefined in 1986, to the public's increasing predilection for holding term deposits in building societies.

Three targets could perhaps be expected to overcome the single aggregate problem encapsulated in Goodhart's Law, where any aggregate targeted by the authorities automatically becomes subject to distortions which render its control difficult. Hitting the bull with one arrow was hard; surely three arrows aimed together at an easier target could be expected to hit home?

The new strategy extended for only three years, compared with the earlier four. And one reason advanced for this, the fact that the beginning of the 1984/5 financial year would mark the end of the government's maximum term of office before a General Election, was a half-hearted one. A government wanting to win the confidence of the financial markets presumably also had to display confidence in its own re-election prospects.

There was a once-bitten, twice-shy tone about the second medium-term strategy, and this was the principal reason for only mapping out a three-year path for monetary growth. Perhaps most importantly of all, the new monetary targets, unlike their predecessors, were not to be regarded as sacrosanct.

In March 1980, the Treasury had stressed that 'there would be no question of departing from the money supply policy', whatever might be necessary to achieve it. In March 1982, on the other hand, there was to be no question of sticking to monetary rules that circumstances had rendered inappropriate. According to the Financial Statement and Budget Report, 'The ranges for 1983/4 and 1984/5 will be reconsidered nearer the time, and will take account of structural and institutional changes which may affect the economic significance of the different aggregates.'

Finally, the behaviour of the pound, which had already shown itself to be important in guiding interest rate decisions, was formally given a new prominence. 'Interpretation of monetary conditions will continue to take account of all the available evidence, including the behaviour of the exchange rate,' the Treasury said.

The scene was set for a repeat of the abortive 1981 attempt to drive interest rates down. Indeed, this was stated explicitly: 'The government intends to pursue a fiscal policy that will leave room for a fall in interest rates within the overall financial discipline needed to reduce inflation.'

And so, just as it is possible to find a quote in the Bible to fit every situation, there appeared to be something in the new, broader and looser medium-term financial strategy to satisfy the financial markets that everything was proceeding according to plan. If the exchange rate was weak, ministers could point to the behaviour of one or more of the monetary aggregates. And if these were misbehaving, then not to worry – as long as sterling was firm.

The changed approach was neatly summed up by John Fforde, then an adviser to the Governor of the Bank of England and, according to William Keegan's entertaining account in *Mrs Thatcher's Economic Experiment*, one of two Bank officials lambasted by Mrs Thatcher in the summer of 1980 for allowing sterling M3 to grow too fast. In a speech called 'Setting Monetary Objectives', delivered in New York in May 1982, he said:

> In brief, the UK monetary authorities again confirmed that while the counter-inflationary strategy remained unaltered in substance, their presentation of the money supply as an intermediate target in pursuit of that strategy had been modified in the light of experience since 1979. It remains to be seen how this relatively pragmatic approach will evolve, both in its practical application and its intellectual and political presentation. But it clearly represents a rather greater emphasis on empiricism in the monetary policy field.

And he concluded:

As may now be visible, this means that setting objectives for the money supply, and endeavouring to carry them out, has become a more humble pursuit. It does not lack resolve, or a clear sense of direction, but it recognizes once more that the successful execution of monetary policy requires the exercise of judgement, and of a constantly interpretative approach to the evolving pattern of evidence. Except in some grave emergency, or in the initial phase of a novel strategy, the abandonment of judgement in favour of some simple, rigid, quantitative rule about the money supply does not reliably deliver acceptable results.

It could hardly have been further removed from Milton Friedman's non-discretionary monetary rules.

Electioneering and Exchange Rate Crises

Economic policy in Britain follows an observed cycle closely related to the timing of General Elections. In the first two years of a parliamentary term, judgement day at the ballot box is sufficiently far away as to be effectively disregarded, provided that the government has a sufficiently large majority in the House of Commons. By the end of the third year, bearing in mind that few governments stay for their allotted five years, the next election has begun to loom rather large. This was the case in March 1982.

The first priority of the Conservative government was to win back the support of its natural constituency among businessmen and industrialists, battered by the 1979–81 recession. The main method of achieving this was the stated one of reducing interest rates. Following the rise to 16 per cent early in October 1981, base rates had been eased down cautiously to a still high 13.5 per cent by Budget day, 9 March 1982. There was a further half-point cut in the week of the Budget, followed by regular reductions in subsequent months. By November 1982, base rates stood at 9 per cent, just over half their level the previous autumn.

In the Budget, Howe announced a reduction in the national insurance surcharge, the 'tax on jobs' introduced by Denis Healey in the form of additional employers' national insurance contributions, and reviled by the Confederation of British Industry. The reduction, with a first-year cost of £1 billion, took precedence over reductions in personal tax, which could wait until rather nearer the election. Income tax was reduced only modestly, by raising personal allowances and thresholds by 14 per cent, rather than the 12 per cent needed to compensate for inflation.

For the first time since taking office in 1979, things appeared to be moving Mrs Thatcher's way in the economy, as they were politically as a result of the Falklands war. To the considerable surprise of the Treasury, and of any

Fig. 4 UK inflation

— Inflation rate
(retail prices)

number of monetarist forecasters in the City, inflation began to fall rapidly, notwithstanding earlier strong growth in broad money. The Treasury's Budget prediction was for 9 per cent inflation by the fourth quarter of 1982, but the final figure, partly due to declining oil and commodity prices as the United States economy entered a down-turn, was 6.2 per cent.

Growth in the economy was becoming a little clearer, albeit with a modest 1.9 per cent rise in gross domestic product in 1982, and manufacturing output flat. Even so, growth of any sort was in welcome contrast to the declining US economy.

Unemployment remained the black mark. The 'headline' total, including school-leavers, rose above three million in the summer of 1982, for the first time since the 1930s. But there were faint glimmers of hope here too. The rise in the adult total was 285,000 in 1982, less than half the 660,000 increase in 1981.

Recognizing that nothing could be done to make substantial inroads into the unemployment total before the election, the government chose to concentrate on the majority of voters who were still in work, and fashion a good old-fashioned pre-election boom. Much has been made of Sir Geoffrey Howe's fiscal rectitude when in sight of the election. The tax cuts that were made, both in 1982 and 1983, were relatively modest. The public sector borrowing requirement in 1982/3, at £8.9 billion, was actually a shade under the £9.5 billion target.

But there is more than one way of skinning a cat, and the Treasury was able to discover other ways of generating a consumer spending boom. Hire-purchase controls had traditionally been used by post-war Chancellors as a means of regulating spending in the economy. When the economy appeared to be overheating and the balance of payments was running into difficulties, controls would be tightened, for example by requiring a greater proportion of the price of a car or television set to be laid down as a deposit. Alternatively, when the economy showed signs of slackening, the controls were loosened.

On 26 July 1982, Howe did not merely loosen hire-purchase controls, he abolished them. In a period of falling interest rates, this could only mean a big increase in sales of cars and consumer goods, financed on the 'never never'.

The sharp 1982 fall in inflation had not just taken the Treasury and the City by surprise. Union wage negotiators, reconciled in a period of rising unemployment to at best compensating their members for inflation, suddenly found that they had done rather better than they expected.

With inflation down to just over 6 per cent by the end of 1982 and average earnings rising at just under 8 per cent, those who had escaped the dole queues found that they were enjoying rising real incomes. And the fall in inflation, together with lower interest rates, encouraged people to save less and spend more. The saving ratio – the proportion of income that people save – declined from 16.3 per cent at the end of 1980 to 11.4 per cent in the third quarter of 1982 and further, to 10.6 per cent, in the first quarter of 1983.

A consumer spending boom, neatly timed for an election that looked certain to take place during 1983, was guaranteed. In the first half of 1983, consumer spending in real terms was 4 per cent higher than its level a year earlier.

The Chancellor, however, left nothing to chance, and even this was not considered enough to ensure the appearance of robust, election-winning economic recovery. In his autumn statement in November 1982, in what looked like a straightforward piece of Keynesian pump-priming, Sir Geoffrey Howe exhorted local authorities and nationalized industries to ensure that they met their capital spending targets. Local authorities were encouraged to release home improvement grants, worth up to 90 per cent of the cost of improvements – a bonanza for self-employed builders and for the middle classes 'gentrifying' Victorian and Edwardian houses.

Whether it was this last move, or the too-rapid rundown of interest rates, or the approaching election and the consequences of a Labour victory, or – more likely – a combination of all three, the financial markets began to get very nervous around this time. Peter Shore, Labour's Chancellor-designate, suggested that a 30 per cent sterling devaluation was needed to allow British industry to compete in world markets, and that this was what a Labour government, if elected, would be seeking to achieve. Terry Burns, the government's Chief Economic Adviser, said in evidence to the Commons

Treasury and Civil Service Committee that a 5 to 10 per cent depreciation of sterling would not be regarded as a major devaluation, remarks interpreted to mean that this was the sort of fall the Treasury was seeking.

Currency dealers had seen it all before, and sold the pound. The sterling index measure of its average value fell from 92.5 in October to just above 85 in December, an 8 per cent drop. The pound fell against all major currencies.

The new, catch-all versions of monetarism offered little comfort. Sterling M3 for once behaved itself, increasing at a rock steady 2.2 per cent quarterly rate during 1982 because, paradoxically, lower interest rates made putting money on deposit with the banks less attractive. But narrow money, M1, was accelerating for the same reason, rising by 2.3 per cent in the second quarter of 1982, 3 per cent in the third and 4.7 per cent in the fourth.

There was no alternative but to push up interest rates, and blame the Opposition for it. Having moved all the way down to 9 per cent by early November, base rates were back up to 10 to 10.25 per cent by the end of the month, and to 11 per cent in January.

It was a lesson that was going to be repeated on several occasions. The government had moved away from single-target simple monetarism, be it in fact or just in presentation. But by throwing more things into the monetary policy stew, the authorities could not prevent the financial markets from focusing on one ingredient, in this case the exchange rate, with damaging consequences.

At this point, it is worth considering what steps a monetarist government, committed to reducing inflation still further, should have been taking early in 1983. The exchange rate was still falling, in spite of higher interest rates. By February the sterling index was down to 80, a further 6.5 per cent fall. All three monetary aggregates were rising at a rate above the official 8 to 12 per cent target range in the first quarter of 1983 – M1 at an annualized rate of over 14 per cent, sterling M3 at a 17.5 per cent rate and PSL2 at a 21 per cent rate.

The message seemed clear: monetary policy had to be tightened further. But the party managers had their eyes on a summer election, at which point, according to advice received from Treasury ministers, inflation would have fallen substantially, albeit to a temporary low. So monetary policy was relaxed, with interest rate cuts in both March and April, and any problems that this stored up for the future could be tackled later.

In the same way, the March 1983 Budget contained its share of pre-election handouts within an overall package which, while presented as an example of the government's financial responsibility and resolve, contained the most suspect Budget arithmetic seen for a long time. The Chancellor was able to cut income tax, again through the preferred method of raising allowances and thresholds by more than inflation – they were increased by 14 per cent, against a 'required' 5.5 per cent. He was also able, or rather forced by the Prime

Minister, against the advice of Treasury officials, to increase the upper limit on mortgage loans eligible for interest tax relief from £25,000 to £30,000.

This was a politician's move. The Conservative Party, largely through the sale of council houses at generous discounts, had presided over a big increase in home-ownership. The property-owning democracy now extended into all social classes, and the Conservative decision to raise the amount of tax relief available for home-owners stood them in good stead when set against Labour plans to abolish it. Economists have tended to argue strongly against this particular fiscal privilege, resulting as it does in a concentration of funds in property rather than in productive investment. Bank of England calculations showed that a large proportion of mortgage money, on which tax relief was available, was withdrawn from the housing market through the process of property sale and purchase, and used to finance consumer spending.

Sir Geoffrey Howe, in what was to be his last Budget, was also able to ensure that excise duties increased only slightly, so as not to upset the path of inflation, headed for 3.7 per cent in May 1983. And all this was achieved within a target for the public sector borrowing requirement of £8 billion for 1983/4.

The sums were indeed suspect. The Chancellor had reduced the contingency reserve, the amount set aside for additional calls on public spending during the fiscal year, from £2.5 billion to £1.1 billion, for no good reason. There was also a curious assumption that government departments and local authorities would underspend, releasing £1.6 billion into the Chancellor's hands.

The City knew that the figures were suspect, but was unwilling to rock the boat so close to an election and risk a victory by the Labour Party, led by Michael Foot. The foreign exchange markets, encouraged by the Conservatives' strong showing in the opinion polls, decided that the pound's fall had been overdone. By election day, 9 June 1983, the sterling index was back up to 85 and the pound was above $1.55 against the dollar.

Not surprisingly, there was a sizeable borrowing overshoot in 1983/4. The PSBR turned out to be £9.7 billion, in spite of action to cut it back by Howe's successor as Chancellor, Nigel Lawson. By then, however, the Conservatives had gained a second term in office.

Changing the Pilot

Margaret Thatcher's second term was won in even more striking fashion than her first, with a majority of 144 seats over all other parties compared with 43 in 1979. One senior Conservative, Francis Pym, expressed concern over the excessive freedom at the disposal of a party with a parliamentary majority of this size, and was exiled to the back benches for his trouble.

Certainly it looked likely that, after over a year of gearing economic policy to the task of getting re-elected, steps would have to be taken to put it back on the monetarist straight and narrow. Sir Geoffrey Howe was moved, at his own request, to the Foreign Office. His replacement at the Treasury was Nigel Lawson, the architect of the medium-term financial strategy.

The contrast between the two could hardly have been more striking. Howe, soft-spoken, undemonstrative and apparently unflappable, had earned the grudging respect even of his political opponents for his tenacity. He had also earned the trust both of his party and the City. The financial markets knew not to expect fireworks from Howe, but rather the reliable, reassuring manner of the family solicitor. He rarely gave the impression of having come up with the ideas or *bons mots* himself but, like the Queen's Counsel that he was before taking up ministerial office, he always learned his brief flawlessly.

Lawson's reputation was rather different. A former journalist (he was City Editor of the *Sunday Telegraph* and Editor of the *Spectator*), the impression he usually gave was of being too clever by half. As a result, he was not particularly popular among the MPs of his own party, and still less among his opponents.

Howe's approach in the House of Commons, unless greatly provoked, tended to be gentlemanly, whereas Lawson was caustic and aggressive. There was no denying, however, that Lawson was a man of imagination and ideas, even if he was likely to get bored with them rather quickly. He had also emerged, among senior Conservatives, as the chief thinker about economics in general and the practicalities of monetarism in particular. While Sir Keith Joseph and Margaret Thatcher had set in train the generality of monetarism, Lawson had delved into the detail of monetary theory and of the various monetary aggregates. He could comfortably hold his own with specialist economists, and did not suffer fools gladly.

Lawson returned to the Treasury as Chancellor of the Exchequer after two years as Secretary of State for Energy. At Energy he was credited with, among other things, presiding over the huge build-up in coal stocks at power stations which was to play such an important part in the government's victory over the miners in the 1984/5 coal strike.

The initial impression given by Lawson was that economic policy would indeed be pushed back towards more rigid adherence to monetarist ideals, or at least those ideals as they had emerged between 1979 and 1981.

It is a commonplace that incoming governments frequently have to act quickly to clear up the mess left by their predecessors. Usually this occurs when their predecessors happen to be the other party. In Lawson's case, one of his earliest acts as Chancellor was to attempt to inject some plausibility into the PSBR projections he inherited from Howe. The manner in which he did this was typical.

On 7 July, less than a month after the election, he informed the Cabinet that there had to be an emergency package of spending cuts of £500 million, plus extra sales of state assets of a similar amount, to put the PSBR back on course.

The cuts, hastily agreed by the Cabinet because of the solid support for Lawson by the Prime Minister, infuriated other ministers. Their fury was intensified by the fact that the only warning was provided by a leaked story in *The Times* on the day of the meeting. The brunt of the cuts, £240 million, was borne by the Ministry of Defence, and the Secretary of State, Michael Heseltine, did not easily forgive Lawson for presenting him with such an unwelcome *fait accompli*.

The other element of the package, raising an extra £500 million through asset sales, in this case by selling part of the government's shareholding in British Petroleum, deserves some explanation. One of the Conservatives' declared aims, given emphasis in the 1983 manifesto, was to return large parts of the nationalized industries, as well as council houses and land owned by the New Towns, to the private sector. Such asset sales fortunately fitted in well with the larger aim of controlling public borrowing and reducing spending. Sales of assets reduce the PSBR and, in Treasury accounting conventions, are defined as 'negative' public expenditure.

In the government's first term, sales of parts of the nationalized industries raised around £500 million a year, and had little impact on the overall sums for public borrowing and expenditure. But as the asset sales programme accelerated from 1983, Lawson was charged not only with selling the family silver, but also with fudging the PSBR figures.

There were mixed feelings in the City about Lawson's £1 billion emergency package. The corrective action on government borrowing was welcomed. But in style the package recalled the frequent economic adjustments of Denis Healey, rather than the steadying hand of Howe. Lawson was to have a love–hate relationship with the financial markets from that time on.

Lawson, the party thinker on monetarism, was clearly not going to be happy blindly following his predecessor's line. Changes were inevitable, and in October 1983 they came. By this time inflation had risen to 5 per cent from the election-time low of 3.7 per cent. Lawson made clear, in a major speech at the Lord Mayor's dinner for bankers,* that 5 per cent was not good enough and that the government's goal was price stability.

He also revealed that, since being appointed Chancellor, he had been undertaking a major review of monetary policy. 'I thought it worthwhile to re-examine some of the technical aspects of the operation of policy,' he said, 'and in particular to examine the balance between rules and discretion; and between monetary and fiscal policy; and whether we are taking account of the most useful indicators, with appropriate weights, in judging monetary conditions.' He described what was, in his view, the role of monetary targets: 'They have

* The Chancellor's Mansion House Speech, 20 October 1983 (H. M. Treasury).

Fig. 5 Public sector borrowing

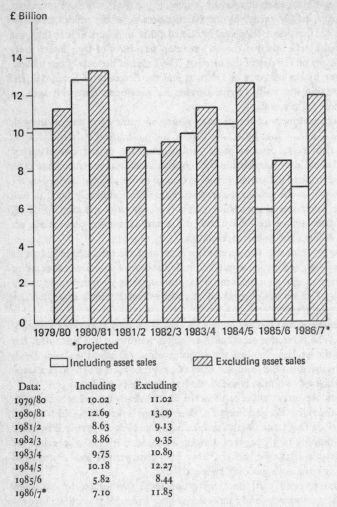

Data:	Including	Excluding
1979/80	10.02	11.02
1980/81	12.69	13.09
1981/2	8.63	9.13
1982/3	8.86	9.35
1983/4	9.75	10.89
1984/5	10.18	12.27
1985/6	5.82	8.44
1986/7*	7.10	11.85

not been, nor have ever intended to be, a form of automatic pilot. Over the years we have adjusted the targets themselves; and we have always sought to take account of shifts in the demand for money, whether due to financial innovation or to institutional change.'

Lawson reviewed the advantages and disadvantages of broad money, sterling M3, and recalled that in 1982 the decision had been taken to target explicitly a narrow money measure, M1. But M1 had shown itself to be subject to some of the distortions of sterling M3, because it contained an interest-bearing component. Thus a search had been conducted for a more reliable measure of narrow money 'for short-term interest rate decisions'. And the search had hit on M0, the so-called wide monetary base.

M0 – notes and coin, bankers' till money and bankers' balances at the Bank of England, immediately christened 'Little M0' in the City – thus achieved prominence. It was, after all, a measure of the monetary base. Did this mean that, two years on, the monetary base control lobby had won the policy debate? Not according to Lawson. 'The remarks I have just made should not be taken to mean that I am advocating a move to monetary base control,' he said. 'The present methods of market management have served us well and I do not intend to institute any changes.'

Lawson's Mansion House speech of 1983 was an important one. It appeared to tidy up many of the loose ends of pragmatic monetarism left by Howe. The new target measure for narrow money, M0, would guide the authorities on interest rates, while broad money, sterling M3, would be important in determining fiscal and funding policy (the sale of government stock). And all the time a watchful eye would be kept on, but no target set for, the exchange rate.

We will see shortly how this worked out in practice. The Lawson line was that policy as stated in October 1983 was fully consistent with what had gone before, since 1979. This simply did not wash. In his Zurich speech of January 1981, referred to in the previous chapter, Lawson had been dismissive of narrow money. 'Narrow money has the advantage of being easier to control,' he had said, 'but it suffers from being almost too easy to control. In particular, a rise in interest rates ... will inevitably lead to a marked switch from non-interest-bearing sight deposits to interest-bearing time deposits, thus sharply depressing the growth of narrow money far beyond any true change in underlying monetary conditions.'

Lawson's Crises

Lawson's honeymoon period lasted almost exactly one year. Growth in the economy in 1983, helped by buoyant consumer spending, was the highest for ten years, with gross domestic product rising by 3.3 per cent. And the momentum was maintained in the first half of 1984. Unemployment did not fulfil the new Chancellor's election-time prediction and actually fall, but the rise in the adult total between mid 1983 and mid 1984 was only 110,000, the smallest increase since the Conservatives took office in 1979.

Lawson was able to bring down interest rates, from 10 per cent in June 1983 to 8.5 per cent by March 1984, and the inflation rate was held at 5 per cent. In his first Budget, delivered on 13 March 1984, he was able to announce considerable success in the achievement of the government's financial targets.

Sterling M3 rose by 8.2 per cent in 1983/4, below the middle of the 7 to 11 per cent target range. The very narrow money measure, Mo, rose by a modest 5.7 per cent. The old narrow money target aggregate, M1, increased by a less respectable 12.6 per cent, but that had now been downgraded in policy.

Emboldened by this success, he announced target ranges for monetary growth stretching five years ahead, although again with the proviso that the targets were subject to revision. The targets for sterling M3 were for steadily falling growth, from 6 to 10 per cent in 1984/5 to 2 to 6 per cent in 1988/9. Narrow money, Mo, was given a similar profile but starting from a lower base – running from 4 to 8 per cent in 1984/5 to 0 to 4 per cent in 1988/9.

Table 3 The Medium-Term Financial Strategy, March 1984: Targets

	1984/5	1985/6	1986/7	1987/8	1988/9
Narrow money (Mo), per cent growth	4–8	3–7	2–6	1–5	0–4
Broad money (£M3), per cent growth	6–10	5–9	4–8	3–7	2–6
PSBR, as percentage of GDP	2.25	2	2	1.75	1.75

Source: Financial Statement and Budget Report, 1984, HMSO

The PSBR, in spite of the previous July's emergency action, overshot the original £8 billion target by £1.7 billion, but that did not prevent bold fiscal action from the Chancellor. There was a radical reform of corporate taxation, with the abolition of the stock relief introduced during the high inflation of the mid 1970s, and capital allowances phased out. In return, the rate of corporation tax was to be reduced from 52 per cent to 35 per cent by 1986/7. There was also a cut in personal income tax, with allowances and thresholds raised by 12.5 per cent, rather than the 5 per cent required to compensate for inflation.

It was all to do, as Lawson explained to another City audience,* with the enterprise culture. Post-war policy-makers had got it wrong, he said, in attempting to generate growth through macro-economic policy, and in particular through fiscal policy, while preventing inflation through micro-economic policy – incomes policies and price controls. The correct ordering, he claimed, was precisely the opposite: 'It is the conquest of inflation, and not the pursuit of growth and employment, which is or should be the objective of macro-economic policy. And it is the creation of conditions conducive to growth and employment, and not the suppression of price rises, which is or should be the objective of micro-economic policy.'

* 'The British Experiment', the 5th Mais Lecture, 18 June 1984.

If there was a disappointment for Lawson, it was that the financial markets had failed to take to his narrow money target, M0. 'Little Mo' was not taken seriously in the City. Both broad and narrow money targets, he said, 'have equal weight in guiding policy decisions – a point which I suspect has not yet been fully grasped by market commentators'.

Very soon he was to have other worries. Sooner or later the pound has intervened to upset even the best-laid plans of British Chancellors. And so it was in July 1984. The pound had been weakening gradually since shortly after the June 1983 election, for a variety of reasons. One was the Chancellor's slightly too obvious determination to reduce interest rates; a second was the strength of the dollar; and a third was the industrial action in Britain's coal mines, which began as an overtime ban in November 1983 and became a strike early in 1984.

The pound's fall was at first gentle enough not to merit major concern. Even so, by the spring of 1984 the sterling index had fallen back to 80, more than 6 per cent below its election level. In May, a drop in the index below 80, and the pound's fall below $1.40, brought forth a half-point defensive rise in interest rates, taking base rates to 9 or 9.25 per cent, depending on which clearing bank you chose.

In July, with the same factors at play and in a month which has often been one when the pound had displayed vulnerability, sterling's gentle decline turned into a steeper slide. The index fell to 78, and against the dollar, the pound began to tumble towards $1.30. Adding to the difficulties, the June money supply figures, published early in July, showed a 1.7 per cent jump in sterling M3.

The Bank of England attempted to hold the line but was finally forced to concede a steep increase in interest rates. The banks, by now all charging 9.25 per cent, raised base rates to 10 per cent on Friday 9 July. But this was not enough to stem the tide flowing against the pound, and on the following Tuesday rates were raised to 12 per cent.

For the markets, it was lesson number one in Lawson's economics. The suspicion was that interest rates had been raised in a traditional defence of sterling, but the performance of the monetary aggregates left enough room for the view that domestic as well as external factors had prompted the increase. Even M0 had risen by 1 per cent during the June banking month.

Lesson number two was to come very quickly. The July jump in interest rates succeeded, temporarily, in steadying sterling, enough for the Chancellor to embark on a policy of reducing them. Despite the weakening pound and broad money growth at the top of its 6 to 10 per cent target range, interest rates were reduced swiftly. By the end of November, base rates were back down to 9.5 to 9.75 per cent, and the pound had fallen below $1.20 – less than half its level during 1980. The sterling index was below 75, another 5 per cent down compared with its July 'crisis' level. The rationale for lower interest rates was that Lawson was following his Mansion House dictum to the letter, and that the well-behaved performance of M0, showing twelve-month rates of increase of 5 to 6 per cent, in the middle of its target range, provided excuse enough.

There were, however, important ulterior motives. The strike by the majority of members of the National Union of Mineworkers was still in progress, and reaching a crucial stage. Most independent outside observers predicted, wrongly, that the strike would result in damaging power cuts over the winter months. It was important for the government's propaganda purposes that the economy should give every appearance of 'business as usual', and one way of achieving this was to provide a stimulus through lower interest rates. At the same time, if the pound was weakening, partly because of the strike, partly because of lower world oil prices, and largely as a result of dollar strength, then no one was attributing the fall to the laxity of monetary policy.

A second ulterior motive was related to the privatization programme. The sale of just over half the government's stake in British Telecom, to raise £4 billion in three stages, was due to start in November. It was important that the sale was a success, both because it pointed the way for future sell-offs and because of its importance to the government's finances. Steadily falling interest rates, with one reduction early in November, were used to keep the stock market in a receptive mood for the sale.

It was all to end in tears. The November money supply figures, published on 11 December, initially showed a rise in sterling M3 of 2.75 per cent, later revised to 2.2 per cent. The Bank of England's reassurances that the sharp rise was due to the distorting effects of the British Telecom sale – with large numbers of people writing out cheques in unsuccessful applications for the heavily over-subscribed issue – were not fully believed. Stories circulating in Whitehall, that the Chancellor was planning £3 billion of tax cuts the following March, come what may, added to the impression that financial irresponsibility had taken over. By Christmas, the pound was in a sorry state, having dropped to new lows against the dollar and on the sterling index. Early in January, it was clear that the situation had all the makings of a full-blown sterling crisis.

Every year, the Chancellor of the Exchequer, the other Treasury ministers and senior Treasury civil servants, meet for a weekend in January to discuss the broad shape of, and priorities for, the Budget. The 1985 meeting, over the weekend of 12–13 January at snow-bound Chevening in Kent, was a miserable affair, and one not greatly concerned with Budget matters.

On Friday 11 January, in response to the tumbling pound and rising money-market interest rates, the Bank of England reluctantly informed the clearing banks that it was prepared to see base rates rise by a point, to 10.5 per cent. But the move, regarded as 'too little too late' in the foreign exchange markets, and condemned as an example of the government's incompetence by Opposition politicians, did not prevent the pound falling to new lows, dropping below $1.12 against the dollar.

The Treasury watched anxiously from its country retreat in Kent. It was just possible, as things looked on the Saturday morning, that the storm would blow over by Monday, the pound would steady and another rise in interest rates would be avoided. But by Sunday this was no longer an option. The Sunday newspapers had come out with markedly different stories about the government's intentions on the exchange rate. The *Observer* said that the government would raise interest rates to prevent the pound from falling further. The *Sunday Times*, on the other hand, reported that the Prime Minister was willing to allow market forces to prevail, and let the pound fall to unity with the dollar, if necessary. The *Sunday Telegraph* was on the side of the *Sunday Times*, saying that the government was not prepared to throw away millions in futile intervention on the foreign exchanges in order to shore up the pound.

The confusion had arisen in the pre-weekend briefings for the Sunday newspapers in Whitehall. At this time the Treasury was highly cautious in its press relations, having been stung by a major leak of the Budget proposals in the *Guardian* in the previous March. The official line was thus left for 10 Downing Street, in the person of Bernard Ingham, head of the Prime Minister's press office and the most senior Whitehall information officer, to put across.

His line was indeed that the government saw massive intervention in support of the pound as futile, as dutifully reported by the *Sunday Telegraph* and built upon by the *Sunday Times*. The *Observer*'s political editor, Adam Raphael, checked out this official guidance with William Keegan, the paper's economics editor. Keegan, a former Bank of England economist, was immediately suspicious, particularly since interest rates had already been lifted on the Friday in defence of the pound. The *Observer* thus emerged with something like the correct version. The Downing Street line was right, but only on the narrow question of intervention. Its guidance did not preclude a dramatic raising of interest rates to save the pound.

Mrs Thatcher was furious, and the Treasury was fired into action. Economics writers on the daily newspapers were contacted on the Sunday with the message that there was no question of allowing the pound's free fall to continue, and that interest rates would be raised further if necessary. It was just possible that this, if stated clearly enough, would deter the speculators, come Monday morning.

It was not to be. The weekend confusion over policy merely added to the vulnerability of the pound and pushed money-market interest rates up sharply. Discussions between the Chancellor and the Governor of the Bank of England, Robin Leigh-Pemberton, had come up with a contingency plan were this to be the case. And so the Bank of England announced that minimum lending rate, suspended three and a half years earlier, in August 1981, was to be revived. The rate, coincidentally the same as when it was suspended, was 12 per cent.

The aim was twofold. Firstly, the authorities wished to give the clearest possible message to the foreign exchange markets that it was leading and not merely acquiescing in an interest rate rise; secondly, there was a clear desire not to allow the panic to push interest rates even higher than 12 per cent.

Having delivered its message, the board at the Bank of England announcing minimum lending rate was duly curtained off again. As the dust settled, analysts of both the political and the financial scene assessed the damage. The pattern had been the same as that in July 1984. One sterling crisis was forgivable. Two in the space of six months smacked of carelessness and incompetence. This time, however, there was worse to come. The rise in interest rates brought a few days of grace for the pound, but by 28 January, with a quarrelsome meeting of the Organization of Petroleum Exporting Countries under way in Geneva, a fall in the sterling index to just above 70 produced a further two-point rise in interest rates, to 14 per cent. Minimum lending rate was not needed on this occasion; the message was clear enough.

By a neat accident of timing, at the end of the week in which interest rates had been raised to 14 per cent, there was a scheduled hour-long interview between Margaret Thatcher and Peter Jay, on the Channel 4 programme 'A Week in Politics'. It was an encounter which promised great things, featuring one of the voices who, in the 1970s, had been responsible for the rise of monetarism, and the politician who had run with it as a powerful political idea.

Asked about the 4.5 point rise in interest rates in the space of two weeks, the Prime Minister explained it thus: 'Interest rates, as you know very well, are a weapon which you have to use now and then. We don't like using them, we don't like putting interest rates up, but the situation you saw was one in which we needed to do so to restore confidence.'

But the most fascinating part of the interview, as far as the history of monetarism is concerned, came later, in the following exchange.

Peter Jay asked: 'Monetarist economists again believe in something called the natural rate of unemployment, which is supposed to be the rate at which inflation stops or ceases to accelerate. Now do you think that we, Prime Minister, with all-time record unemployment figures this week, have yet reached that natural rate, even though inflation is still proceeding sufficiently to halve the value of money every fifteen years?'

Mrs Thatcher replied: 'It's not a doctrine to which I've subscribed. It's one which I think actually came in with Milton Friedman. I used to look at it, I used to look at it and not adopt it. It's a theory to which I've never subscribed. At the moment in spite of three and a quarter million unemployed, we have a current-account surplus – we've had a current-account surplus for five years in a row.'

And that, despite further questioning by an incredulous Jay, was that. A central element of monetarism was dismissed in a few short sentences and a *non sequitur* about the balance of payments. And Friedman was no longer the man whose ideas had shaped a party's economic philosophy. Those ideas, apparently, had been considered and rejected.

January 1985 was the turning-point. At the end of 1984 the Conservative government could claim that, in name at least, its monetarist policies were still intact. By the time a cold and snowy January had passed, Britain's monetarist experiment had been consigned to the dustbin of history and Conservative politicians were already amending the records.

Mrs Thatcher's rejection of the Friedmanite concept of the natural rate of unemployment was also a rejecfion of the monetarist ideas she had nurtured during four years as leader of the Opposition, and which she had vigorously attempted to put into practice on her election as Prime Minister in May 1979.

Lawson's second sterling crisis rammed home a fundamental truth about the British economy. Six years of monetarist experimentation had left the pound as vulnerable to damaging waves of selling pressure as it had been under Denis Healey in the mid 1970s. Only the happy accident of North Sea oil, which permitted a big build-up in Britain's foreign exchange reserves during the early 1980s, allowed the government to escape an embarrassing recourse to the International Monetary Fund.

Monetarism is Dead – Official

The January 1985 sterling crisis has been described at length because it marked the changeover point from pragmatic monetarism to pragmatism. The Conservatives had acted in the manner of all post-war governments in response to a sterling crisis. But there were no new rabbits that could be pulled out of the hat to convince the markets that the pound could be taken on trust. This meant that, irrespective of the performance of the monetary aggregates or the recorded inflation rate, interest rates had to be kept high.

During February, the pound almost achieved unity with the dollar, falling to a low of $1.0370. But the dollar's peak was near and it was soon falling against all currencies, helped by a policy change in Washington, which favoured driving it down. The danger passed, but the pound retained its central role in monetary policy.

The crisis also affected Lawson's standing in the Cabinet. In his 1984 Budget speech he had promised that the major reform of corporate taxation he was unveiling would be followed a year later by personal tax reforms. It transpired during the approach to the 1985 Budget that one area where such reform was intended was in the taxation of pensions, and the generous tax relief available on them. But, faced with vocal opposition from within his own party, Lawson was unable to carry the Prime Minister with him.

The Budget did contain imaginative changes in national insurance contributions, intended to boost employment, although the evidence that they did so is scanty. But for Lawson it was a cautious package. The target ranges for monetary growth, 5 to 9 per cent for sterling M_3 and 3 to 7 per cent for M_0, were trotted out. But the general impression was of a Budget for sterling, including a planned reduction in public sector borrowing from a coal strike-boosted £10.2 billion in 1984/5 (against a £7 billion target) to £7 billion in 1985/6.

The target for sterling M3, if it was ever intended to be taken seriously, quickly became meaningless. In the weeks following the Budget, interest rates were reduced, but entirely in response to the rising value of the pound, which by the summer was back up to 80 on the sterling index. In July, just a few days after the publication of money-supply figures showing a 2 per cent rise in sterling M3, to take its twelve-month rate of increase to 12 per cent compared with the 5 to 9 per cent target range, the Bank of England actually led the clearing banks into a base rate cut.

The game had changed. Sterling M3, which by late summer was 14 per cent above its level a year earlier, clearly did not matter. M0, in the eyes of the City, never had. It was the exchange rate and nothing more which was guiding the government, it appeared.

In October, two years after the Mansion House speech in which he had launched M0, Lawson delivered an even more important address on the same stage.* There were two important monetary policy statements in the speech. One was to do with the technical conduct of policy. In its efforts to hold down sterling M3, the Bank of England had been forced to resort to overfunding – selling more government stock than was required to fund public sector borrowing. It was a clumsy way of going about things. Broad money growth was boosted chiefly by bank lending but then reined back, largely for presentational purposes, by overfunding. A consequence of this was the so-called 'bill mountain' at the Bank of England. Until the late 1970s, the Bank would normally act to relieve temporary shortages in the money markets by buying Treasury bills from the banks.

Overfunding the PSBR involved ever greater sales of government debt – gilt-edged securities – outside the banking system, to the insurance companies and pension funds, to individuals and to overseas buyers.

The monetary system is like a balloon in that squeezing in one place results in pressure and a danger of a rupture elsewhere. Increasing sales of government debt, long-term paper, tilted the money markets, the markets for short-term paper, out of equilibrium. The temporary liquidity shortages in the money markets became larger, and took on an appearance of permanence.

Had the Bank of England decided to do nothing about it, the result would have been higher and more volatile short-term interest rates. And the consequences of this would have been higher interest rates charged by the banks, more expensive mortages and, presumably, another summons to Number

* The Chancellor's Mansion House Speech, 17 October 1985 (H. M. Treasury).

10 Downing Street for Bank of England officials, to explain themselves.

So the Bank had to relieve these money market shortages which could be as much as £1 billion a day. The difficulty was that the size of the shortages was far greater than the banking system's holdings of Treasury bills. The earlier cosy relationship, whereby the authorities sold more official long-term paper and bought back official short-term paper, was no longer possible.

The Bank of England was therefore forced to buy in another type of bill, that issued by companies. The Bank bought commercial bills, and held them. During 1985 these commercial bill holdings, the 'bill mountain', climbed above £15 billion.

The Bank's willingness to take on commercial bills also increased the possibilities for bill arbitrage, or round-tripping, whereby companies could borrow from their banks on overdraft and re-lend in the money markets by issuing bills. This clearly countered some of the good achieved by overfunding by boosting broad money growth from another direction. Hence Lawson's decision to end systematic overfunding.

But the bombshell in the speech was the announcement that the target for sterling M3 was suspended for the remainder of the financial year. The target, of 5 to 9 per cent, had been set too low at the time of the Budget seven months earlier, Lawson said. To try to bring it back within its target range – it was then growing at a twelve-month rate of 14 per cent – would mean an excessive tightening of monetary policy.

A clearer statement of the fact that pragmatism now ruled could not have been made. The *Financial Times* had no doubts, the following day running a leading article, written by Anthony Harris, under the heading 'Monetarism is Dead – Official'. The paper's principal economics commentator, Samuel Brittan, was unwilling to see it written off so readily, claiming in his own signed commentary a week later, that monetarism was far from dead.

To all intents and purposes, however, monetarism was dead. Sterling M3, the symbol, rightly or wrongly, of the British monetarist experiment, had disgraced itself so much that it had to be sent from the field. Narrow money, M0, apart from fulfilling Lawson's 1981 claim that it was almost too easy to control, had failed to gain acceptance since it was introduced as a target two years earlier.

This left the exchange rate, which clearly had featured in interest rate decisions, and any number of other factors which the 'seat of the pants' approach to economic policy pushed to the surface. Lawson was certain which was the most important of these. 'The acid test of monetary policy,' he said, 'is its record in reducing inflation. Those who wish to join in the debate about the intricacies of different measures of money and the implications they may have for the future are welcome to do so. But at the end of the day the position is clear and unambiguous. The inflation rate is judge and jury.'

This was a curious about-turn. The man who had made the intricacies of monetary policy his speciality was dismissive of those who now did so. The essence of monetarism, to deliver not just a low inflation rate now, but continuing low inflation, was missing from the new pragmatism.

And there it may have rested. There was a repeat in January 1986 of at least the early stages of the sterling crisis of a year earlier, this time on the rather stronger grounds of a collapse, and not merely a weakening, of oil prices. The spot market price of North Sea oil fell from more than $30 a barrel in the autumn to less than $20 in January, and further, to under $10 a barrel, in the spring of 1986. But interest rates in Britain started from a high position, and the Bank of England permitted only one increase in base rates, early in January, from 11.5 to 12.5 per cent.

Between the mini-crisis of January and a further fall in the exchange rate in the summer, there was a curious event. The City, having seen the pragmatic approach work reasonably smoothly over the winter, decided that the suspension of sterling M3 would become permanent. The Chancellor had said in his Mansion House speech that he would consider what target to set for sterling M3 for 1986/7 in his March 1986 Budget. Most people took this to mean that he would consider it, and then set no target at all. But Lawson, perhaps stung by the response to his October speech, with some commentators fearing a return to the monetary laxity of the Heath/Barber years of the early 1970s, did set a target. It was just for one year, 1986/7, and it was for sterling M3 growth within the very generous target range of 11 to 15 per cent.

Unless the intention was the Machiavellian one of weaning the financial markets off sterling M3 for ever, the effect was the opposite to that intended. It quickly became clear, as the broad money measure surged in the months immediately following the Budget, that even the apparently generous 11 to 15 per cent target range was too low. Following the May banking month, when sterling M3 grew by 3 per cent after a 3.2 per cent April rise, the twelve-month rate of growth of broad money was 19.5 per cent. Its annualized growth rate over three months was just under 40 per cent, a figure not seen before, even in the broad money explosion of the early 1970s. And yet, through it all, the government felt able to reduce interest rates, from 12.5 per cent in January to 10 per cent by the end of May.

It was back to the old, pre-monetarist days. Whenever the exchange rate allowed, interest rates were cut, partly to boost a flagging economy. And inflation did appear to be the judge and jury, not only of the success of monetary policy, but also of decisions on interest rates.

As the effects of lower oil prices for consumers fed through to the retail price index, coupled with lower mortgage rates compared with a year earlier,

Fig. 6 The money supply, 1982–6

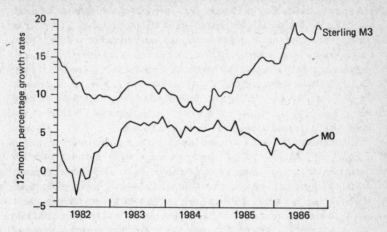

the inflation rate fell to less than 2.5 per cent in the summer of 1986, from 7 per cent a year earlier.

Even inflation at such a low rate was not enough to persuade financial markets of the government's resolve. In August, the National Institute forecast a current account deficit of nearly £6 billion for 1987, and a sterling crisis began to rumble again. The markets were looking beyond the temporary dip in the inflation rate to the inevitable upturn, and 18 to 20 per cent broad money growth provided them with good reason for doing so.

The Bank of England intervened heavily on the foreign exchange markets to support sterling, on occasion calling in the German Bundesbank to help out. The official reserves were topped up with a $4 billion Euromarket loan to help in the support effort. But it was of little avail; the pound continued to fall, the sterling index dropping to well below 70.

Interest rates were held until after the Conservative Party Conference early in October, but then had to be raised. Lawson blamed the Labour Party and the fall in oil prices for the pound's weakness. In his October 1986 Mansion House speech, Lawson was happy to fall into the trap that, in 1981, he had criticized the Heath government for failing to avoid – seeking reassurance from narrow money growth. The sharp increases in broad money and credit were not inflationary, he said.

Few believed it. The monetarist experiment, by now ancient history in the markets, had left no legacy of goodwill with its proponents. Interest rates in double figures, when set against inflation rates of comfortably less than 5 per cent, were testimony to that.

There were two further demonstrations that autumn of the fact that monetarism had fallen. In October the Governor of the Bank of England, Robin Leigh-Pemberton, delivered a lecture at Loughborough University in which he admitted that 'it cannot be said that our experience with our chosen framework for operationg monetary policy has been satisfactory'.

Reviewing the factors that had rendered the control of broad money, sterling M3, difficult, he conceded that the record of control, when set against the targets, had been poor. But the case for automatic policy rules had never been strong, the Governor added, and it was now time to consider whether it was worth setting targets, certainly for broad money, at all.

The Governor's speech knocked another nail in the coffin of British monetarism. As a technique for guiding monetary policy, monetary rules had become obsolete. The Chancellor of the Exchequer, in his Autumn Statement the following month, provided a body blow for monetarism in a wider sense.

The British monetarist experiment, as it had evolved, placed great importance on the control of public expenditure. At first the aim was to achieve absolute cuts in real public spending. This gave way to the more modest ambition of holding spending constant in real terms.

In November 1986, with his eyes firmly on a forthcoming General Election that the Conservatives looked in danger of losing, Nigel Lawson suddenly became convinced of the virtues of public spending. The previous targets for public spending were scrapped and no less than £7.5 billion was added to spending on programmes for the 1987/8 fiscal year. The planning total for spending was raised by more than £10 billion over the two years 1987/8 and 1988/9.

It was electioneering, and of a more blatant kind than Sir Geoffrey Howe had embarked upon in 1983. The biggest real increase in spending, of more than 2 per cent, was planned for 1987/8, where it would have the greatest electoral impact. But it was also rather more than traditional pre-election pump-priming. Yet another plank of the economic policy programme embarked upon by the Conservatives seven years earlier had been knocked away. Even a post-election squeeze on spending would not change that.

Lawson claimed, as might be expected, that there had been no change in policy. It had never been the aim of the government either to cut or to hold constant real public spending, he said. History was being re-written on fiscal policy as it had been on monetary policy. In neither case did the claim of consistency in policy fit the facts.

9

REAGANOMICS, MONETARISM AND THE DOLLAR

The year 1979 was a vintage one for monetarism. Not only was the Thatcher government elected in Britain, but in the United States economic policy turned distinctly monetarist. The change, which can be timed exactly to the adoption by the Federal Reserve System of new operating procedures and monetary policy priorities in October 1979, occurred well over a year before Ronald Reagan became President.

In Britain, it is possible to draw distinctions between the 1976–9 version of monetarism under Labour, and the Thatcher experiment from May 1979 onwards. In the United States, a single monetarist experiment spanned two administrations. It started under Jimmy Carter and it ended under Ronald Reagan.

And, even more than in Britain (as might be expected in the home of monetarism), the United States' experiment resulted in a furious debate between monetarist economists and their opponents. American monetarists chose to fight their corner on the argument that, despite the rhetoric of policy, which appeared to be strongly monetarist, the actual conduct of policy was not. The same argument has been applied to Britain, but with rather less force. British monetarists tended to recognize that, however impure the experiment, it was probably the best they were going to get.

The October 1979 Changes

The background to the 1979 shift towards monetarism in the United States is familiar. Following the first oil crisis of 1973/4, there had been a gradual return to the traditional policy goal of fostering economic growth. The starkest example of this was at the economic summit of the major industrialized nations in Bonn in the middle of 1978 when, egged on by the United States, Germany – in modern times the last bastion of sound money – was persuaded into a fiscal expansion to act as a 'locomotive' for the rest of the world.

In the United States itself, monetary targets were in place but the money supply was allowed to exceed target because of fears of recession. As the Organization for Economic Co-operation and Development reported in 1979, reflecting on the conduct of US monetary policy in 1977 and 1978: 'Indications of rapid growth of the monetary aggregates tended to be discounted since an imminent decline in real growth was feared, yet in retrospect the growth of the aggregates was giving more accurate information on strong growth and accelerating inflation than was thought at the time.'

During 1979, inflation became the main policy concern in the United States. The second oil crisis, sparked off by the Iranian revolution late in 1978, produced a 60 per cent rise in posted oil prices by the summer. The United States, partly insulated from the first oil shock by the decision to keep down the price of some domestically produced oil, was more vulnerable to the second. The rise in oil prices came as inflation was on a rising trend and President Carter's non-monetarist counter-inflationary strategy was breaking down. From 6.5 per cent in 1977, consumer price inflation rose to over 11 per cent in 1979.

On 6 October 1979, the Federal Reserve Board announced a series of changes in monetary policy designed to reduce inflation and relieve pressure on the sharply falling dollar. The 'Fed', under the chairmanship of Paul Volcker, a man as tall as a basketball player and rarely seen without a cigar in his mouth, thus became practical, if not totally committed, monetarists.

The aim was to place considerable emphasis on bringing the rate of growth of the money stock, variously defined, within pre-set target ranges or 'cones'. In return for this, the Federal Reserve was prepared to cede some of its traditional control over short-term interest rate fluctuations. It was a practical statement of the proposition, learned by monetarists in the cradle, that you can control the money supply or you can control interest rates, but you cannot control both simultaneously.

The practical details of the policy shift, in brief, were a move by the authorities to control the supply of bank reserves, the so-called 'non-borrowed' reserves, while allowing the Federal funds rate, and short-term interest rates in general, to move more widely than had previously been permitted. Before 6 October 1979 the permitted range for fluctuations in the Federal funds rate between meetings of the Federal Open Market Committee, the policy-making body, was one percentage point or less. After the change, the permitted range was widened to four or sometimes six percentage points.

As in Britain, prominence was given to one monetary aggregate. Unlike Britain, the measure selected was a narrow monetary aggregate, M1. It was set to grow within a range of 4 to 6.5 per cent in 1980, and it was supplemented with targets for the wider money measures, M2 (6 to 9 per cent), and M3 (6.5 to 9.5 per cent). The Federal Reserve Board signalled its determination to meet the newly emphasized monetary targets by announcing, alongside the new operating procedures, higher official interest rates.

The discount rate was raised by a point, in line with already sharply rising market interest rates, and following a one-and-a-half-point discount rate increase during the third quarter of 1979. By early November the Federal funds rate, freed from its former constraints, was four points above its level immediately prior to the changes of 6 October. The major American banks charged their best corporate customers nearly 16 per cent on loans. Five months earlier, prime rates had been less than 12 per cent.

As well as higher interest rates, special reserve requirements were imposed on the banks, to restrict the growth in Eurodollar borrowing and large time deposits. It was a formidable armoury, and one which could hardly have made the intentions of the authorities clearer. The majority of monetarists were prepared to accept that, at least in the design of the new monetary policy, the Federal Reserve had embarked on a monetarist experiment.

The initial stages of the experiment were accompanied by recession and rising inflation. But the recession was mild – gross national product declined by a mere 0.2 per cent in 1980 before rising by 1.9 per cent in 1981. Inflation, measured by consumer prices, rose from just over 11 per cent in 1979 to 13.5 per cent in 1980, before subsiding to less than 10.5 per cent in 1981. While the macro-economic effects of the experiment, at least in the early stages, were comparatively muted, the instabilities ushered in in the financial markets were not.

In London, the financial markets can glean information on the likely course of narrow money, M0, from the weekly returns of the Bank of England. But complete information on M0, and indeed anything more than market estimates of the broader aggregates, has to wait until the publication of the monthly money supply figures, between two and three weeks after the end of the period. In New York, the official information available to market operators comes more frequently. One consequence of the October 1979 changes was that the weekly M1 data became the focus for the markets.

Far from moving smoothly within its target path, it soon became clear that M1 was behaving in a highly erratic fashion. In the time-honoured manner, encapsulated in Goodhart's Law, the very act of targeting M1 appeared to increase its volatility. Some broad trends could be discerned between the erratic weekly movements. By February 1980, in spite of the high interest rate regime in place, M1 growth was well above its target range. A slowdown then occurred, following a special package of credit controls in March, to take it below the range by the early summer. And then it was off again, so that by the autumn it was well above the target range set a year earlier.

This was not at all what the monetarists had in mind when advocating

Fig. 7 Volatile money in the United States

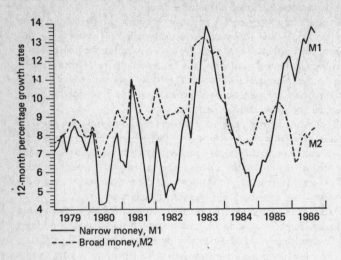

monetary rules. As Friedman was to comment later: 'A monetarist policy involves not only targeting monetary aggregates but also – as a major and central element – achieving a steady and predictable rate of growth in whatever monetary aggregate is targeted. By this essential criterion, the experiment was anti-monetarist.'

Reaganomics

The eminent American economist Arthur Okun, writing in 1970 about the consequences of monetarism, said: 'What is most important and most dangerous about the monetary rule is its implicit precept: ignore fiscal policy. Carried to its ultimate conclusion, the monetarist position would justify a totally unconstrained federal fiscal policy. Now I know a few people in Washington who would love an intellectual justification for fiscal irresponsibility. Some day they are going to discover the most important message of the monetarist view. And then we will see some fireworks.' This was exactly what happened in 1981 and 1982, following the election of Ronald Reagan as President.

The story, probably apocryphal, is told of the day that Reagan's team of economic advisers met up to devise policy. On one side of the table were the monetarists, favouring stable growth of the money stock within pre-set target ranges. On the other side were the supply-siders, wanting large tax cuts to restore incentives and foster enterprise. Waiting in the wings was the most powerful lobby in Washington which wanted, and got, large increases in defence spending.

Supply-side economics, as presented to the American public in the run-up to the November 1980 presidential election, was a magical thing. The approach, generally associated with Arthur Laffer who began developing it at Chicago, and Robert Mundell of Columbia University, was popularized by Jude Wanniski in the *Wall Street Journal*.

Supply-side economics, a term coined by Professor Herbert Stein of the University of Virginia, was initially taken up by such heavyweights as Martin Feldstein, later Chairman of President Reagan's Council of Economic Advisers. It produced the economic policy equivalent of the Holy Grail – popular and incentive-restoring tax cuts which paid for themselves. This principle was encapsulated in the Laffer curve.

According to Arthur Laffer, there came a point at which tax rates were so high that they reduced overall tax revenues by removing incentives and depressing the economy. Revenues at tax rates of 100 per cent will be the same as at tax rates of 0 per cent – zero – because no one has any incentive to work just for the benefit of the government. At some point between tax rates of 0 and 100 per cent, it was claimed, overall revenues will decline when rates are increased because of incentive effects, and vice versa.

The supply-sider could point to the tax cuts under Presidents Harding and Coolidge in the 1920s and, more recently, under Presidents Kennedy and Johnson in the 1960s. In both cases, lower tax rates appeared to boost overall revenues.

Supply-side economics came like manna from heaven to the Republican Party in the 1970s, badly in need of re-invigoration following Watergate. It was taken up by Congressman Jack Kemp of Buffalo, New York, and Senator William Roth of Delaware. The Kemp–Roth bill, introduced in 1977, which formed the basis for Reagan's 1981 tax cuts, called for 30 per cent across-the-board reductions in income tax rates. Reagan himself, having come to the White House from California, where the citizens had energetically supported the Proposition 13 reductions in property taxes, needed little persuasion.

From the start it was clear that there would be friction between monetarism and supply-side economics. The actual income tax cuts introduced by the Reagan administration were a 5 per cent reduction in October 1981, 10 per cent in July 1982 and a further 10 per cent in July 1983. The effect, other things being equal, was to reduce tax revenues by $750 billion over the period from 1981 to 1986. Defence expenditure over the same period was boosted by $237 billion, while cuts in non-defence spending, of $585 billion, were planned.

The gap between reductions in taxes and net reductions in spending was, again other things being equal, $400 billion. Of course, the essence of the supply-side approach was that other things would not be equal, and that lower tax rates would produce offsetting increases in revenues.

When it became clear that this was not coming about, and the consequence of large tax cuts was a sharply rising budget deficit, the policy-makers in Washington began to fall out. The Federal budget deficit increased to more than $200 billion by 1983. In the 1970s, deficits of more than $50 billion were considered high. The figure rose from 1.1 to 5.6 per cent of gross national product between 1979 and 1983.

To the supply-siders this did not contradict any of their principles. Rather, the Federal Reserve, in its dogged pursuit of monetary targets, was putting a lid on the economy which prevented the benefits of the tax cuts from coming through in stronger growth and higher tax revenues.

Paul Volcker, the Chairman of the Federal Reserve Board, was no great believer in supply-side miracles. Far from monetary targets thwarting tax cuts, he argued, it was the other way round. As he was to say later, in one of his politer observations on the budget deficit:

> The actual and prospective size of the budget deficit inevitably complicates the environment within which we work. By feeding consumer purchasing power, by heightening scepticism about our ability to control the money supply and contain inflation, by claiming a disproportionate share of available funds, and by increasing our dependence on foreign capital, monetary policy must carry more of the burden of maintaining stability and its flexibility, to some degree, is constrained.

By 1982, Volcker was under pressure from all sides. The economy had made a weak recovery in 1981 but started to head downhill again in 1982. Gross national product fell by 2.5 per cent during the year. The White House was becoming increasingly irritated with the Federal Reserve Board, having decided that the blame lay with excessively tight monetary policy. Meanwhile, Volcker was under attack from monetarist hard-liners for failing to deliver the smooth, month-to-month growth of the money supply they had expected following the October 1979 policy shift.

The Federal Reserve had been caught out by something which, according to the monetarist textbooks, was not supposed to happen – sudden and unexpected shifts in the demand for money. The demand for narrow money, M1, fell sharply in 1981 and then increased, equally sharply, in 1982. The monetary targets set by the Federal Reserve thus erred on the loose side in 1981 but became very tight in 1982.

The experiment, started in October 1979, ended abruptly. As Professor James Pierce of Berkeley described it: 'In the second half of 1982, with the economy in disarray and with growing concern about the ability of the financial system to withstand further strain, the Federal Reserve abandoned its new operating procedures. There was a shift back to the more "comfortable" world of stabilizing fluctuations in the Federal funds rate.'

The experiment ended on 9 October 1979, three years, almost to the day, after it had begun. Volcker announced that the target for M1 was to be given less emphasis in policy decisions and that it would be abandoned temporarily. Underlying this was a shift in monetary policy priorities. Hitting the targets and bearing down further on already sharply declining inflation – in 1982 consumer price inflation was a little over 6 per cent; in 1983 the rate virtually halved to just over 3 per cent – was less important than accommodating much-needed economic growth and preventing financial collapse.

The 1979–82 Experiment Assessed

In assessing the 1979–82 experiment, economists fell into two distinct camps. Those who were out of sympathy with monetarism from the beginning concluded that it had been tried but had failed lamentably. The monetarists, on the other hand, were unwilling to concede that what had been attempted was monetarism, let alone accept the charge of failure.

British monetarism ran into trouble in 1980 and 1981 because of excessive reliance on the performance of a broad monetary aggregate, sterling M3, which was heavily influenced by the public sector deficit. In the United States this was clearly not the case – monetary and fiscal policy pursued conflicting courses. Nevertheless, extreme difficulties arose. Somewhere between the two there may have been an appropriate fiscal policy for smooth and unflustered growth in the money stock. But it was not obvious what it was.

Assessing monetary policy is no less difficult. Growth in the M1 money stock in the United States slowed sharply between 1979 and 1981, but with highly erratic month-to-month movements. M1 growth, 7.5 per cent in both 1979 and 1980, fell back to 5 per cent in 1981, before increasing by 9 per cent in 1982.

But the broader M2 measure showed steadily rising growth from 1979 to 1981, before edging back in 1982. The paths of money growth shown by the two aggregates carried very different messages for policy. M1 implied tightening in both 1979 and 1980, loosening in 1981, and tightening again in 1982. The message from M2, relative to its target range, was modest tightening in 1979, 1980 and 1981, followed by loosening in 1982.

The difficulty was created by changes in the velocity of circulation, the counterpart of demand for money changes, and the fact that velocity shifts for broad and narrow money did not occur in parallel. The velocity of M1, after

Fig. 8 Velocity of Money* in the United States

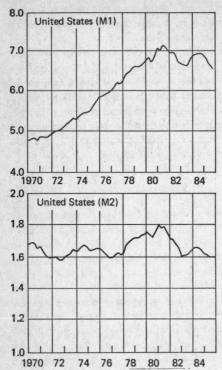

* Nominal GNP divided by the money stock
Source: International Monetary Fund

rising sharply but predictably during the 1970s, began to jump around as soon as it became the key target variable. The velocity of M1 at the end of the experiment was little changed from its level at the beginning, but in the intervening period it had recorded a number of sharp changes. M2 velocity rose initially but then fell steadily, to end lower than in October 1979.

The most popular explanation for the sharp shifts in the velocity of M1 was that they were the result of high and volatile interest rates and financial innovation. During the period 1979 to 1982, short-term interest rates varied from 8 to 18 per cent. But acceptance of the argument that interest rate changes caused sharp velocity shifts was difficult for monetarists, implying as it did that the demand for money was highly responsive to interest rates, virtually to the exclusion of other factors.

Financial innovation during this period included the development of interest-bearing checking accounts with deposits withdrawable on demand, notably NOW (negotiable order of withdrawal) and sweep accounts, where idle deposits could be automatically swept in to become interest-bearing. NOW accounts, originally available only in New England, received nationwide authorization during this period, and from January 1981 became available throughout the United States.

Significant though financial innovation was in the years 1979 to 1982, it was questionable whether the period represented a clear enough break in the trend of financial innovation, which had been progressing briskly for a number of years, usually to sidestep government controls on the banks.

And so the main monetarist critique of the 1979–82 experiment centred firmly upon the Federal Reserve Board, and the operating procedures it had adopted to try to control the money supply. By focusing on non-borrowed reserves, it was argued, the authorities had virtually guaranteed monetary volatility. According to Friedman:*

> The real experiment was in the operating procedures adopted – the use of non-borrowed reserves as the instrument. In effect, that meant a reversion to the 'free reserves' approach of the 1920s. Combined with lagged reserve requirements, the new approach enhanced volatility in monetary growth and, as a consequence, in both interest rates and economic activity. As a citizen, I deplore these results which . . . included imposing a much higher cost for the achieved reduction of inflation than was necessary.

It was a familiar Friedman theme. As in Britain, central bank incompetence was responsible. But, as Kaldor observed later, 'It was nowhere stated in the writings of Friedman or any of his followers that the quantity theory of money only holds in countries where the monetary authorities are sufficiently "competent" to regulate the money supply.'

The Friedman critique, that the 1979-82 experiment was not monetarist because it involved greater monetary volatility than before – indeed, greater than in any three-year period since 1945 – begged the question of whether it was possible to produce the smooth growth of the money stock required by the monetarists. Did the quantity theory relationships uncovered by Friedman and his co-workers over a hundred years and more of data only apply when the money stock was not being actively targeted?

However little the monetarists had to say in praise of the conduct of the 1979–82 experiment, they were less than happy with its relaxation and abandonment. 'The increased rate of monetary growth in the 1981–83 biennium

*American Economic Review: Papers and Proceedings of the 96th Annual Meeting, May 1984.

suggests that we have passed the trough in inflation and that inflation will be decidedly higher from 1983 to 1985 than it was from 1981 to 1983,' Friedman predicted.

No one would have made much money from following his forecast. Inflation was actually lower in 1983–5 than in 1981–3.

Table 4 Money and Inflation in the United States

	1978	1979	1980	1981	1982	1983	1984	1985
Money Stock *								
M1	8.2	7.5	7.5	5.1	8.7	10.4	5.3	11.9
M2	8.0	8.1	9.0	9.3	9.1	12.2	7.9	8.6
Inflation †								
GNP deflator	7.3	8.8	9.1	9.6	6.5	3.8	4.1	3.3
Consumer prices	7.6	11.3	13.5	10.4	6.1	3.2	4.3	3.5

* Change, end-year on end-year
† Change on previous year
Source: International Monetary Fund

The Deficit and the Recovery

Friedman's inflation prediction was wrong mainly because he ignored one of his own precepts. Even if the quantity theory works perfectly, with no inconvenient changes in velocity, then it can only convey information about the path of national income expressed in money terms (nominal GNP in the United States, money GDP in Britain). It says nothing about how that increase in money income will be divided between real growth and higher prices.

Following the adoption, or rather the re-adoption, of a pragmatic approach to monetary policy by the Federal Reserve Board, the economy did not need to lose out in the battle between the budget deficit and monetary targets. The monetary authorities became prepared to adopt a more accommodative approach, and there was nothing to hold the economy back.

Monetarists, while condemning the Federal Reserve's more relaxed attitude to monetary targets, could explain the recovery in the economy which started in 1983 in terms of the power of money. A mistakenly tight policy had given way to a looser one, so recovery, at least in the short term, could be expected, although there were dangers of higher inflation later.

The supply-siders saw their 1980–82 criticism of the Federal Reserve as vindicated by the onset of recovery, which began with 3.5 per cent GNP growth in 1983 and accelerated to a breakneck 6.5 per cent expansion in 1984. The 1983/4 recovery was the fastest since the early 1960s. As the supply-siders had said, the incentive effects of tax cuts could not work through as long as the economy was held back by tight monetary policy and high interest rates. When this constraint was removed, the economy started performing. The failure of the deficit to exhibit any self-correcting tendencies was an inconvenience. But it was early days, and the rising budget deficit could as well be blamed on public expenditure as on taxation.

Those who took a more old-fashioned view of fiscal policy, the Keynesians, saw things in simpler terms. Federal budget deficits were straightforward injections of demand into the economy, and growth, not surprisingly, ensued. According to the International Monetary Fund, the structural budget deficit in the United States, that is after allowing for inflation and cyclical factors, increased by the equivalent of 2.3 per cent of GNP between 1980 and 1985. The only other major economy with a similarly expansionary fiscal policy over this period was Canada, where the structural budget deficit rose by 2.9 per cent of GNP. In all other major economies the opposite occurred; fiscal policy exerted a contractionary influence.

Table 5 Growth and the Deficit

	1979	1980	1981	1982	1983	1984	1985
Fiscal balance*	−1.1	−2.3	−2.4	−4.1	−5.6	−4.9	−5.9
Fiscal impulse†	−0.8	0.4	0	0.3	1.6	0.4	1.0
GNP growth (per cent)	2.5	−0.2	1.9	−2.5	3.5	6.5	2.2

* Central government fiscal balance as percentage of GNP; minus equals deficit
† Influence of fiscal policy; plus equals expansionary, minus equals contractionary, as percentage of GNP
Source: International Monetary Fund

It is fair to describe US monetary policy during the recovery as accommodative, but it would be wrong to describe it as irresponsible. Paul Volcker had been disappointed with the 1979–82 experience, but he was determined not to throw the baby out with the bath-water by abandoning monetary targeting completely. The Federal Reserve's tactics immediately after October 1982 were to allow a once-for-all increase in the money stock, but then to proceed, albeit more pragmatically, with monetary targets.

For a few months, the lid was taken off. Financial innovation continued; NOW accounts developed into even more attractive super-NOW accounts, with unrestricted interest rates. Other interest-bearing checking accounts, notably money market deposit accounts, emerged. And so for a few months the money supply was allowed to expand at a fast pace.

By the spring of 1983, the three main monetary aggregates, M1, M2 and M3, all showed double-figure percentage rises on a year earlier. In the six months to May 1983, annualized growth of M1 was over 14 per cent, and of M2 more than 16 per cent. Interest rates fell sharply – the Federal funds rate dropped from nearly 15 per cent in the middle of 1982 to just over 8 per cent by early 1983.

The worst of the monetary bulge appeared to have passed by the middle of the year and, in July 1983, new re-based targets were announced for the money supply. The M1 target for 1983, of 5 to 9 per cent annualized growth, started from a second-quarter base. Similarly, the bases for M2 and M3 growth, February–March 1983, were selected on the argument that this was after most of the sharp winter rise had occurred. On these, admittedly artificial, criteria, the Federal Reserve was able to claim some degree of success. Annualized M1 growth between the second and fourth quarters of 1983 was 8.5 per cent, just within target; M2 was in the middle of its 7 to 10 per cent range, also growing at an annualized 8.5 per cent; only M3, up 10 per cent (6.5 to 9.5 per cent), spoiled a perfect record.

The important point was that the US authorities, while allowing enough money into the economy to keep the recovery going, indeed accelerating, and also, by 1979–82 standards, keeping interest rates low, managed to convey the impression that monetary policy was tighter than it was. And impressions are very important in the foreign exchange markets.

The Gravity-Defying Dollar

The world economy was dominated in 1983 and 1984 by something which, on the face of it, should not have been happening at all. The dollar, which in 1980 had been a highly vulnerable currency, rose in a way that put sterling's earlier sharp climb in the shade. And it occurred in spite of the fact that, on the traditional method of assessing a currency's prospects – the balance of payments – the United States' position was deteriorating rapidly.

At its peak in February 1985, the dollar's average value was 70 per cent above its 1980 level. And this occurred against the background of a damaging shift into deficit on the US current account. From a position of small surplus in 1980 and 1981, the current account moved into $8 billion deficit in 1982, widening to over $40 billion in 1983 and more than $100 billion in 1984.

Clearly, the forces that were pushing the dollar up were not operating through the current account – trade in goods, services and net earnings on overseas investment. The answer lay with the huge inflows of capital into the United States over this period, and the explanation for these inflows lay with the peculiar mix of fiscal and monetary policy, a mix characteristic of Reaganomics.

Fiscal policy in the United States was clearly very loose. Budget deficits of $200 billion a year had a direct impact on the dollar. Funding the deficit through the issue of Treasury debt required a major take-up of this debt by foreigners, if the crowding-out pressures on the American financial system were not to become unbearable. There were, therefore, direct flows across the exchanges into dollars as foreigners – particularly the Japanese – took up US debt instruments.

A more powerful factor was the interaction of the deficit with monetary policy. The implication, to the financial markets, of large budget deficits was that they would result in strong growth and higher borrowing. There was a risk of higher inflation, through 'monetization' of the deficits (financing them by printing money). But the view was that, with Volcker in charge at the Federal Reserve Board, this would not be allowed to happen.

In any case, the dollar's rise was itself acting as a forceful restraining influence on US inflation, by reducing the cost of imported goods. Foreign exchange speculators appeared to be offered something which they were hardly going to pass up, a one-way option on the dollar. As long as the dollar was on the way up, there need be no risks on inflation, which traditionally sends investors scurrying for the exits. To the already attractive yields available on dollar assets could be added the near certainty of currency gains. And at the heart of it was the mix of relatively tight monetary and clearly loose fiscal policy.

There was an obvious reluctance in the White House, in the run-up to the November 1984 Presidential election, to see the dollar's rise as in any way unsustainable, or as a child of irresponsible fiscal policy. President Reagan saw the US economy as 'like a greyhound' which was outpacing the rest of the world. The old economies of Europe, with their hidebound traditions and obsolete institutions, were no longer up to it. The dollar's rise, he averred, was occuring because the US economy was so much stronger than any other.

The Treasury Secretary, Donald Regan, stung by one too many international criticisms of the budget deficit, set a team of Treasury economists combing through the evidence on the links between budget deficits and interest rates. The results proved, he said, that whatever else might be the cause of historically high world interest rates and the rising dollar, it was not the US budget deficit.

At the Federal Reserve, Paul Volcker was unwilling to correct the imbalance between fiscal and monetary policy by relaxing monetary policy further. The movement, he argued, had to come from the side of fiscal policy. Monetary policy in 1984 continued where it had left off in 1983. Strong growth in the monetary aggregates in the first half of the year was met with a tightening of policy in July. When this appeared to work rather too well and signs of economic slow-down emerged later in the year, the Federal Reserve cut interest rates and increased the supply of reserves to the system.

The guiding light of monetary policy was to sustain domestic growth. With a GNP rise of 6.5 per cent in 1984, it worked remarkably well. The strong dollar was someone else's problem.

Bursting the Dollar Bubble

Almost from the time it began its dramatic rise, economists were predicting that the dollar was riding for a fall. The current account deficit, once established above $100 billion, would exert itself and send the dollar sliding, it was said. And once the currency began to fall, foreign investors would take fright and the whole house of cards would tumble down. The forecasters, or at least the majority of them, were right on direction, eventually, but wrong on timing. The dollar's climb lasted longer and reached far greater heights than anyone had predicted.

Four main factors can be cited in the dollar's slide which, when it came, began in February 1985 and progressed rapidly, far quicker than its earlier rise.

The first was a swapping of jobs in the US Administration between Donald Regan, who moved from the Treasury to become White House Chief of Staff, and James Baker, who became the new Treasury Secretary. On the face of it, this was a reshuffle which should have sent the financial markets reeling. Donald Regan came into the Reagan Administration from the giant Wall Street investment house Merrill Lynch, and clearly knew a lot about finance and economics. But James Baker had come to the White House with a long pedigree in Republican politics, a background as a Texan lawyer, but no obvious credentials for the job of Treasury Secretary. Regan, however, was a financial market man who had lost the confidence of the financial markets. His dogged determination to provide intellectual justification for $200 billion-plus budget deficits had not just infuriated his counterparts in other countries; it had got Wall Street worried.

Baker was clearly not an expert on the financial markets, but he knew a lot about what was happening in the real economy. He could see that, for all the talk of an economic miracle, large sections of American industry and agriculture were dying on their feet, killed off by the soaring dollar. It soon became clear that the new Treasury Secretary wanted a hands-on approach to the dollar, and one that would bring it down to more realistic levels.

The second factor was that, as economists had predicted, the current account deficit began to weigh down on the US economy. It was one thing for newspaper reports to describe the sorry state of the old smokestack industries, or even the newer industries which could not compete with the dollar at almost twice its 1980 level. It was another when the current account, through the net exports component of gross national product, began to produce a sharp slow-down in America's growth rate. This happened from the second half of 1984 onwards – growth slowed from 6.5 per cent in 1984 to 2.2 per cent in 1985 – and the view that dollar strength meant a strong economy began to have a false ring to it.

Thirdly, the long-awaited action to rein back the budget deficit started in earnest in Reagan's second term. After lengthy negotiations between the administration and Congress, cuts of $55 billion in the proposed budget deficit for the 1986 fiscal year were passed in August 1985. This was backed up by the passage in December of the Gramm–Rudman–Hollings amendment to the bill to increase the country's debt ceiling. The amendment imposed automatic deficit-reducing actions on the US government. The aim was for a balanced budget by 1991.

The action on the deficit was to come later, but it was an important straw in the wind early in 1985. There were grounds, therefore, on at least three counts, for expecting dollar weakness. But the timing of the dollar fall, which had fooled the experts before, remained in doubt.

Such doubts might have remained had it not been for the fourth factor – large-scale central bank intervention on the foreign exchanges to drive down the dollar. In January, the finance ministers of the Group of Five countries – the United States, Britain, Japan, Germany and France – had met in Washington and reaffirmed the principle of intervening in disorderly currency markets. The principle had originally been agreed at the world economic summit in Williamsburg, Virginia, two years earlier.

The significance of the January 1985 reaffirmation of this principle was not, however, fully appreciated. It was widely seen as a friendly gesture to help the pound, by then under severe pressure, without actually spending any money. For most of February, it seemed as if nothing had changed. At a Congressional hearing, Paul Volcker spoke with scepticism of the powers of currency intervention. President Reagan, maintaining his pre-election style, said that the United States was 'a nation renewed ... a great industrial giant is reborn. Our economy is not getting older and weaker, it is getting younger and stronger.'

Then on 27 February, with a suddenness which left the foreign exchange markets reeling, central bank selling sent the dollar sharply lower. In two hours the dollar fell almost 20 pfennigs from its peak of just above DM 3.45. In the space of a few days the central banks, led by the German Bundesbank, sold in excess of $10 billion.

As an initial raid it was successful, but serious question-marks remained in the minds of foreign exchange dealers. Would the trick be repeated, given the prevalent official view that intervention was only to be used in emergencies? And would Paul Volcker at the Federal Reserve Board be willing to stand by and allow the dollar to fall, a fall which carried the risk of rekindling inflation?

The answer to the latter question came fairly quickly. In May, the Federal Reserve cut the discount rate, in spite of above-target monetary growth, because of signs of economic weakness. It signalled that neither missed monetary targets nor the falling dollar would stand in the way of lower interest rates in the United States. The moves to curb the budget deficit had produced, in the eyes of the financial markets, a shift on one side of the fiscal and monetary policy mix; now the evidence started to mount that a shift was also taking place on the other side.

Tighter fiscal policy was mirrored by easier monetary policy, to produce something that was beginning to move, albeit very slowly, towards a consistent middle ground. During 1985, the M1 money measure was allowed to grow well above its target path, recording an increase of nearly 12 per cent, against a target of 4 to 7 per cent, raised and widened to 3 to 8 per cent in mid year.

Further evidence of the administration's intentions towards the dollar came in September. On 22 September, James Baker called the finance ministers and central bankers of the Group of Five to the Plaza Hotel in New York. The meeting, a key one in the economic history of the period, set in train further large central bank sales of the dollar, this time with the United States, through the Federal Reserve Bank of New York, playing a full part.

For the rest of September and in October, another $10 billion was spent driving the dollar down, $3.2 billion of it by the United States. This time, the foreign exchanges got the message. The dollar, which had paused in its slide, began to fall again. A year after the Plaza meeting, in September 1986, the participants could look with some satisfaction on what had been achieved. The dollar was close to DM2 against the mark, over 40 per cent below its February 1985 peak; and $1.50 against sterling, a dollar fall of more than 30 per cent. The Japanese authorities had prevented the yen from falling too much against the dollar during its sharp climb, but acceded to it rising strongly against a falling dollar. The dollar fell from 265 in February 1985 to 150 in September 1986. And the chorus of protest shifted from America's industrial heartlands, across the oceans to industrialists in Japan and Germany, who were complaining that they could not live with their currencies at such levels.

The official view of US monetary policy during the 1985/6 period of deliberate dollar depreciation was that there had been no change in priorities. According to the Federal Reserve Bank of New York: 'Monetary policy in 1985 sought to encourage sufficient money and credit growth to sustain the economic expansion against a background of relatively well-contained inflationary and cost pressures.'

The means by which economic growth could be sustained had, however, changed. It now required the extra ingredient of a declining dollar, and the main aim of monetary policy became that of securing a substantial, but not uncontrolled, dollar fall.

Thus, in December 1985, the Federal Reserve deliberately held interest rates up in the United States to give the dollar time to pause for breath. The Plaza accord had been almost too successful. On 23 September, the day after the meeting, the dollar fell by more than 5 per cent against most currencies.

The Bank for International Settlements in Basle, reviewing US policy during this period, described it thus:

> The Plaza Agreement was evidently interpreted in the market as an indication that a tightening of monetary policy in the United States was not in prospect. Once the dollar began to weaken, however, US policy seems to have been influenced by the possibility that in time excessively rapid depreciation, while stimulating output, could push up the US inflation rate. In addition, a weakening of foreign demand for dollar investments could put upward pressures on interest rates in the United States, given the need to finance the large Federal government budget deficit. By late 1985 interest rate policy appeared to be geared largely to preventing a precipitous decline in the dollar.

Policy became a subtle blend of achieving a lower dollar without risking a damaging crash-landing. In the spring of 1986, co-ordinated action on the dollar by the major industrialized countries switched to co-ordinated action to reduce interest rates, with reductions in the United States, Germany, Japan, Britain and France.

The dollar dominated policy. The United States, traditionally the most insular of the major economies, had had to switch to a policy under which the exchange rate took precedence over domestic monetary targets.

Later in the year, co-operation on interest rates turned into a poker game between Washington, Bonn and Tokyo. The United States, through aggressive interest rate cuts, attempted to pressure other countries into reducing their rates, with a further dollar fall as the consequence of not doing so.

As monetary targets, while still dutifully published, took on a secondary role, so the monetarist experiments of the earlier part of the 1980s became a distant memory. It is easy to see why. The long-term relationships which formed the basis of monetarism had been built up over a period when, by and large, exchange rates were fixed or semi-fixed. In the case of the United States, the closed economy assumption of simple monetarist models was appropriate for most of her economic history, but increasingly inappropriate as the 1980s progressed.

The neatly declining paths for growth in the money stock; the lags between money changes and those in nominal GNP; the ease with which the authorities could control the money supply – all had been based on a huge under-estimation of the scale and effects of major and rapid exchange rate shifts. The idea of formal monetary targeting being replaced by informally managed exchange rates was anathema to Friedman. His advocacy of freely floating exchange rates was almost as strong as that of monetary rules. But with the Treasury Secretary, James Baker, talking of the possibility of an eventual return to something like the Bretton Woods system of fixed exchange rates, and with the Federal Reserve Board a willing participant in the new era of informal exchange rate management, in the United States, too, Friedman's views had clearly fallen from grace.

IO

AFTER MONETARISM

Monetarism has been around, in one shape or another, for 300 years. Ten turbulent years of practical monetarism, and imperfect practical monetarism at that, could be dismissed by the determined monetarist as a short and irrelevant interlude. But the problems of the set of economic policies labelled monetarist have raised serious doubts about the underlying theory.

The experience of monetarist policies has persuaded many people, even those sympathetic to monetarist ideas, that the quantity theory is, at best, only interesting and useful as a long-run relationship.

There is an analogy with the theory of purchasing power parities for exchange rates. Over a large number of years, the evidence is that currencies do indeed tend towards levels which reflect relative inflation rates between countries. The problem is that, in the short term, as clearly happened in the floating-rate era of the 1970s and 1980s, exchange rates can move wildly away from their 'correct' purchasing power parity levels.

So with the relationship between the stock of money and money national income. The debate over the direction of causation aside, the majority of economists would concede that there is a long-term relationship between changes in the money stock and changes in gross domestic product, expressed in money terms. The difficulty faced by the practical exponents of monetarism was that, for months or even years, the relationship was highly volatile, and hence untrustworthy as a guide to policy.

Economic policy, whether it is labelled monetarist or Keynesian, is more often pragmatism tinged with a particular theoretical bias. In certain circumstances, fixed ideas will take hold of policy, pushing pragmatism temporarily out of the way. This is perhaps the best way in which to view the monetarist experiments of the 1970s and 1980s.

Fashions in economics come and go. Around the world, and not just in Britain, the parties in opposition are advocating, not a return to rigorous monetary targeting, but a variety of other formulations of economic policy. Monetarism is last year's economic policy model; it is no longer fashionable.

Monetarism has, however, made a lasting contribution. No longer is it possible for politicians to say that money, meaning monetary policy, does not matter. Equally, the simplistic view that if the money supply is controlled then everything else falls into place is no longer tenable, partly because it begs the question of whether money can actually be controlled.

The Lessons of the Monetarist Experiments

(i) 'Catch 22'

Friedman's monetary rule, expressed in his 1967 presidential address to the American Economic Association, implied the abandonment of discretion in policy:

> My own prescription is still that the monetary authority go all the way in avoiding such swings by adopting publicly the policy of achieving a steady rate of growth in a specified monetary total. The precise rate of growth, like the precise monetary total, is less important than the adoption of some stated and known rate. I myself have argued for ... something like a 3 to 5 per cent per year rate of growth in currency plus all commercial bank deposits.

If necessary, Friedman argued, governments should be required by law to publish and abide by the monetary rule. But there is a difficulty here, and it is one that came to the fore during the monetarist experiments. Politicians will be willing to comply with monetary targets when it suits them, but will also relax monetary policy and jettison targets when there are enough political pressures on them to do so. And for governments to be legally constrained in the area of monetary policy: that requires politicians to do something which goes against the grain – to hand over power to some other authority, in this case the central bank.

The 'catch 22' of the monetary rule is that it is imposed on politicians by politicians, and they have to be prepared to subject themselves to it when it may act to their political disadvantage to do so. Sir Terry Burns, the government's Chief Economic Adviser in Britain, has argued that the very act of publishing monetary targets implies a presumption that they will be met. Politicians who want to relax or abandon monetary targets then have to provide a robust justification for doing so.

This was true, but with monetary targets at best imperfectly understood by the general public, at worst not at all, it was not difficult for the politicians to come up with good reasons for not sticking to pre-announced monetary plans, particularly when the electorate was baying for blood. In some cases, targets were relaxed or abandoned for sound technical reasons; in others, because it was politic to do so.

(ii) Velocity Shifts

The biggest single difficulty faced by practical monetarists has been that the demand for money, or the velocity of circulation (the one is the reciprocal of the other), far from being stable or at least predictable, has been unstable and highly unpredictable.

It is easy to see why this was problematical by reference to the simple $MV = PY$ quantity theory equation. To achieve the desired result for PY (money national income), by controlling M (the stock of money), it is necessary to know what is happening to V (the velocity of circulation). And *not* knowing this proved to be the bane of policy-makers. Long before the monetarist experiments of the 1970s and 1980s, Keynesian critics of the quantity theory argued that its weakest point was the assumption of stable or predictable velocity. They said that the demand for money was a 'will o' the wisp' which was likely to flit about in any direction at any time.

Friedman's response to this was typically robust: 'A numerically constant velocity does not deserve the sneering condescension that has become the conventional stance of economists.' The assumption of stable demand for money, he argued, was far closer to the truth than the extreme, will o' the wisp alternative.

Friedman's results, it may be recalled, showed that the demand for money tended to rise slowly and steadily in the long run. In the short term, it would tend to rise during cyclical upswings and fall during downswings. In both cases it was, however, predictable.

The British econometrician David Hendry, in collaboration with Neil Ericsson, subjected Friedman's claims to close testing in 1983. In fact, the testing did not need to be too rigorous. Describing Friedman and Schwarz's 1982 work, *Monetary Trends in the United States and the United Kingdom*, Hendry wrote:

> A wide range of claims concerning the behaviour of monetary economies was made by Friedman and Schwarz and they asserted that these claims were consistent with the long-run historical evidence. A remarkable feature of their book is that none of the claims was actually subjected to test. Rather, equations were reported which did not manifestly contradict their theories and this non-contradiction was taken for 'corroboration'.

Friedman and Schwarz's claim of a stable demand for money function was easily tested. Hendry split the sample period in two and checked the equations generated for the two periods against one another for statistical fit. They did not fit well. The results rejected the claim that there existed 'stability of the demand for money as a function of a small number of arguments'. Hendry and Ericsson's work was published, perhaps appropriately, by the Bank of England

Panel of Academic Consultants. It knocked holes in many of the empirical planks of Friedman's monetarism, and Friedman has yet to offer a response to it.

In 1985, Hendry turned his attention to the post-1979 behaviour of monetary models. He found that the sharp shifts in the velocity of circulation were mainly due to financial innovation. Each new financial instrument, offering more attractive terms, or a combination of high returns and convenience, was likely to influence the demand for money, he said. According to Hendry, 'Money demand models remain useful if it is thought, or known, that financial innovation will not occur; or if innovations do occur but their quantitative effects can be anticipated.' Financial innovation did indeed occur during the monetarist experiments but its effects were difficult, if not impossible, to predict.

The sharpest movements in velocity have occurred in those measures of the money stock most actively targeted. In Britain, the velocity of circulation of broad money, sterling M3, rose steadily throughout most of the 1960s and 1970s. A continuation of this trend, for a 1 to 1.5 per cent a year rise in velocity, was a reasonable assumption in setting out the medium-term financial strategy in March 1980. Unfortunately, velocity went into an abrupt reversal at about that time, probably as a result of the abolition of the corset controls on the banks and the removal of exchange controls.

Over the period 1980 to 1985, sterling M3 velocity – measured by the rise in money GDP divided by the rise in sterling M3 – declined by an average of 2.5 per cent a year. The monetary targets devised in 1980 were thus unintentionally tight.

The effects of financial innovation and liberalization are more typically on narrow money. The relatively stable velocities experienced for the major monetary aggregates in Germany and Japan – although short-term movements were still important – may be explained by the fact that the financial systems of these countries were much more tightly regulated. The de-regulation and financial liberalization generally favoured by monetarists may carry with it the penalty that the stable economic relationships which form the basis of monetarism break down.

The difficulty with shifts in velocity is that they only become apparent long after remedial action can be taken. Most calculations of velocity are a form of economics shorthand, measuring this year's rise in the money stock against this year's money GDP increase. This is because the lags in monetarist relationships have always been admitted to be variable. This year's rise in the stock of money may therefore be correctly associated with next year's money GDP rise, or that of the following year. It is only possible to be wise about velocity well after the event.

Fig. 9 Velocity of money* in Britain

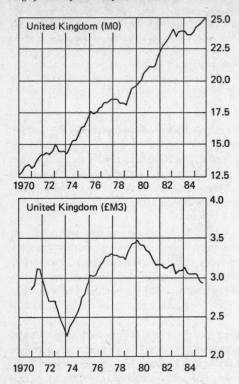

* Money GDP divided by the money stock
Source: International Monetary Fund

(iii) Controlling Money

Perhaps the most basic presumption of monetarism, so basic that it hardly merited attention initially, was that money could be controlled. Monetarists, when they were in the policy wilderness, always assumed that achieving a steady rate of growth of the money stock was in the gift of the monetary authorities, if only they had the will to do so. As David Laidler put it in the *Oxford Review of Economic Policy*, Spring 1985:

> Though adamant that controlling money growth was the key to controlling inflation, monetarists prior to the 1980s paid little attention to the choice of the monetary

aggregate in terms of which to implement their policies. Different people had different preferences but there was agreement that the matter was of secondary importance. The consensus belief was that, if the growth rate of one aggregate was pinned down by policy, then that of the others would be brought into line by the stable portfolio behaviour of the private sector and all would be well. Incredibly, we failed to notice that, although this position might be perfectly adequate to characterize steady states in which relative rates of return on various monetary assets were not changing, it was grossly inadequate as a guide for anyone seeking to change the long-run time path of monetary policy.

In Britain, the failure to achieve control over what was originally the favoured monetary aggregate, sterling M3, was a major blow for the monetarist experiment. Professor Charles Goodhart, the Bank of England's specialist adviser on monetary economics from 1968 to 1985, was sensitive to the criticism that this failure of control occurred because the Bank was not trying hard enough or, to paraphrase Friedman, because it did not believe in monetarism enough to have the determination to make it work.

He tested the speed of the central bank's reaction to above-target monetary growth in Britain, as compared with the response times of the monetary authorities in the United States, Germany and Canada. His conclusion, contained in his book *Monetary Theory and Practice*, was that: 'Far from appearing as "unbelieving monetarists", these results would suggest that the authorities in the UK acted relatively more forcefully and vigorously to attain their targets.'

The difficulties with sterling M3, according to Professor Goodhart, lay elsewhere. The two main counterparts of sterling M3 are bank lending and the public sector borrowing requirement. The Bank of England could and did exert fairly tight control over the public sector counterpart through its funding policy – the sale of gilt-edged securities. If the public sector borrowing requirement is fully funded, in other words if enough government stock has been sold to cover it, then it exerts no expansionary influence on sterling M3. Indeed, if it is overfunded the public sector exerts a contractionary influence, and this was often the case.

Controlling bank lending was rather more difficult. The weapons at the Bank's disposal were credit controls, either formal or informal, and interest rates. With the abandonment of exchange controls in 1979 and the corset in 1980, the task fell to interest rates to control bank lending, and they did not do so. In the recessionary conditions of 1980, higher interest rates actually boosted bank lending, by increasing the amount of distress borrowing by troubled companies already burdened with debt. But even in the easier economic conditions later, high interest rates did not restrain lending. In 1985 and 1986 real interest rates were at historically very high levels of, on average, 6 or 7 per cent.

Even so, by the summer of 1986 bank lending was rising fast enough to push up sterling M3, on its own, by 2 per cent a month. Controlling bank lending through price alone was difficult, if not impossible.

Monetarists saw one problem of policy as confusing credit, of which the broad money aggregates clearly contained a great deal, with money proper. Even narrow money, measured by M1, contained a substantial proportion of credit, or interest-bearing deposits, in both Britain and the United States. The mistake, on this view, was in not controlling the monetary base.

There is, therefore, a nagging doubt about the monetarist experiments. Would they have worked if monetary base control – the control of cash plus bankers' balances at the central bank – had been adopted? Professor Goodhart suspected not. He wrote:

> Strict control of the base ... would continually threaten frequent and potentially massive movements in interest rates, if not complete instability. Changes in the base would inevitably carry implications for interest rates, and the greater the emphasis on control of the base, the less the possibility that the central bank could intervene to ameliorate any interest rate fluctuations ... Indeed, it is doubtful whether such a system could possibly work, mainly because of the time it would take for markets to adjust to the interest rate changes induced by the banks in their attempts to meet their reserve requirements.

Slotting in the monetary base as an additional indicator for policy – as was done by the Chancellor of the Exchequer, Nigel Lawson, in 1983 – clearly sidestepped such difficulties. But it could never have been a short-term palliative. Several years of experience with the monetary base as an indicator would have been required before firm judgements could have been made on the basis of its behaviour.

(iv) The External Factor

In the areas of financial innovation and the practical difficulties of controlling money, it can be conceded that monetarism was a little unlucky. It is easy to be wise after the event and it is perhaps understandable that, before monetarism became a serious policy proposition, its proponents did not focus on these potential problems.

This was not the case, however, with the monetarist failure to grasp the significance of the exchange rate, and the major distortions and pressures on policy that would be created by massive and destabilizing currency shifts.

The era of floating exchange rates which began in 1973 was, from the start, one in which currencies did not move smoothly from one equilibrium to another. Rather, the large flows of short-term capital between the major financial centres were often totally unrelated to the underlying economic fundamentals of relative inflation and trade performance. They produced long periods of over-valuation or under-valuation for the different currencies, followed by excessively large corrections. One could search long and fruitlessly for evidence that the currency market in the era of floating rates was a stable one which tended towards equilibrium.

Most monetarist models in the United States and Britain ascribed only a minor role to the exchange rate. Monetarist models in which the exchange rate was prominent, including those developed by Peter Jonson and his colleagues at the Reserve Bank of Australia in the mid 1970s and the international monetarist approach of the London Business School in Britain, tended to assume that currencies would follow a smooth adjustment path, in line with relative rates of monetary growth.

For the majority of countries, including all the smaller economies in Europe, the luxury of pursuing independent monetary targets and leaving the exchange rate to find its own level was simply too expensive. Even before the 1979 monetarist experiments in Britain and the United States, in 1978 Switzerland had been forced to abandon her monetary targets temporarily to prevent the Swiss franc from rising too far and too fast.

Given Britain's post-war history of currency pressures, it was incredible that it took several years and two Conservative Chancellors before it was admitted that the pound was, after all, more important than domestic monetary targets. In the United States, traditionally the least vulnerable of the major economies to outside pressures, the omission was less surprising, but no more tenable.

As Ralph Bryant of the Brookings Institution put it in his book *Controlling Money*, following the 1979–82 US experiment:

> The international issues stem from the growing financial openness of the American economy. When the Federal Reserve takes a policy action, a modest – but an increasingly less modest – part of the effects of the action leaks out to foreign nations. When foreign nations take policy actions or when non-policy disturbances originate abroad, an increasingly greater part of the effects spills over into the United States. As a consequence of the growing interdependence of the American economy and the economies of other nations, the policy decisions of the Federal Reserve and of other central banks become more difficult to make and more uncertain in their consequences.

The elevation of the dollar in US monetary policy was gradual. In some cases, shifts occurred rather more suddenly. The government of Canada, vainly attempting to operate an independent monetary policy in the shadow of the United States, announced in November 1982 that monetary targets were to be abandoned completely. Japan, as is clear from the relatively muted movements of the yen against the dollar in the early 1980s, never allowed the exchange rate to become a residual item in monetary policy.

The countries of the European Monetary System – the original six members of the European Community plus Ireland and Denmark – operated under an exchange rate constraint, although this was less obviously so in the case of France in the early years of President Mitterrand's time in office.

Of the major economies, this left Britain and the United States to pursue monetary policies which were, initially at least, free from any limitations imposed by the exchange rate. In each case, the consequences were felt in large and damaging currency shifts which exacerbated the effects of policy errors in monetary targeting.

Manufacturing industry, on both sides of the Atlantic, was dealt a blow from which much of it would never recover. Great emphasis was placed by the political proponents of monetarism on the benefits that would accrue from stable, non-inflationary economic conditions. In the key area of exchange rates, monetarism only helped to generate damaging instability.

The Success with Inflation

Most monetarists would argue that, whatever the imperfections of the monetarist experiments; whatever the record in exactly hitting monetary targets; whatever the difficulties with volatile velocity of circulation, monetarism did achieve its stated aim of bringing down inflation.

Inflation in the industrialized countries of the Organization for Economic Co-operation and Development fell from nearly 13 per cent in 1980 to an estimated 3.5 per cent in 1986. In Britain, retail price inflation touched nearly 22 per cent in 1980 before falling sharply to less than 2.5 per cent in the summer of 1986.

As Nigel Lawson said in October 1985: 'The acid test of monetary policy is its record in reducing inflation ... The inflation rate is the judge and jury.'

David Laidler, writing in 1985, noted that: 'Monetarism's most basic claim was that, in order to slow down inflation, money growth needed to be curbed. Over the last five years, on average, money growth has been more restrictive than it was in the 1970s, and inflation has fallen markedly.' His main concern was that: 'Though the inflation rate has been reduced significantly since 1980, the cost of doing so has been much higher than anyone expected.'

To the critics of monetarism, this view raised more questions than it answered. Did the inflation rate come down as a direct consequence of monetary targeting and control, or merely as a side-effect of an economic slump imposed by over-restrictive monetary, and outside the United States,

Table 6 Consumer Price Inflation, 1979–86

	1979	1980	1981	1982	1983	1984	1985	1986*
Britain	13.4	18.0	11.9	8.6	4.6	5.0	6.1	4.0
United States	11.3	13.5	10.4	6.1	3.2	4.3	3.5	2.8
Germany	4.1	5.5	6.3	5.3	3.3	2.4	2.2	0
Japan	3.6	8.0	4.9	2.7	1.9	2.2	2.1	0.5
OECD average	9.8	12.9	10.5	7.8	5.2	5.2	4.5	3.5

* estimate/forecast
Source: OECD

fiscal policies? If so, was the low inflation of the mid 1980s sustainable as and when the major economies returned to anything like full capacity?

It is possible to construct a plausible explanation of the great inflation of the 1970s and early 1980s which does not ascribe a central role to money. Thus the two recent peaks for OECD inflation, in 1974/5 and 1980/81, followed sharp rises in the price of oil and other commodities. Shifts in the balance of power between commodity producers and consumers have clearly had an influence on the profile, at the very least, of Western inflation over the past twenty years.

But, monetarists argue, the sharp fall in inflation since the second oil crisis is testimony to the effectiveness of measures taken to control the money supply. Inflation did indeed fall more sharply from 1981 onwards than it did between the two oil shocks.

Money is, however, only one explanation. Between the two oil price hikes there was a softening but not a collapse in the oil market. Prices weakened but did not plunge. After the second price rise, oil prices collapsed as the Organization of Petroleum Exporting Countries fell into disarray. There was a clear shift in the balance of power back to commodity consumers.

In the same way, the huge increases in unemployment in the 1980s, particularly in Europe, tilted the labour market in favour of the buyers of labour, employers, and against the sellers, workers. On the simple Phillips curve relationship, the sharp rises in unemployment – in Britain the rate rose from less than 5.5 per cent in 1979 to nearly 14 per cent in 1986 – could be expected to exert a major restraining influence on inflation. But even on Friedman's natural rate approach, unemployment could have been expected to constrain real wages.

The other non-money reason for the sharp fall in inflation in the 1980s was tight fiscal policies. According to calculations by Professor Marcus Miller of the University of Warwick, there was only one year between the two oil shocks, 1977, when Britain ran a 'true' structural surplus. The true structural balance is arrived at by adjusting the public sector's financial balance for inflation and cyclical factors.

The larger the structural surplus, the tighter is fiscal policy. In 1977, the year of the greatest impact of the International Monetary Fund's emergency measures, the surplus was equivalent to 0.3 per cent of gross domestic product. It was surrounded by deficits, ranging from 1 to 3 per cent of GDP. In the 1980–84 period, in marked contrast, Britain ran a structural surplus every year, ranging from 1.1 to 6.1 per cent of GDP. Fiscal policy, after allowing for inflation and the scale of the recession, was very much tighter than in the earlier period.

The calculation rather overstates the actual tightness of policy, because in the latter period the government was enjoying major revenue flows from North Sea oil, but the general conclusion still holds.

An explanation of the inflation of the 1980s which ignores the role of restrictive monetary policies is clearly an incomplete one. But it illustrates the fact that there were other powerful factors at work, some intended, some fortuitous.

The unkindest cut of all for monetarists is that the onset of low inflation did not make the task of controlling the money supply any easier. Apart from the fact that governments around the world came under increasing pressure, and in some cases responded to that pressure, to switch their attention from the control of inflation to the reduction of unemployment, monetary aggregates continued to misbehave, even in a low inflation era. In Britain in the summer of 1986, broad money, sterling M3, albeit of limited interest by then to the authorities as a target aggregate, was growing at nearly 20 per cent alongside an inflation rate of less than 2.5 per cent. In Germany, despite zero inflation, the central bank money stock, the main target aggregate, grew at an above-target 7 per cent during 1986, the first overshoot for eight years.

The important question, given that governments in most countries decided to give the greatest priority to reducing inflation in the 1980s, is whether the methods adopted to do so were the best available. Here, there is an unusual consensus among the proponents and critics of monetarism. No one would argue that anti-inflationary policy, as it evolved, was very near the optimum.

The starkest evidence of this, of course, lies with unemployment. In Britain, unemployment rose from 1.2 million in 1979 to 3.2 million in 1986. In the Western industrialized countries of the OECD, the average unemployment rate rose from 5 to 12 per cent over the same period. By 1986, over 32 million people were out of work in the industrialized nations.

There has been a tendency, in Britain perhaps more than anywhere else, to absolve monetary policy and the monetarist experiment from the blame for this. Unemployment, it is said, is a consequence of imperfections in the labour market and the fact that large and unwarranted real wage rises have occurred for those in employment, to the detriment of the unemployed.

Monetarists should blush at such assertions. The big rise in unemployment in Britain occurred between 1979 and 1981, during the period when monetary policy was mistakenly tight. Subsequently, looser monetary policy has fuelled large increases in pay. But the rhetoric has not shifted as much as the policy, and employers, believing that the monetary reins have been held tight, have held back from taking on extra manpower.

Was there a policy mix which could have generated low inflation without the heavy costs in unemployment? Any such mix would clearly have had to avoid the initial 'short, sharp shock' of monetarism. It would also have needed to ensure that the consequences of looser monetary policy were felt in higher employment rather than in higher pay.

In Britain, attention has again turned to forms of incomes policy, such as those which operate through tax incentives and penalties. The Chancellor of the Exchequer, Nigel Lawson, floated a scheme in 1986, based on the ideas of Professors Martin Weitzman and James Meade, under which tax relief was offered on that proportion of pay which is directly linked to profits.

The difficulty with such ideas is that they smack of locking the stable door after the horse has bolted. Palliatives of this nature could have helped prevent the sharp rise in unemployment, assuming that the mistakes of policy had been avoided. They may be less effective in correcting the economic consequences of earlier monetarist errors.

Stateless Money

In the earlier discussions on the velocity of circulation, financial innovation loomed large. The emergence of new financial instruments and the breaking down of barriers between different types of financial institution as de-regulation occurred have generally been analysed in a narrow sense. As long as policy-makers could make sufficient allowance for such developments in setting monetary targets, it was assumed, then they would not go too far wrong.

In fact, the logical consequence of financial innovation and de-regulation is that, even for the major economies, pursuing an independent monetary policy is no longer a tenable proposition. As money increasingly becomes stateless and divorced from the banking systems of individual countries, so the whole paraphernalia of monetary targeting, which operates upon those domestic banking systems, becomes obsolete.

In April 1986, the Bank for International Settlements in Basle published the report of a special study group set up to examine the consequences of international financial innovation.* It said:

A sharp acceleration in the pace of innovation, de-regulation and structural changes in recent years has transformed the international financial system in important ways. Major new financial instruments – mostly taking the form of off-balance sheet commitments – have either been created or have dramatically increased their role in the financial structure: international credit flows have shifted away from loans through large international banks into direct credit markets; the volume of daily transactions has multiplied; financial markets have become far more closely integrated worldwide; capital has become much more mobile.

The study group discerned three main trends in financial innovation. The first was securitization, the process by which bank loans are packaged into a form of security which can be bought or sold. Securitization can range from the grand to the more mundane such as, in the United States, the securitization of house mortgages amd car loans. The effect is to transfer the ownership of credit from banks – under the control of a particular country's central bank – to institutions outside that control. Traditional banking controls, operating through credit or liquidity ratios, become difficult, if not impossible, to enforce.

The evidence of securitization is provided by a major shift from bank credit to the international securities markets. Between 1981 and 1985, there was a fall from $100 billion to $25 billion in syndicated Euro-bank loans. Over the same period there was a rise, from $44 billion to $160 billion, in international bond and note issues.

The second trend identified was a sharp increase in the off-balance sheet activities of the banks; bank business which does not involve booking assets and taking deposits. Among examples of these are note issuance facilities (NIFs), currency and interest rate swaps and options, and forward rate agreements. All provide banks with the means of hedging interest rate risks, while leaving their balance sheets and capital ratios untouched.

The third trend was, of course, the worldwide integration of financial markets. The obvious sign of this has been the increased responsiveness of markets, in both bonds and equities, to events in other markets. Financial operators in Britain can no longer content themselves with the daily diet of domestic financial, economic and political news. An event in Tokyo, New York or Frankfurt is just as likely to move the market.

These developments have far-reaching implications for policy. Monetary policy which operated through credit controls may now, more than ever, be

* 'Recent Innovations in International Banking', Bank for International Settlements, Basle.

doomed to failure. There is now an endless variety of methods, and a large and growing number of international routes, to by-pass such controls. And with the growth in the availability of interest rate hedges, changes in interest rates may be slow to act on monetary aggregates, if they are effective at all.

Finally, and most importantly, these developments have laid the ghost of independence in monetary policy. Most notably from the Plaza Hotel meeting of the Group of Five countries in September 1985, economic policy has been seen in an international context. In an ideal world, the fiscal and monetary policies of the major economies would dovetail into an optimum framework for non-inflationary growth. The practicalities are rather more difficult. And, if money is becoming increasingly stateless, it is by no means certain that such co-ordination would solve the problems. It is, however, one obvious way forward.

Buffer Stock Money

An important development in monetary theory which has dealt a further blow to the idea that it is possible for governments to adopt a benign 'hands-off' approach to monetary policy, and simply set monetary targets and stick with them, has come with the 'disequilibrium money' approach in the academic literature.

There are many variants on the approach, developed partly to explain why previous monetary relationships had broken down, and partly by followers of Keynes, such as James Tobin, to provide a further rebuttal to Chicago monetarism. The one which has most appeal is the treatment of money as a buffer stock.

Imagine the economy as a sort of grand Victorian plumbing system. Under simple monetarism, the money supply taps are turned on at one end and the water flows out, in the form of higher money income, at the other. But suppose that, all along the way, there are pipes running off the main, along which people are emptying or filling their own stocks. The end result then becomes far less certain.

A money supply shock, either a sharp increase or a decrease, can be accommodated by individuals adding to or running down their buffer stocks of money. Only when they are certain that the shock to the system is permanent will they make the necessary adjustment to their stocks.

Because everyone will have different perceptions about when a temporary shock has become permanent, the adjustment may be long and unpredictable. It may be thought, at first blush, that this is nothing more than the long and variable lags of monetarism. It can indeed be nothing more than this, but it can also have far greater implications for the conduct of policy.

Buffer stock holdings complicate monetary policy in a number of ways. An expansion of the money supply may have little effect on the economy because it is simply absorbed into higher stocks. In the same way, a tightening of policy may be ineffective, because individuals respond to it by running down their buffer stocks of money. Perhaps most importantly, there can be a sudden and inflationary release of money into the system because, for some reason which may be unconnected with policy, large numbers of people have decided to reduce their stocks of money.

Those monetarists who have attempted to accommodate the buffer stock approach argue that, if major changes in stocks occur after monetary shocks, the important thing is to avoid such shocks. The gradualist approach to monetary targeting is therefore underlined.

However, most proponents of the disequilibrium approach argue the opposite. Rigid monetary targeting, even if the path of money is a gradual one, will, in combination with unpredictable shifts in money holdings, produce volatility in interest rates and instability in financial markets. The approach thus pushes policy even more firmly along the discretionary route. It may even be that monetary policy has to act, not in response to changes in the money stock, but to changes in the behaviour of holders of money.

Some evidence of this approach at work was provided by the British authorities in 1986. After a long period of rapid growth in broad money in the economy, the Bank of England began to sound warnings about the creation of a glacier of liquidity. The Bank's view was that there was no cause for concern as long as this liquidity was willingly held at existing interest rate levels; as long, in other words, as the glacier did not begin to melt. But, the Bank said,

> It remains possible that, at some point, the process by which liquidity holdings have been built up could be reversed and that where held by industrial and commercial companies the funds could help to finance high pay settlements; that where held by financial institutions they might be switched abroad; and that where held by households they might seep into additional consumption.

The trigger for action would not therefore be the behaviour of the broad money aggregate itself, but evidence of its later damaging release into the system, through an acceleration of pay settlements, a fall in the exchange rate brought about by movements of capital overseas, or a consumer spending boom.

The Bank of England was on the side of those arguing that the disequilibrium approach renders monetary targeting inappropriate. The Governor of the Bank of England, Robin Leigh-Pemberton, suggested in a lecture at Loughborough in October 1986 that there was a case for abandoning the targeting of broad money and, indeed, for dispensing with monetary targets entirely.

The disequilibrium money approach takes us almost back to where we started, to the attack by Keynes on the quantity theory in the 1930s. It is possible for monetary policy to be ineffective, in the manner of 'pushing on a piece of string', if an expansion of the money supply simply adds to stocks of money.

The approach also fits the facts of the monetarist experiments rather well – apparently sensible and stable goals for the money supply can be damaging and highly destabilizing because of the unpredictability of those making decisions in the economy.

After Monetarism

The attitude of monetarists to the monetarist experiments of the 1970s and 1980s is rather similar to that of the Keynesians, following the breakdown of the Keynesian consensus in the early 1970s. Both schools blamed errors in policy and unhelpful external factors for the shortcomings of their ideas when put into practice. Post-war demand management, said the Keynesians, was not the practical application of the ideas of Keynes but the economic policy equivalent of muddling through. The experiments of the late 1970s and early 1980s, monetarists said, were experiments in bastard monetarism.

There is some truth in both claims. But the economist who is waiting around for the perfect practical application of his ideas will have to wait a long time. Laboratory experiments in economics, conducted in clinical conditions, do not take place in the real world.

The Keynesian/monetarist debate, or the New Classical/neo-Keynesian debate, or any other variant of the long-standing disputes between economists, are thus essentially sterile. The important thing is to learn from what has happened and attempt to improve upon it.

The first question is one of priorities. In the 1980s, in virtually all countries (Sweden is a notable exception), the full-employment objective was dropped in favour of the objective of reducing inflation. Nigel Lawson has said that the control of inflation is the only realistic objective of macro-economic policy, with growth and employment the proper concerns of micro-economic policy. It would be a lot easier for finance ministers if things were as simple as that. Clearly, however, as monetarists now admit, macro-economic decisions on the level of taxation and government spending have important implications for growth and employment.

Let us assume that the priority of policy has switched, or is switching, from the straightforward goal of defeating inflation, almost irrespective of the real economy costs, to that of preserving low inflation while generating more growth – and reducing unemployment substantially. It was once argued, and occasionally is still argued, that low inflation in itself will be sufficient to bring down unemployment in the industrialized countries. But even those who espouse this would concede that any such fall in unemployment will not be a mirror image of its rise. The fall will be a long time coming.

A more widely held view is that, in many countries, unemployment is now so deeply ingrained in the economic system that the scope for such automatic correction is limited. In 1986, the long-term unemployed – those out of work for more than a year – accounted for nearly half of male unemployment in Britain, and a third of female unemployment.

So, how to achieve the twin aim of preserving low inflation while sharply reducing unemployment? There is, as far as it is possible in economics, a consensus that, while monetary policy cannot handle economic policy alone, money does matter. It is therefore necessary for actions by governments to take account of the monetary and inflationary consequences.

It is not, however, at all necessary, or even desirable, that this should be achieved by rigid adherence to monetary targets. Central bankers see their essential role as guardians of the currency. The fact that, in many cases, it is the central bankers who have rebelled against the straitjacket of targets should say something to those theoretical monetarists who still yearn for rigid targeting.

Responsible monetary policy can operate in a number of ways. Policy action on, say, interest rates can be triggered by other things than growth in the money supply. It can act, and in most countries is acting, on the basis of movements in a diverse range of indicators, including the exchange rate, shifts in asset markets, unit labour costs and indicators of final inflation. One of the lessons of the monetarist experiments is that apparently responsible policy, based on monetary targets, can be both irresponsible and unsustainable.

A consequence of the monetarist experiments was that, in the majority of countries but demonstrably not in the United States, monetary targeting proceeded in train with efforts to cut back budget deficits. As things had developed by the 1970s, it is probably true that corrective action on government deficits was needed. Most countries, again excluding the United States, had achieved what could reasonably be regarded as respectable reductions in their structural budget deficits by the mid 1980s. Any further action smacked, and for those who are still doing it smacks, of the hair-shirt.

There is no consensus for massive, catch-all reflation through fiscal policy. The composition of unemployment, with its bias towards the long-term unemployed, means that large numbers of the unemployed have effectively dropped out of the labour market. There is a 'core' of the labour market, and there is a periphery. Suppose that, in Britain's three million-plus unemployed, there are 250,000 people with the right skills, and in the right place, to take advantage of any strong upturn in demand. A general reflation aimed at restoring full employment would quickly pull in the 250,000 but the remainder of the unemployed would not be so readily accommodated in employment. The reflation would therefore lead to a small fall in unemployment and a large increase in inflation, by pulling up the wages of those already in employment.

The answer, as Professor Richard Layard has suggested, is to finely target any fiscal action towards the unemployed, and in particular the long-term unemployed, through training, job subsidies and tax breaks for employers taking on the long-term jobless – as long as they are also recording a net increase in employment.

The question of whether or not such action should be backed up by some form of incomes policy is a more difficult one. It has been the case, in Britain in particular, that real incomes for the employed have risen strongly while unemployment has been increasing. The challenge for those who argue for a return to incomes policies is to prove that the benefits of such policies would more than compensate for any adverse effects on growth and incentives. Incomes policies may have a better chance of success when introduced at a time of low and stable inflation than when, as has been the tradition, they are used to attempt to put a cap on sharply rising inflation.

Finally, there has to be a very large international dimension to policy. The major industrial countries have been moving, albeit slowly and argumentatively, towards setting mutually compatible objectives for policy, in an effort to eliminate the sharp and destabilizing currency shifts and payments imbalances which have built up since the break-up of the Bretton Woods system of fixed exchange rates in 1973. Whether this can be formalized into a workable quasi-Bretton Woods system, based for example on target zones for exchange rates, remains to be seen. The success of the European Monetary System, which started life in 1979, and which has survived the second oil shock and associated economic disturbances, gives some cause for hope.

That said, there have to be meaningful constraints on countries' policy actions. There is the 'free rider' problem in which one country can profitably pursue its own line as long as all the others are obeying the rules. Some would say that this characterized US economic policy in the first half of the 1980s. There is also the 'catch 22' that the international policy co-operation agreed upon by the current set of politicians may prove less acceptable when they have an election to fight, or not at all acceptable to the next set of politicians to take office. It may also be that the international capital markets are now too powerful, even for the concerted actions of governments.

We have come a long way from the quantity theory of money of David Hume and John Locke. We should have learned a lot from the monetarist experiments of the 1970s and 1980s. It is important that those lessons are not easily forgotten.

THE DEVELOPMENT OF THE QUANTITY THEORY

Early Monetarists

It is generally agreed that the father of modern economics was Adam Smith, in the second half of the eighteenth century. But a Scots near-contemporary of Smith, the philosopher David Hume, is usually credited with the birth of monetarism, although some would cite earlier writers such as John Locke, at the end of the seventeenth century. Hume's essay 'Of Money', published in 1750, contains the following description of the effects of an increase in the quantity of money: 'At first, no alteration is perceived; by degrees the price rises, first of one commodity, then of another; till the whole at last reaches a just proportion with the quantity of specie which is in the kingdom.'

The language is different, but the message from Friedman, writing in the 1960s, is the same: 'The central fact is that inflation is always and everywhere a monetary phenomenon. Historically, substantial changes in prices have always occurred together with substantial changes in the quantity of money relative to output. I know of no exception to this generalization . . .'

These two statements, two centuries apart, give the flavour of monetarism. Monetarists believe that money is the driving force in the economy. There are, they say, well-defined relationships between changes in the stock of money and other economic variables. And these relationships are not just theoretical claims. According to Friedman and his co-workers, they have stood the test of time and have lasted throughout measurable economic history.

The central concept is that of the quantity theory of money. The terms 'monetarist' and 'quantity theorist' are usually, but not always, interchangeable. The quantity theory of money postulates a stable and predictable relationship between changes in the stock of money and changes in national output and prices.

The main policy recommendation emerging from this is that if low and steady rates of growth of the money stock can be achieved, stable economic growth without inflation should result.

In the first half of the nineteenth century, culminating in the vigorous debate between the currency and banking schools at the time of the Bank Charter Act for the Bank of England in 1844, the quantity theorists operated with a tenacity that has been inherited by their intellectual descendants. By 1829, the Oxford economist Nassau Senior was describing the quantity theory in modern terms: 'The general doctrine is, that the value of money depends partly on its quantity, and partly on the rapidity of its circulation.'

Economists of the currency school, such as Robert Torrens and Lord Overstone, took their lead from the earlier arguments of David Ricardo. He said that, in a paper-money economy in which banks can create credit, credit must be made to behave as if it was metallic money. Mechanical rules would thus be required to control credit.

The banking school, in contrast, said that, in a credit economy, the central bank should be allowed to operate according to its discretion. John Stuart Mill, the economist and philosopher, advocated subtle monetary management, conditioned by the 'feel' of the market. Thomas Tooke, whose views contain hints of the approach adopted by one of the most effective modern critics of monetarism, the late Lord Kaldor, said that changes in the note issue follow, rather than precede, changes in the price level. John Fullarton, also somewhat ahead of his time, inveighed against the notion of controlling money, as defined by the Bank of England note issue, because, with growing financial sophistication, transactions by cheque could grow at a far faster rate than the quantity of bank notes in circulation.

The currency school won, at least in the battle over the institutional structure of the Bank of England. To this day, the Bank is divided into an issue department and a banking department. The currency school's victory may have been a pyrrhic one, for the actual practice of the Bank of England was more in line with the banking school's recommendations, but it underlined the importance of the quantity theory in economic thought.

In the latter part of the nineteenth century and the early twentieth century, economies were believed to be self-stabilizing at full employment. Say's Law, named after the French economist Jean-Baptiste Say, whereby supply creates its own demand at the macro level, held sway. Falling prices were as likely to occur as inflation; macro-economics took second place to the micro-economics of individual markets. But the macro-economic debate, such as it was, favoured the quantity theory.

Alfred Marshall, who was responsible for establishing the Cambridge tradition in economics, wrote: 'If everything else remains the same, then there is this direct relation between the volume of currency and the level of prices, that if one is increased by 10 per cent, the other will also be increased by 10 per cent.'

He was followed in this by, among others, Arthur Pigou, Denis Robertson and, until his dramatic change of view, Keynes, who taught the quantity theory at Cambridge.

The Fisher Equation

It was an American economist, the Yale professor Irving Fisher, who first formalized the quantity theory in 1911. Fisher set down in equation form the fact that the total money value of transactions in the economy must equal the money value of goods sold. If M is the quantity of money in circulation and V the number of times it changes hands, this multiplied together must equal the product of the price level P and the number of transactions T. Or, more neatly, $MV = PT$.

To move back from this to the more familiar, non-mathematical forms of the quantity theory, Fisher looked a little more closely at T, transactions, and V, the velocity of circulation. Under the conditions of full employment assumed and experienced by pre-1914 economists, Fisher could realistically take T, the total number of transactions within a given period, to be constant. Similarly, V, the number of times a certain amount of money changes hands, was seen as determined by the unchanging or slowly evolving economic framework – the structure of the banking system, the frequency with which people are paid – and could also be assumed to be constant.

This left M, money, and P, the price level. For the identity to hold, changes in the quantity of money have to equal changes in the price level. Fisher's formalization of the quantity theory left open the question of the direction of causation. Changes in the quantity of money could be the force bringing about price changes. But the relationship could just as well be the other way round, whereby an increase in the price level called forth extra money from the banking system. However, this latter possibility, which had been raised by the earlier banking school economists, was generally thought to defy commonsense. The quantity of money determined the price level.

Fisher set off a vigorous academic debate, not mainly on the implications of his equation, but on whether it best specified the quantity theory. The first response to Fisher was directed at the rather hazy notion of transactions, in an effort to take the quantity theory closer to the real world. The number of transactions, T, and the velocity of circulation, V, posed insuperable measurement problems, out of which came the income version of the quantity theory.

This took money and prices as before, but re-defined velocity and introduced, instead of transactions, the national income of the economy in real terms, Y. Then, V became the income velocity of circulation, or the number of times each unit of money is used for making a transaction that represents someone's income, and Y is total national income, in real or inflation-adjusted terms. So, the amended version of the theory was $MV = PY$.

As with Fisher's version, the income variant of the quantity theory reduced to the familiar relationship whereby changes in the quantity of money match changes in the price level. Income velocity, like transactions velocity, was determined by the institutional structure of the economy and could be assumed to be stable. Real national income was fixed at its full-employment level. But, as before, there was no satisfactory explanation of why money changes lead to price changes and not vice versa. This left the quantity theory open to the criticism that it was merely a truism, offering no useful guidance on the direction of causation between money and price changes.

The Cambridge Cash Balance Approach

This criticism was tackled in yet another formulation of the quantity theory, the Cambridge cash balance approach associated with Marshall and Pigou in particular, and also with Robertson and Keynes. The starting-point was the notion that people wish to hold a certain amount of cash to cover the transactions they expect to make, as well as some precautionary holdings of cash for unforeseen circumstances. The level of these cash balances would be determined by habit and experience and could be expected to form a stable proportion of income. No holdings of idle, or speculative, balances were allowed for in this approach. Rather, the level of cash balances was believed to be stable, rising only when people became better-off in real terms.

Having established this principle, the Cambridge economists could then proceed with a robust explanation of the link between changes in the quantity of money and prices. Suppose that the Bank of England decided to double the number of notes in circulation. The effect is to push more cash into the hands of the community than it wishes to hold. Actual cash holdings have increased to twice the desired level. In these circumstances, people have no option but to go out and spend. Now – and remember that the economy was thought to be operating under the classical condition of full employment – this extra spending cannot push up real national income. What it does is to raise prices in the economy. The process works its way through until a point is reached when cash balances have returned to their desired proportion of income. This happens when prices, like the quantity of money in circulation, have doubled.

The Cambridge cash balance variant of the quantity theory sidestepped problems of measuring the velocity of circulation. Instead a new variable, which in practice could be taken as constant, was introduced. This was k, usually known as the Marshallian k, the desired proportion of income held in cash. With M, P and Y as defined in the income version of the quantity theory, the more sophisticated Cambridge approach specified it as $M = kPY$.

The terms on the right-hand side of the equation represent the demand for money. For the quantity theory to hold, this must equal its supply, as represented by the single term M. It will be immediately obvious that taking k to the other side of the equation restores the earlier quantity theory, where income velocity, V, is equivalent to the reciprocal of the Marshallian k, or $1/k$. But the Cambridge approach was much more than mere algebraic juggling. It offered a version of the quantity theory which did not merely set up an accounting identity. It also, within strict, self-imposed limitations, provided an explanation.

Friedman's Modern Quantity Theory

The Keynesian revolution in economic thought dealt two body blows to the quantity theorists, one specific, the other more general. The general attack launched by Keynes was his demolition of the classical idea that full employment was the equilibrium condition for economies. With this assumption no longer tenable, the quantity theory ideas about links between money and prices could and did break down. An expansion of the money stock could as well be reflected in higher employment and output as in higher prices.

But Keynes, with a more specific attack on the quantity theory, was able to show that monetary policy was not the appropriate weapon to use in conditions of high unemployment. In Keynes's scheme there existed, as well as the traditional transactions and precautionary demands for money, a speculative demand for money, which was related to the rate of interest.

Money could be substituted for bonds. Keynes postulated a liquidity preference schedule upon which each individual would base his or her relative holdings of money and bonds. When interest rates were low and bond prices high (the two are inversely related), the demand for money would be strong – because most people expected a fall in bond prices and a rise in interest rates. Conversely, when interest rates were high, the demand for money would be low.

The demand for money would therefore not be stably related to income, as in the Cambridge cash balance version of the quantity theory; instead it would be very sensitive to interest rate changes. Keynes postulated a situation, the so-called liquidity trap, in which interest rates were low enough to produce the maximum demand for money, but still too high to encourage investment in the economy. Any expansion of the money supply would be ineffective – 'pushing on a piece of string'.

Like all good campaigners, Friedman used his enemy's strengths to his own advantage. But to provide a complete version of Friedman's quantity theory, it is first necessary to define the concept of permanent income.

This came out of another strand of his work, on consumption. The income received by individuals, he postulated, consists of two parts – permanent and transitory. Suppose an unexpected bonus is received, or a lottery prize. It is not regarded as permanent income on which to base spending decisions; these will continue to be determined by that part of income regarded as permanent. In the opposite situation where there is a temporary drop in income, perhaps because a person is put on short-time working, consumption is unlikely to fall in response. Rather, it will continue to be based on permanent income. At some stage, of course, what was first taken as a temporary change in income becomes permanent. Friedman suggested a three-year time horizon for transitory elements to be incorporated into permanent income.

Armed with permanent income, we can see how it fitted into Friedman's redefinition of the quantity theory. For his version of the quantity theory, while supporting the same conclusions, is a very different animal from its predecessors. It drew much, as stated above, from Keynes's monetary analysis. This distinction was laid down by Friedman in 1956, when he wrote: 'The quantity theory of money is in the first instance a theory of the demand for money.'

The central question that Friedman sought to answer was: What determines the demand for money? Keynes, it will be recalled, said that the demand for money depended both on income and the rate of interest, because money can be held idly or used to buy bonds. Friedman agreed with Keynes, that money should properly be regarded as an asset which can be substituted for other assets, but argued that Keynes's formulation was much too restrictive in defining only financial assets – bonds – as substitutes for money. 'The most fruitful approach is to regard money as one of a sequence of assets, on a par with bonds, equities, houses, consumer durables,' he wrote. In this wider approach, money is only one way in which wealth can be held, along with a large number of other assets.

But what is wealth, other than accumulated income? And how is it measured, other than by reference to actual income? There was another measure, Friedman said, which did not suffer from the volatility of actual income, his own idea; that of permanent income.

Wealth, as well as the quantities of the long list of assets outlined, is also human wealth – the earnings potential of the individual. So this too had to be included in the demand for money. Friedman was not finished yet. As well as being dependent on wealth, the proxy for which was permanent income, and the ratio of human to non-human wealth, the demand for money would also depend on the rates of return on different assets. The return on money is the convenience and security of holding it. To the individual, the value of that convenience and security will be related to the price level and expectations about further price changes. The return on a financial asset is an easily measured financial return. But how do you measure the return on a washing-machine? Even here, Friedman said, it is possible to derive some measure of the satisfaction obtained from owning and using the machine.

There was method in Friedman's apparent madness of putting everything, including the kitchen sink, into the demand for money. The rate of interest, so important in Keynes's approach, with possible dire consequences such as the liquidity trap, becomes only one of a number of elements in the restated quantity theory.

In a more familiar form, Friedman's quantity theory boils down to the statement that the demand for money, M, depends on the price level, P, wealth as defined by permanent income, Y, and the whole host of other factors described above, which we can denote $1/V$. Thus the quantity theory becomes $M = 1/V(PY)$, or, in rather neater form, $MV = PY$.

It all fitted into place, providing the transmission mechanism from changes in the money stock to income and prices. An increase in the money supply leads to individuals having more money in their portfolio of assets than they wish to hold. The response would be to shift this money into the rest of the portfolio, including bonds and equities, but also – and this is the key point – washing-machines and other goods. The shifts occur until the rates of return to the individual on the different assets are equalized.

The process continues until money is resorted to its equilibrium share of total assets. And the sum of these purchasing decisions is a higher level of money income than we started with. Changes in the money stock produce changes in money national income.

GLOSSARY

BRETTON WOODS SYSTEM   The post-war system of fixed exchange rates, which collapsed in 1973, so called because it was set up following a conference in Bretton Woods, New Hampshire, in 1944. Since 1973, currencies have been allowed to float against each other, although not always freely.

BROAD MONEY   Money can be defined and measured in a number of ways. Measures of broad money are essentially measures of credit and liquidity. Sterling M3, a broad money target, was the main money target originally selected by the Thatcher government. It is defined as notes and coin plus all sterling sight and time deposits held by the banking system (current and deposit accounts).

COMPETITION AND CREDIT CONTROL   Changes in methods of monetary management introduced by the Bank of England in 1971 and superseded ten years later. The aim was to replace the previous credit restrictions and ceilings with a system which would place greater reliance on competition and interest rates. The removal of quantitative restrictions on bank lending provided one reason for the sharp money-supply increases under Edward Heath and Anthony Barber.

DEMAND FOR MONEY   Monetarists believed that the demand for money represented a stable proportion of income: the better-off people become, the more cash they wish to hold. Keynesians said that the demand for money was unstable and highly sensitive to changes in interest rates. The experience of the 1970s and 1980s suggested that the monetarists' belief in a stable demand for money did not hold, at least in the short term. The demand for money is the reciprocal of the velocity of circulation, so volatile money demand implies volatile velocity.

MONETARY BASE   Banks create credit on the basis of money deposited with them. The monetary base is the source for credit creation, and monetarists have argued that controlling the monetary base will also exert control over wider measures of credit and liquidity. This assumes stable behaviour by the banks. In Britain the monetary base, M0, has been used as a monetary target, here defined as notes and coin in circulation and in bank tills, plus bankers' balances at the Bank of England. It has been criticized, because the banks are under no obligation to limit the amount of credit they can create in respect of cash in circulation or in their own tills.

MONETARY RULES The requirement that the monetary authorities set and adhere to rigid rules for the growth of the money stock. Friedman was a powerful advocate of monetary rules, and they formed the basis of the British government's medium-term financial strategy, launched in 1980.

MONEY GDP Gross domestic product, or national income, is measured in three ways. It is the total value of all expenditures in Britain on domestically produced goods, plus foreign expenditures on British goods; it is the total of all incomes in the economy; and it is the sum of the values of all goods and services produced in Britain. The three methods of measuring GDP should come up with the same result, although in practice there are discrepancies. Money GDP is simply gross domestic product in current prices. GDP and GNP (gross national product) are generally but not precisely interchangeable, as are money GDP and nominal GNP. The key monetarist relationship is between the stock of money and money GDP, or nominal GNP.

MONEY SUPPLY The stock of money, which can be measured in a number of ways, is the amount existing in the economy at any one time. The money supply is the increase in that stock.

MO A measure of the monetary base, it is described as the wide monetary base. It comprises notes and coin in circulation and held in bank tills, plus banks' deposits with the Banking Department of the Bank of England. These deposits are of two kinds: some are placed there for operational purposes, the rest so that the banks can maintain appropriate cash ratios.

M1 A measure of narrow money. In Britain it is defined as notes and coin in circulation plus all private-sector sight deposits (that is, withdrawable on demand) in sterling. At any one time, a large proportion of these sight deposits are on the move between different bank accounts as cheques are written. The Bank of England includes 60 per cent of these so-called transit items in measuring M1.

M2 A measure of the money stock which attempts to assess the amount available at any one time for transactions purposes. In Britain it comprises notes and coin in circulation with the public, plus non-interest-bearing sight deposits with the banks (current accounts), plus so-called retail deposits, which bear interest, with the banks, the building societies and the National Savings Bank. It measures that money which the public can readily obtain in order to spend.

NARROW MONEY Measures of money which, typically, only contain a small proportion of interest-bearing deposits. M1, in both Britain and the United States, is regarded as a narrow money measure.

NATURAL RATE OF UNEMPLOYMENT Milton Friedman postulated a natural rate of unemployment for the economy, determined by the structure of the labour market: trade union power, the ease with which people can change jobs, and minimum wage and social security legislation. Attempts to drive unemployment below its natural rate by expanding the economy would automatically result in inflation, he said.

NAIRU The non-accelerating inflation rate of unemployment; another, more precise way of describing the natural rate of unemployment. It is that level of unemployment prevailing at any one time at which there is no tendency for the inflation rate to increase. Its proponents say that attempts to drive unemployment below the NAIRU through fiscal or monetary expansion will result in higher inflation.

NEW CLASSICAL ECONOMICS A second wave of monetarism which arrived during the 1970s. Essentially the embodiment of the belief that you cannot fool all of the people all of the time, it claimed that the use of fiscal policy for expanding the economy had been rendered redundant. People would see through the fiscal expansion to the inflation that would follow.

PERMANENT INCOME A concept invented by Friedman to explain consumption behaviour. People based spending decisions on their long-run, stable income, he said, and would not move spending around in line with windfall gains or unexpected income losses. Friedman used the concept of permanent income to explain away the volatility of the demand for money in relation to actual income.

PHILLIPS CURVE The belief that there exists a trade-off between unemployment and inflation, operating through wages. Wages increase rapidly when unemployment is low, but are held back by high unemployment. The trade-off was formalized by Professor Alban Phillips.

PSL2 The widest of all the monetary aggregates in use in Britain. It includes notes and coin in circulation with the public, all private sector sight and time deposits with the banks (current and deposit accounts), private sector holdings of bank certificates of deposit in sterling, private sector holdings of money market instruments and certificates of tax deposit, and deposits with the building societies and the National Savings Bank, less holdings by the building societies of money market instruments and bank deposits. PSL2 goes beyond money as a measure; it is the total private sector liquidity in the economy.

PUBLIC SECTOR BORROWING REQUIREMENT One measure, some way from being the best, of the British government's budget deficit. It is the amount that has to be borrowed each year to cover the difference between public expenditure and tax revenues.

QUANTITY THEORY OF MONEY The basis of monetarism. The stock of money, M, together with the number of times each unit of money is used – its velocity, V, is equivalent to the number of transactions in the economy, T, and the price level at which such transactions take place; or $MV = PT$. Later versions of the quantity theory have specified a relationship between the money stock, velocity and money national income, or money GDP; or $MV = PY$.

RATIONAL EXPECTATIONS   The belief that everyone acts in a rational manner on the basis of information available to them. Originally developed to explain the behaviour of the financial markets, it was extended in the 1970s to explain all economic behaviour. It was used to demonstrate the impotency of fiscal policy, because people would see through the short-term expansionary effects of any fiscal boost to the resulting inflation.

STERLING INDEX   A measure of the pound's average value against other currencies, weighted according to the importance of other countries in Britain's overseas trade. The base date for the index is 1975, when the index would have stood at 100. Thus, if the sterling index stands at 70, the pound is worth 70 per cent of its 1975 level.

STERLING M3   The measure of money that was the cornerstone of the Thatcher experiment in monetarism. It comprises notes and coin in circulation with the public, together with private sector sterling sight and time deposits with the banks (current and deposit accounts) and private sector holdings of sterling bank certificates of deposit. It is a measure of broad money.

SUPPLEMENTARY SPECIAL DEPOSITS SCHEME   The Supplementary Special Deposits Scheme, or 'corset', was introduced by the Chancellor of the Exchequer, Anthony Barber, in December 1973, and used intermittently until it was abandoned in 1980. Banks which exceeded prescribed growth rates in lending were penalized by being forced to place additional non-interest-bearing deposits at the Bank of England.

SUPPLY-SIDE ECONOMICS   In general, a school of economic thought which holds that the actions of governments are important for their micro-economic effects – on, for example, work incentives, savings and investment behaviour; in particular, as supply-side economics emerged in the United States in the 1970s and transferred to Britain in the 1980s, the belief that tax reductions were necessary to promote incentive and an 'enterprise culture'.

VELOCITY OF CIRCULATION   How hard each unit of money works. In the earlier versions of the quantity theory of money there was a transactions velocity of circulation: the number of times each unit of money is used over a given period to make a spending transaction. In later versions, velocity became the income velocity of circulation; the number of times each unit of money forms a part of someone's income. It is usually measured by dividing money GDP by the stock of money.

BIBLIOGRAPHY

AMERICAN ECONOMIC REVIEW, Papers and Proceedings of the 96th Annual Meeting, May 1984

BACON, ROBERT, and ELTIS, WALTER, *Britain's Economic Problem: Too Few Producers*, Macmillan, 1976

BALL, R. J., and DOYLE, PETER (eds.), *Inflation: Selected Readings*, Penguin, 1969

BANK FOR INTERNATIONAL SETTLEMENTS, *Recent Innovations in International Banking*, Basle, April 1986

BANK FOR INTERNATIONAL SETTLEMENTS, Annual Reports, 1985 and 1986, Basle

BANK OF ENGLAND, *Quarterly Bulletins*, 1969–86

BARNETT, JOEL, *Inside the Treasury*, André Deutsch, 1982

BARTLETT, BRUCE, 'Supply-side Economics: Theory and Evidence', National Westminster *Quarterly Review*, February 1985

BECKERMAN, WILFRED (ed.), *The Labour Government's Economic Record, 1964–70*, Duckworth, 1972

BEGG, DAVID, 'The Rational Expectations Revolution', London Business School *Economic Outlook*, Gower Press, June 1982

BLACKABY, F. T. (ed.), *British Economic Policy, 1960–74*, Cambridge University Press, 1978

BLAKE, ROBERT, *The Conservative Party from Peel to Thatcher*, Eyre & Spottiswoode, 1984

BRITTAN, SAMUEL, 'How to End the "Monetarist" Controversy', Institute of Economic Affairs, 1981

BRYANT, RALPH C., *Controlling Money: The Federal Reserve and Its Critics*, Brookings Institution, 1983

BUTLER, EAMONN, *Milton Friedman . . . A Guide to His Economic Thought*, Temple Smith/Gower, 1985

CLOWER, R. W. (ed.), *Monetary Theory: Selected Readings*, Penguin, 1969

CONGDON, TIM, 'Monetarism, An Essay in Definition', Centre for Policy Studies, 1978

DAVIES, GAVYN, 'Where Economists Now Agree', Bass Ireland Lecture, Simon & Coates, London, 1986

DAVIES, GAVYN, 'Governments Can Affect Unemployment', Employment Institute, London, 1985

FEDERAL RESERVE BANK OF NEW YORK, *Quarterly Reviews*

FFORDE, JOHN, 'Setting Monetary Objectives', Bank of England *Quarterly Bulletin*, June 1983

FINANCIAL STATEMENTS AND BUDGET REPORTS, 1972–86, HMSO

FRIEDMAN, MILTON (ed.), *Studies in the Quantity Theory of Money*, University of Chicago Press, 1956

FRIEDMAN, MILTON, *A Theory of the Consumption Function*, Princeton University Press, 1957

FRIEDMAN, MILTON, and SCHWARZ, ANNA, *A Monetary History of the United States, 1867–1960*, Princeton University Press, 1963

FRIEDMAN, MILTON, *Dollars and Deficits: Inflation, Monetary Policy and the Balance of Payments*, Prentice-Hall, 1968

FRIEDMAN, MILTON, *The Optimum Quantity of Money and Other Essays*, Macmillan, 1969

FRIEDMAN, MILTON, 'The Counter-Revolution in Monetary Theory', Institute of Economic Affairs, 1970

FRIEDMAN, MILTON, 'Unemployment versus Inflation', Institute of Economic Affairs, 1975

FRIEDMAN, MILTON, 'Inflation and Unemployment: The New Dimension of Politics', Institute of Economic Affairs, 1977

FRIEDMAN, MILTON, and SCHWARZ, ANNA, *Monetary Trends in the United States and the United Kingdom*, University of Chicago Press, 1982

GOODHART, CHARLES, *Money, Information and Uncertainty*, Macmillan, 1975

GOODHART, CHARLES, *Monetary Theory and Practice*, Macmillan, 1984

HAMILTON, ADRIAN, *The Financial Revolution*, Viking/Penguin, 1986

HENDRY, DAVID, and ERICSSON, NEIL, 'Assertion Without Empirical Basis . . .' etc., Bank of England Panel of Academic Consultants, Paper 22, 1983

HENDRY, DAVID, 'Monetary Economic Myth and Econometric Reality', *Oxford Review of Economic Policy*, Spring 1985

INTERNATIONAL MONETARY FUND, *World Economic Outlook*, Washington, April 1986

JAY, PETER, 'Employment, Inflation and Politics', Institute of Economic Affairs, 1976

JONES, AUBREY, *Oil: The Missed Opportunity*, André Deutsch, 1981

KALDOR, NICHOLAS, 'The New Monetarism', Lloyds Bank *Review*, July 1970

KALDOR, NICHOLAS, *The Scourge of Monetarism*, Oxford University Press, 1985

KEEGAN, WILLIAM, *Mrs Thatcher's Economic Experiment*, Penguin, 1984

KEYNES, JOHN MAYNARD, *The General Theory of Employment, Interest and Money*, Macmillan, 1936

LAIDLER, D. E., *The Demand for Money*, Intertext Books, Aylesbury, Bucks., 1969

LAIDLER, D. E., *The Demand for Money: Theories and Evidence*, Harper & Row, 1985

LAIDLER, D. E., 'Monetary Policy in Britain – Successes and Shortcomings', *Oxford Review of Economic Policy*, Spring 1985

LAWSON, NIGEL, 'Thatcherism in Practice: A Progress Report', Address to the Zurich Society of Economics, 14 January 1981, HM Treasury

LEKACHMAN, ROBERT, *The Age of Keynes*, Penguin, 1967

LONDON BUSINESS SCHOOL, *Economic Outlook*, 1977 to 1986, Gower Press

MAYES, D. G., 'The Controversy Over Rational Expectations', National Institute *Economic Review*, May 1981

MILLER, MARCUS, 'Measuring the Stance of Fiscal Policy', *Oxford Review of Economic Policy*, Spring 1985

MORGAN, BRIAN, *Monetarists and Keynesians – Their Contribution to Monetary Theory*, Macmillan, 1978

NATIONAL INSTITUTE FOR ECONOMIC AND SOCIAL RESEARCH, *Economic Review*, 1966 to 1986

NORTON, PHILIP, *Conservative Dissidents: Dissent within the Conservative Party, 1970–74*, Temple Smith, 1978

ORGANIZATION FOR ECONOMIC CO-OPERATION AND DEVELOPMENT (OECD). 'Monetary Policy in Japan', Paris, 1972

OECD, 'Monetary Policy in Germany', Paris, 1973

OECD, 'Monetary Policy in the United States', Paris, 1974

OECD, *Economic Outlook*, 1977 to 1986, Paris

PEPPER, GORDON T., and WOOD, GEOFFREY E., 'Too Much Money', Institute of Economic Affairs, 1976

PHILLIPS, A. W., 'The Relationship between Unemployment and the Rate of Change of Money Wage Rates in the United Kingdom, 1861–1957', *Economica*, vol. 25, 1958

PLIATSKY, LEO, *Getting and Spending*, Blackwell, Oxford, 1982

SAVAGE, DAVID, 'Monetary Targets and the Control of the Money Supply', National Institute *Economic Review*, August 1979

SHEARSON LEHMAN BROTHERS, *The Monetary–Fiscal Mix: Implications for the Short Run*, Shearson Lehman, New York, May 1986

SMITH, DAVID, 'A Monetary Model of the British Economy, 1880–1975', National Westminster *Quarterly Review*, February 1977

TEW, BRIAN, *The Evolution of the International Monetary System, 1945–77*, Hutchinson, 1977

TREASURY AND CIVIL SERVICE COMMITTEE, Session 1979–80, Memoranda on Monetary Policy, HMSO, 1980

WALTERS, ALAN, 'Economists and the British Economy', Institute of Economic Affairs, 1978

WALTERS, ALAN, *Britain's Economic Renaissance: Margaret Thatcher's Reforms, 1979–84*, Oxford University Press, 1986

WAPSHOTT, NICHOLAS, and BROCK, GEORGE, *Thatcher*, Futura, 1983

WHITEHEAD, PHILLIP, *The Writing on the Wall*, Michael Joseph, 1985

INDEX